IN THE WAKE OF
THE GREAT REBELLION

Manchester University Press

IN THE WAKE OF
THE GREAT REBELLION

Republicanism, agrarianism
and banditry in
Ireland after 1798

James G. Patterson

Manchester University Press
Manchester and New York
distributed in the United States exclusively by Palgrave Macmillan

Published by Manchester University Press
Oxford Road, Manchester M13 9NR, UK
and Room 400, 175 Fifth Avenue, New York, NY 10010, USA
www.manchesteruniversitypress.co.uk

Distributed in the United States exclusively by
Palgrave Macmillan, 175 Fifth Avenue,
New York, NY 10010, USA

Distributed in Canada exclusively by
UBC Press, University of British Columbia, 2029 West Mall,
Vancouver, BC, Canada V6T 1Z2

British Library Cataloguing-in-Publication Data is available

Library of Congress Cataloging-in-Publication Data is available

ISBN 978 0 7190 8556 7 paperback

First published by Manchester University Press in hardback 2008

This paperback edition first published 2011

Printed by Lightning Source

Contents

Acknowledgements

I would like to thank a number of individuals for their support, both academic and personal, in the completion of this project. First, I owe a tremendous debt to my mentor, Dr Nancy J. Curtin. Without her patience and insight over a lengthy period, this work could not have reached fruition. Moreover, she is a valued friend.

Barbara J. Costa, Fordham University's History Department secretary, assisted me in too many ways to be listed. I would also like to thank Dr John McCarthy of Fordham for his help and guidance throughout my doctoral study. The late Drs Donald Frank and William George inspired and advised me during my earlier academic development. I hope they would be pleased.

I offer my sincerest thanks to Steve Ball and Breandán Mac Suibhne. They generously read portions of this work and offered invaluable advice. More importantly, they have gifted me with their friendship. Along the same lines, I must express my gratitude to Tim McMahon, Matt O'Brien, and Brian MacDonald. Also, I would like to thank Ruán O'Donnell, David Miller, and James Donnelly for their generosity over the years.

A number of my colleagues at Centenary contributed their support throughout the final stages of this work. They include: Shane Fitzpatrick, Joe Linskey, Barbara-Jane Lewthwaite, John Autore, Christine Floether, Charlie Frederickson, Steve McHugh, Tim Cleary, Sandy Genduso, Chris Linn, Heather Dunham, Harriet Gaddy, Bryon Grigsby, Candice Chase, Norm Cetuk, Bob Search, Dean Bethea, Amy D'Olivo, Bob Szkodny, Jeff Carter, and Ray Frey.

On a purely personal level, I must convey my appreciation to Steve and Shirley Owens, Sean McEvoy, Dave Flaten, Beth Kunz, David Caldwell, Mark Hannafin, the Kennys, and Tim and Doreen Harness. I especially would like to thank Déirdre O'Dwyer and Shane McEvoy; I truly could not have done it without them.

My parents, Thomas and Muriel Patterson, lent me their unquestioning support throughout their lives. Drew, J. D. and Maggie, my children have kept everything in perspective. Finally, Carol this is for you; words cannot express.

Introduction

In the last quarter of the eighteenth century, long-term grievances over the domination of the Irish parliament by the Imperial government, as well as the subsidiary status of Ireland's economy to that of Britain, led to a movement for reform. Backed by the Volunteers (local military units nominally raised to defend Ireland while much of its regular garrison was engaged abroad during the conflicts centred on the American Revolution), these so-called 'patriots' sought to take advantage of the climate of fear created in Whitehall by the events in America to obtain the lifting of trade restrictions and legislative independence for the Irish parliament.[1] These dual objectives were achieved in 1779 and 1782 respectively. Yet the executive branch of the Irish government remained responsible to the Imperial cabinet. Moreover, the Viceroy retained the ability to manipulate the corrupt Irish parliament through the liberal distribution of patronage. Most importantly, the Reform Act of 1782 failed to address the aspirations of the Protestant middle classes, which largely remained excluded from the political process. By the second half of the eighteenth century, middle-class resentment, particularly amongst the Presbyterians of Ulster, centred on the continued denial of political participation. Influenced by the ideals of the Enlightenment, coupled with the example of the rational government established by the American revolutionaries to whom many of the Ulster Presbyterians had ties of kinship, the irrationality of the Irish political environment became intolerable.

Inspired by the events of the French Revolution, a revived Volunteer movement emerged in 1790, this time seeking not only the reform of parliament, but, in some instances, Catholic enfranchisement. Modern Irish republicanism was born in Belfast and Dublin during 1791 with the foundation of the Society of United Irishmen. The United Irishmen's political thought was a potent combination of classical republicanism, Lockean contract theory and Painite natural rights principles. On a practical level, the organization sought the radical reform of parliament and, more strikingly, complete Catholic emancipation. In the early years, the majority of the United Irishmen's leaders favoured the utilization of moral and popular persuasion to bring about a peaceful reform of the system. Yet from the onset, there existed within the movement an element which believed that only by overturning the ascendancy and severing the British connection would it be possible to effect the necessary political transformation of Ireland.[2]

To prevent an alliance between the radical Presbyterians of the North, who dominated the early United movement and the country's Catholic majority, William Pitt, in the face of strong opposition from the Anglican ascendancy, pushed a series of Catholic Relief Acts through the Irish parliament. These reforms culminated in the Act of 1793, which granted the vote to qualified Catholics. Yet Catholics were still denied the right to sit in parliament or to hold higher posts in the government and military. The declaration of war between England and France in 1793 blocked further Catholic relief as the British government in time of crisis instinctively reverted to its traditional alliance with the Anglican elite.

Indeed, the pressure exerted by the war rapidly transformed Pitt's policy of conciliation to one of repression. The government ordered the Volunteers to disband in 1793, and by mid-1794 the United Irishmen were suppressed. Finally in 1795, a reforming Viceroy, Earl Fitzwilliam, supported a bill in the Irish parliament to remove the final restrictions on Catholic political participation. This endeavour raised howls of protest from the throats of the Protestant establishment. Pitt responded by promptly recalling Fitzwilliam to London. Thus, with all legal avenues of reform blocked, the balance between the moral persuasion and physical force wings of the United Irishmen shifted in favour of the latter. By 1795, the organization had transformed itself into a mass-based, oath-bound, secret society dedicated to bringing about a republican revolution.[3]

In order to obtain the numbers required to successfully challenge the ascendancy and England, the United Irishmen reached out to the Catholic Defender movement. This latter organization had formed in south Ulster in the mid-1780s to protect Catholics from the depredations of lower-class Protestant Peep O'Day Boys (the progenitors of the Orange Order). Defenderism rapidly spread throughout Ulster and into the northern counties of Leinster and Connaught.

The ensuing years saw the United Irishmen focus their efforts on politicizing and mobilizing the population. One of the founding fathers of the movement, Wolfe Tone, travelled to Paris in 1795 in an attempt to persuade the French Republic that the people of Ireland were organized to actively support an invasion. Tone's efforts were rewarded in December 1796, when a French fleet carrying 15,000 hardened veterans appeared in Bantry Bay. However, a providential 'Protestant wind' prevented a landing. The failed invasion nonetheless confirmed the belief that another attempt was inevitable and would probably succeed. Correspondingly, thousands of individuals who had previously waited on the fence rushed to swell the republican ranks. In the aftermath of the near calamity at Bantry Bay, the government made a concerted effort to crush the United Irish–Defender alliance before the French could make another attempt. The formidable Ulster organization was the primary target of this suppression; and by the end of 1797, severe damage had been done to the northern United Irishmen. The ill-treatment of nations 'liberated' by French revolutionary armies on the continent led many ranking United Irishmen to believe that the advantages of an indigenous rising outweighed the risks. Thus, a *coup de main* directed at the capital replaced a supportive rising as the primary objective of the United Irishmen. This transformation necessitated a massive recruitment drive in Dublin and the surrounding counties while inevitably shifting the focus of the national organization southwards from Ulster to Leinster. The final decision to launch a domestic rising was reached in early 1798, although the preparations were, perhaps fatally, disrupted by the arrest of most of the Leinster directory at Oliver Bond's house in Dublin on 12 March. Nonetheless, efforts proceeded. The republicans' seizure of the mailcoaches from Dublin to the provinces signalled the onset of the great rebellion on 23 May.[4]

The rebellion of 1798 tore the fabric of Irish society as no other event, with the exception of the famine, in the period between the Treaty of Limerick in 1691 and the establishment of Ireland's independence in 1921. In Leinster, the risings of Carlow, Kildare, Meath and Wicklow were quickly crushed. Only in County Wexford did the rebels meet with success. They managed to take most of the county, but failed in their efforts to break through and carry the rebellion to the north and west. On 21 June, the decisive engagement of the Wexford campaigning was fought at Vinegar Hill, and the republican army was routed. It is at this point (the brief, if underrated, risings in Antrim and Down having been put down in early June) that the rebellion of 1798 is traditionally considered to have ended.

Yet rebel armies remained in the field until mid-July, while a belated, small-scale French landing at Killala in County Mayo was overwhelmed in September. In reality, resistance in a variety of forms continued in all four provinces through 1803. Moreover, as early as August or September 1798 when the French were in the west, surviving mid-level United Irish officers held a meeting in Kevin Street, Dublin. These men proposed a number of actions, including an attack on Dublin Castle, although ultimately they could reach no agreement.[5] By November, it was clear that some semblance of a republican organization had indeed survived at the national level.[6] In December, word reached Dublin Castle of an active revolutionary structure operating in the confines of the capital and on the nineteenth, Mr Beresford reported to Castlereagh, 'The almost annihilated body of the United Irishmen ... is rising Phoenix like from its ashes. I know from certain information that they are again meeting in the city and its neighbourhood, and are preparing fresh publications to agitate the people.'[7] Similarly in February 1799, William Wickham, the Under Secretary, who was at the time in London, stated that he had obtained 'good information' that the United Irishmen in Dublin were in contact with France. Moreover, the Duke of Portland, the Home Secretary, believed on the basis of intelligence he had received that the United men in London were 'subject to the control and direction of the Executive Committee in Ireland, which has been appointed by such of the state prisoners as originally filled that office and who are now, of course unable to do it.'[8]

In fact, throughout the winter of 1799 the United Irishmen in Dublin strove to re-establish a national executive. The republican leadership drew up a 'New Plan of Organization', which was put forward by February. Along with the establishment of corresponding committees for the maintenance of communications between the executive and the provinces, the plan sought to avoid the major flaws of the old system, namely the prevalence of informers and the tendency of local committees to act independently. The mass-based, participatory organization of the old society was, therefore, altered radically. In its place, a hierarchical structure – where the executive appointed commanders for each county, who in turn designated colonels for each barony and so on down through the ranks of the officer corps – replaced the (at least theoretically) democratic system of the pre-rebellion period. Communications were to be carried by word of mouth, thereby avoiding the use of the written documents that had so often fallen into the hands of the government in the past. All now hinged on the arrival of the French, and lower committees were told to remain dormant until the landing of a sizable invasion force.[9] The rationale behind this policy was laid out clearly in the New Plan of Organization:

> This plunder of arms was always the cause of counties being proclaimed that fruitful source of every crime ... assassination having become frequent, we must disassociate from it; killing the Yeoman or Magistrate wouldn't change the system which is the root and provides justification for repression.[10]

Indeed the New Plan was premised on the assumption that 'the mass of the population of Ireland' was 'panting for emancipation' and would 'most freely follow at any period the Republican talent ... whenever they call[ed] them forth to act.'[11]

Herein lay the fatal flaw in the post-1798 society of the United Irishmen. The official policy of inactivity served to rob the executive of the ability to harness the pervasive discontent existing in much of Ireland between the summer of 1798 and 1803. However, it is essential to recognize that the inactivity and caution of the United Irishmen's leadership did not signify a rejection of republican ideology or a move to loyalism by the majority of the societies' rank-and-file. Instead, reports received by Dublin Castle repeatedly cited the prevalence of popular disaffection.

The identity of the new leadership came into sharper focus in the winter and spring of 1799 largely through the reports of the Belfast informer, James McGucken. These men included Thomas Wright, a surgeon and an active United Irishman since 1791, Henry Baird, the former secretary of the Leinster provincial, Robert Emmet, George Teeling, Mr Wilkinson, Mr Howell, Councillor Lawson and Hugh O'Hanlon, a former officer in Spanish service. Other important names tied to the post-1798 society included Messrs

Quinn and Delaney from Kildare, William Putnam McCabe, a long-time Belfast activist, George Palmer and James Farrell. Significantly, this group maintained contact with and deferred to the movement's original leaders, most of whom now were imprisoned in Kilmainham.[12]

As a result of McGucken's information, much of the reconstituted leadership was compromised, and in early April 1799, the Lord Lieutenant ordered the arrest of Emmet, Wright, O'Hanlon, Baird, Lawson, Howell and Farrell.[13] In due course, the authorities 'took up' Baird, although he claimed he knew 'nothing of a new directory'.[14] They also arrested Wright, whom they compelled to become a double agent, although much of the intelligence he provided was intentionally misleading. Wright did in fact acknowledge his membership in the United Irishman since 1791 yet claimed to have been inactive until late in 1798, thus conveniently avoiding any role in the 1798 rebellion. He also admitted his attendance at a meeting where O'Hanlon was present and the group discussed the feasibility of rising in support of a French invasion. More significantly, Wright claimed that he had met often with Baird, whom he described as 'the confidential agent of the old Directory', whose members were at the time imprisoned in Kilmainham. The informer also pointed to Mr Lawson, who 'seemed to know much', as a member of the original executive and described young Robert Emmet as 'active'. Finally, Wright considered 'the danger in Dublin' to come from the 'clerks and shopmen' and observed: '[although the] masters do not take a part ... they wink at the conduct of their clerks.'[15] This important observation concerning the social composition of the post-1798 organization in Dublin is confirmed by other sources. An earlier report described a local committee in the capital as 'vagabonds [who] form a set constantly together on the United Irish business.' The group met 'twice a week and dined at Brumptons ... and were so secret now that it is almost impossible to come to what they are about.' Charles Smith (an Abbey Street grocer) and a fruit-man named Vaughn were the leaders. Other identified members included Doyle (a tea and sugar merchant), Henry Sweetman (a clerk), Charles Reilly (who ran a dram shop), John Covey and Peter Smith (both grocers), and Tobias Cormick and Sergeant O'Brien of the Rotunda division (the first a merchant and the second a pawn broker).[16]

Ultimately, Robert Emmet and the majority of the other leaders successfully eluded capture and by various means eventually made their way to France, where they joined the United's exile community and actively worked to bring about another invasion. Meanwhile, the state prisoners were transferred to Fort George in Scotland in an endeavour to eliminate the influence they were able to maintain while imprisoned in Kilmainham.[17] Thus by the summer of 1799, Marianne Elliott argues that as a result of '[t]he removal of the state prisoners, coupled with the attempted purge of the new leaders, and the flight of many to escape it, the United Irish leadership was forced into almost total exile.'[18] Additionally, she holds that 'the period between the collapse of the 1798 insurrection and the rupture of the peace of Amiens in 1802 forms a hiatus between two phases of intense United Irish activity.'[19] It will be argued here that continuity at the grass-roots level is in fact an overriding theme of the period between 1798 and 1803.

Indeed, despite the best efforts of the government, it is apparent that middle-level activists successfully maintained some semblance of a national republican structure through 1803. Some hint as to the identity of the surviving core leadership in Dublin was provided by McGucken in the early summer of 1800. He cautioned that Lawson, Richardson, Norris and Baird 'ought not be allowed to remain in the country'. Furthermore, he believed that Wright, although having been 'turned', may in fact have played the role of double agent: '[I] suspect he is not acting the part of an honourable man.' Finally, McGucken said of an Abbey Street printer of known republican sympathies (John Stockdale): 'his house is a general rendezvous for the politicians of the day and he himself I consider a very dangerous person, he constantly communicated with the prisoners at Fort George.'[20] In October 1800, Edward Cooke received information that confirmed the 'old leaders still meet in private [and] entertain the same opinions and past hopes, but that there is no organization.'[21] This intelligence of meetings of leaders taking place, with no corresponding local activity, may in fact reflect the success of the United Irishmen's stated policy of dormancy by the lower ranks of the society.

The collapse of the peace of Amiens in 1802 renewed hope of French assistance among the United Irish exiles. Correspondingly, efforts were soon under way to prepare the disaffected in Ireland for another rebellion. On behalf of the exile community Robert Emmet returned to Dublin in October 1802 and rapidly assembled a hard-core cadre of middle-level activists. These men, many of whom were remarkably talented, included James Hope, William Putnam McCabe, Michael Quigley, William Hamilton, Malachy Delaney and Nicholas Grey. In April, Thomas Russell, a founding father of the United Irish movement as well as its most socially radical member, also returned to Ireland from France. The plans for the rising remained contingent on a French invasion, with the United Irishmen playing an auxiliary role. From March, preparations for the impending rebellion were under way in a number of counties. These efforts utilized links whose re-establishment had begun in 1800. Trusted and highly capable agents were dispatched to a number of key counties where they contacted known republicans. The conspiracy centred on the capital, where Dublin Castle was to be seized by a *coup de main*. Essential support was to be provided by the adjacent counties of Kildare and Wicklow. Yet significantly, contact also was established, albeit tenuously, with sympathizers in all four provinces. In fact, it is apparent that Emmet believed that he could count on some support in at least nineteen counties.

By early spring of 1803, the United Irishmen were expecting to rise in conjunction with a French invasion scheduled to arrive in August. As the result of an accidental explosion on 16 May at one of the United Irishmen's clandestine munitions depots in the capital, the conspiracy was thrown into chaos. With the government thus alerted, the rebels were forced to move quickly before the inevitable countermeasures could be implemented. On the evening of 23 July 1803, a hastily conceived attempt, known since as Emmet's rebellion, was quelled rapidly in the streets of Dublin.

On Monday 19 September 1803, the most significant trial in the history of Ireland took place in Dublin. No legal precedent was set, nor was the question of guilt or innocence ever in doubt. At the dock stood Robert Emmet, a twenty-five year old former Trinity student and a doctor's son. He was being tried for heading the rebellion of 23 July 1803. Far more than the rising itself, it is his closing 'Let no man write my epitaph' speech that insured his place in the nationalist pantheon. The iconic power of Robert Emmet in Irish history cannot be overstated. His name and that of Wolfe Tone are the best remembered of the United Irishmen today. Undeniably, the romantic notion that his blood sacrifice purified the Irish nation, thereby making it worthy of independence, is directly mirrored in Pearce's Easter rising of 1916. Yet Emmet's rebellion, although symbolically of the highest relevance is, in practical terms, still frequently dismissed as an organizational fiasco. Moreover, the years between the great Irish rebellion of 1798 and Emmet's rising often are ignored by historians. This perception of the 1803 rebellion as an isolated phenomenon robs it of its proper context and is patently false. In reality, like the great rebellion, Emmet's rising is part of a complex process of radical politicization and revolutionary activity extending from 1791 through 1803 and beyond. It is the critical five-year period between 1798 and 1803 that is the primary focus of this study.

Although Robert Emmet looms large in republican narratives of the past, the rising he led remains to be fully contextualized, and a comprehensive history of the aftermath of the rebellion of 1798 remains to be written. The work of Jim Smyth and Nancy Curtin on politicization, which has done so much to further our understanding of the 1790s, is concerned predominantly with the period leading up to the great rebellion.[22] Marianne Elliott's groundbreaking *Partners in revolution* is the only work that attempts to place the pivotal years between 1798 and 1803 in a national context, but the focus of her study is the entire revolutionary period between 1795 and 1803. Moreover, although she offers an excellent account of the activities of the surviving United Irish leadership, her primary concern is the relationship between the republican and Napoleonic governments of France and the United Irishmen. Elliott describes a new, inexperienced leadership emerging with a nearly unanimous view on the need for French aid in any renewed attempt at rebellion. In order to prevent government penetration of the organization (perceived as a major flaw in the mass-based pre-1798 society), the new leaders blocked all activity below the highest level and put their trust in French promises of impending invasion. This policy handcuffed the United Irishmen to a foreign power while denying the still pervasive local discontent a republican leadership. To Elliott, the resultant vacuum led to the channelling of permanent disaffection into Defenderism and religious hostility. This in turn caused the movement's leaders to distrust the rural Catholic masses and increase their efforts to obtain French assistance.[23]

The only monographs solely concerned with the post-rebellion period are Ruán O'Donnell's excellent, comprehensive two-volume study of Robert Emmet as well as his *Post-rebellion insurgency in Wicklow, 1799–1803*.[24] Important articles by Thomas Bartlett, Daniel Gahan and Michael Durey, as well as the concluding chapter of Liam Chambers' *Rebellion in Kildare, 1790–1803*, largely complete the extant historiography. What differentiates this study from the work of O'Donnell and Elliott is that their primary concern is military and political history, while my focus is on grass roots politicization in the form of paramilitarism and secret society activity.[25]

The primary sources utilized in this study include the massive Rebellion Papers and State of the Country Papers housed in the Irish National Archives. These collections consist of the correspondence of government officials, military officers, informers, local magistrates and gentry. Other noteworthy manuscripts include the Kilmainham Papers, containing reports from general officers stationed in the provinces to the military undersecretary at the Royal Hospital, as well as the Luke Cullen Papers, comprising eyewitness accounts taken from surviving rebels and others in Counties Wicklow and Wexford during the first half of the nineteenth century. A number of estate and personal papers have been utilized as well.

Also heavily drawn from are the sizable Home Office Papers, the communications between the Irish executive in Dublin Castle and its counterparts in Whitehall. Although these documents frequently overlap with the Rebellion Papers, they provide an invaluable filter that may be applied to the often exaggerated claims of local magistrates and informers. This is particularly useful in view of the highly problematic nature of sources pertaining to post-1798 popular disaffection. By necessity, the historian of the period is largely reliant on the intelligence reports garnered from informers, which fall into two broad, overlapping, categories. The first were United Irishmen, who were 'turned', frequently under the threat of capital prosecution, after the government obtained evidence against them. The second category comprised a number of mercenary spies who had penetrated the society. In both instances, the informers were under pressure to provide intelligence to their handlers, and exaggeration and outright fabrication were often the result. Equally problematic are the even greater volume of reports generated by local magistrates and gentry. While many of these individuals appear to have been as objective as the circumstances permitted, others clearly exaggerated the nature and extent of disaffection due to local political and economic considerations. For this work a key problem is the tendency of the magistracy in disturbed parts of Munster and Connaught to attribute political motivations to acts of apparently traditional agrarian resistance. Invoking political conspiracy allowed local elites to seek government assistance while excusing their own inability to deal with the problem. Finally, the general climate of fear – often shading into outright paranoia – that followed the rebellion made elements of the loyalist population and government highly vulnerable to rumour and innuendo. Every effort has been made to confirm the veracity of such sources by following the path of analysis from the local sources on to the national and imperial levels. In other words, if a report, generated by a local magistrate, was passed on with supporting comments by regional military commanders to Dublin Castle, where ranking officials including the Viceroy assessed and confirmed its validity, there is a good chance that the information was accurate. Another important consideration is the fact a conspiracy can exist without ever manifesting itself in overt incident. A prime example of this phenomenon is the extensive United Irish organization that has been proven by David Dickson to have existed in the south Munster region in the 1790s.[26] Until very recently, the regional failure to rise was viewed as proof positive that republicanism in the region was weak.

It must be stated at the outset that this study is not a political narrative of the events in Ireland between 1798 and 1803. Instead, individual counties or regions in each of the four provinces of Ireland are examined. The selection process is based on several criteria. The areas most involved in the rebellion of 1798 are the obvious starting point. This holds true for Counties Antrim and Down, the only counties to rise in the province of Ulster, as well as Galway and Mayo in Connaught. Yet in Leinster, the province most active in 1798, other considerations come into play. Kildare, at the forefront of the radical movement through 1803, is excluded because of the work of Liam Chambers. His study of that county from 1790 to 1803 effectively covers the post-1798 period in its final chapter. Similarly, Ruán O'Donnell thoroughly examines pre- and post-rebellion Wicklow. For Leinster, I examine southern Carlow and west Wexford, because this region is reflective of the state of disaffection that prevailed through much of the southeast in the years following 1798.

Part I (Chapters 1–4) challenges the still pervasive historiographical consensus that the Presbyterians of Counties Antrim and Down, who were at the heart of the republican movement from its inception in 1791, made the rapid transition from rebel to loyalist, abandoning their Enlightenment-influenced, non-sectarian ideals in the process. In fact, it is apparent that a large number of northern dissenters, particularly of the lower orders, were co-opted into the hitherto predominantly Catholic Defender movement, where they continued to actively resist until 1801. The Presbyterians of Antrim and Down, contrary to traditional historiographical interpretation, actively resisted through 1801. Moreover, the sympathies of many northern dissenters remained radical well beyond 1803.

Chapter 5 addresses the activities of a band of rebels headed by Joseph Cody and James Corcoran, who successfully operated in south Carlow and western Wexford between 1798 and 1804. It is argued here that this group is reflective of several further key aspects of post-1798 resistance.

Most significantly, the support the group received from the local population demonstrates the extent of the widespread animosity towards the state that existed in southern Leinster. In turn, this disaffection is not primarily attributable to an atavistic desire on the part of local peasants to support 'social bandits'. Instead, it resulted from efforts by the United Irishmen to politicize the region from 1797 on. An additional central role was played by the counter-revolutionary 'white terror', which persisted in much of south Leinster through 1801. This phenomenon, which had both political and sectarian aspects, ultimately crippled Dublin Castle's efforts at reconciliation with the defeated rebels. In fact, the sectarian focus of the continuing terror, combined with the excesses that preceded the rising and the horror of the rebellion itself, served to void the legitimacy of the state in the eyes of the majority of the population of south Leinster.

On 22 August 1798, prophesies of a French invasion were apparently fulfilled with the appearance of a small squadron in Killala Bay. Unfortunately, the great rebellion of 1798 had been suppressed several weeks earlier. Nonetheless, the tiny French army was joined by thousands of Irish volunteers. In the succeeding 200 years, historians have failed to explain satisfactorily what drove as many as 10,000 supposedly complacent Irish peasants to partake in such an apparently ill-conceived endeavour. Chapter 6 argues that such views oversimplify a highly complex situation. In reality, the west had experienced a period of prior politicization by the Defenders and United Irishmen, which in turn was shaped by pre-existing, regionally specific socio-economic and cultural factors. More precisely, the existence of an underground Catholic gentry with long-term connections to the continent and the interrelated presence of a pervasive smuggling culture, coupled with traditional agrarian discontent, had produced a deeply rooted, albeit unfocused, anti-state *mentalité* into which the radical organizations tapped. Additionally, the chapter closely examines the massive wave of agrarian agitation manifested itself in the region during the winter of 1798–1799. This phenomenon took the traditional form of 'houghing', or the hamstringing of cattle. Yet the existence of pockets of rebels operating in the same geographical area, coupled with evidence that at least some of the houghers believed they were acting under the auspices of the United Irishmen, makes it extremely difficult to tease out the motivational forces that underlay post-1798 agrarian agitation in west Connaught.

Chapter 7 centres on the activities of groups preoccupied with, apparently, traditional agrarian concerns in Munster. My work suggests that these post-1798 'white boys' continued to address the issues of tithes, rents, evictions and middlemen. Yet the impact of the events of the preceding turbulent decade had fundamentally transformed the secret societies in parts of Munster and Connaught. This alteration is graphically illustrated in the dramatic increase in the level of physical violence utilized by the post-1798 agrarian movements. Moreover, the long-term presence of radical emissaries in the region, combined with the heightened anticipation of a French invasion, lent ominous political undertones to these traditional acts.

Ultimately, I hope to do for the early 1800s what Smyth and Curtin did for the 1790s – to view politicization and political action in as broad a context as possible, beyond formal organizations.

Notes

1 For the Volunteer Movement, see P. D. H. Smyth, 'The Volunteers and parliament, 1779–1784', in Thomas Bartlett and D. W. Hayton (eds), *Penal era and golden age: Essays in Irish history, 1690–1800* (Belfast, 1979), 113–36, and Ian McBride, *Scripture politics: Ulster Presbyterians and Irish radicalism in the late eighteenth century* (Oxford, 1998), particularly chapters 5 and 6.

2 Nancy J. Curtin, *The United Irishmen: Popular politics in Ulster and Dublin, 1791–1798* (Oxford, 1994); Marianne Elliott, *Partners in revolution: The United Irishmen and France* (New Haven, 1982); Jim Smyth, *The men of no property: Irish radicals and popular politics in the late eighteenth century* (New York, 1992); Kevin Whelan, *The tree of liberty: Radicalism, Catholicism and the construction of Irish identity* (Cork, 1996).

3 Curtin, *The United Irishmen*.

4 Ibid.; Elliott, *Partners*; Smyth, *Men of no property*; Whelan, *Tree of liberty*.

5 The National Archive (formerly, Public Record Office; hereafter TNA), Home Office Papers (hereafter HO) 100/86/301–3, information given by Thomas Wright, Surgeon, Dublin, May 1799.

6 William Wickham to Lord Castlereagh, Whitehall, 14 Nov. 1798, C. Stewart (ed.), *Memoirs and correspondence of Viscount Castlereagh, second marquis of Londonderry*, 4 vols (London, 1848–1849), vol. 1, 444. For Doyle, also see Elliott, *Partners*, 254.

7 Mr J. C. Beresford to Castlereagh, 19 Dec. 1798, Stewart, *Memoirs Castlereagh*, vol. 2, 50.

8 Wickham to Castlereagh, Whitehall, 28 Feb. 1799, Stewart, *Memoirs Castlereagh*, vol. 2, 193.

9 For the 'New Plan of Organization', see National Archives Ireland (hereafter NAI), Rebellion Papers (hereafter RP) 620/47/100, examination of Robert Henry, County Antrim, 23 July 1799; NAI RP 620/7/74/6, James McGucken, 2 Feb. 1799; ibid. 620/7/74/11, John Pollock, 15 Feb. 1799; ibid. 620/7/74/15, McGucken to Pollock, 19 Feb. 1799.

10 NAI RP 620/53/39, 'Plan of Organization', n.d.

11 Ibid. 620/53/39, 'Plan of Organization', n.d.

12 Ibid. 620/7/74/6, McGucken, 2 Feb. 1799; ibid. 620/7/74/8, McGucken, 7 Feb. 1799; ibid 620/7/74/9, McGucken, 9 Feb. 1799; ibid. 620/7/74/11, McGucken, 15 Feb. 1799; ibid. 620/7/74/15, McGucken, 19 Feb. 1799; ibid. 620/7/74/22, McGucken, 15 Apr. 1799; ibid. 620/7/74/24, McGucken, 21 Apr. 1799; ibid. 620/7/74/26, McGucken, 27 Apr. 1799; TNA HO 100/86/179, Wickham to Edward Cooke, Whitehall, 23 Mar. 1799; ibid. 100/86/198–9, Wickham to Castlereagh, 26 Mar. 1799, Whitehall; ibid. 100/86/224, Castlereagh to Wickham, Dublin Castle, 30 Mar. 1799. For post-1798 leadership, also see Wickham to Castlereagh, 23 Mar. 1799, Stewart, *Memoirs Castlereagh*, vol. 2, 223–7; Ruán O'Donnell, *Aftermath: Post-rebellion insurgency in Wicklow, 1799–1803* (Dublin, 2000), 110–11; Elliott, *Partners*, 247.

13 TNA HO 100/86/242–3, Castlereagh to Wickham, Dublin Castle, 2 Apr. 1799.
14 NAI RP 620/47/8, information given by Henry Baird, 21 May 1799.
15 TNA HO 100/86/301, information given by Wright, Dublin, 3 May 1799.
16 NAI RP 620/46/150, Dublin, 25 Apr. 1799.
17 For the government's failure to take Emmet, see TNA HO 100/86/325, Castlereagh to Wickham, Dublin Castle, 6 May 1799. For Emmet, also see Elliott, *Partners*, 250–1; O'Donnell, *Aftermath*, 110–12.
18 Elliott, *Partners*, 251.
19 Elliott, *Partners*, 243.
20 TNA HO 100/94/56, secret information from [McGucken?] to Alexander Marsden, June 1800.
21 Ibid. 100/98/82, Cooke to John King, Dublin Castle, 25 Oct. 1800.
22 Curtin, *The United Irishmen*; Smyth, *Men of no property*.
23 Elliott, *Partners*.
24 O'Donnell, *Aftermath*; Ruán O'Donnell, *Robert Emmet and the rebellion of 1798* (Dublin, 2003); Ruán O'Donnell, *Robert Emmet and the rising of 1803* (Dublin, 2003).
25 Liam Chambers, *Rebellion in Kildare, 1790–1803* (Dublin, 1998); Daniel Gahan, 'The "black mob" and the "babes in the wood": Wexford in the wake of the rebellion, 1798–1806', in *Journal of the Wexford historical society* 6, no. 13 (1991), 92–110; Thomas Bartlett, '"Masters of the mountains:" the insurgent careers of Joseph Holt and Michael Dwyer. County Wicklow, 1798–1803', in Hannigan and Nolan (eds), *Wicklow history and society: Interdisciplinary essays on the history of an Irish county* (Dublin, 1994), 390–5; Thomas Bartlett, 'Clemency and compensation: The treatment of defeated rebels and suffering loyalists after the 1798 rebellion', in Jim Smyth (ed.), *Revolution, counter-revolution and union: Ireland in the 1790s* (Cambridge, 2000), 112–13; Michael Durey, 'Marquess Cornwallis and the fate of the Irish rebel prisoners in the aftermath of the 1798 rebellion', in Smyth, *Revolution, counter-revolution*, 128–44.
26 David Dickson, *Old world colony: Cork and south Munster 1630–1830* (Madison, 2005).

Part I
Antrim and Down

1

Antrim and Down: an introduction

Historians have traditionally considered the non-sectarian republicanism of the United Irish movement in east Ulster to have died a sudden death in the wake of the crushing defeat of the rebel armies of Antrim and Down in June 1798. The traditional view also holds that the Presbyterians of the two counties, who had been at the heart of the movement from its inception seven years earlier, made a rapid transition from rebel to loyalist often embracing the Orange Order in the process. Completing this model is the re-emergence of Defenderism, which, with equal speed, reverted to its Catholic sectarian roots.[1] The untimely demise of northern republicanism is attributed to several factors, including the increasing distrust of the methods and motives of the United Irishmen's French allies and the impact of government-sanctioned repression. Yet these factors are of secondary or tertiary importance, the pivotal role being played by the fear engendered by the denominational violence that supposedly dominated the rebellion in the southern counties, particularly Wexford. Ultimately then, the middle-class Presbyterian merchants and farmers of the North abandoned their radical political principles when faced with the prospect of losing their property, and possibly their lives, to a Catholic peasant *jacquerie*. Simply put, the alliance between Presbyterian United Irishmen and Catholic Defenders collapsed under the weight of religious animosity.[2]

Although there are slight historiographical variations, the relatively small numbers of historians who have addressed the period following the rising concur on the major points of interpretation. For example, R. F. Foster believes that news of the sectarian outrages in the South drove a large number of Presbyterians to loyalism, stating: 'when the Wexford pattern was known in Ulster, many insurgents defected or even became yeomen'.[3] Thus, for Foster, the ultimate legacy of the rebellion was sectarianism. As proof that 'the sectarian rationale had triumphed', he cites a Defender toast from 1799 that expressed the desire to mutilate Orangemen and finds that loyalism had become synonymous with Protestantism.[4]

In her ground-breaking study *Partners in revolution*, Marianne Elliott argues that by 1799 the inactivity of the remaining United Irish leadership allowed popular disaffection to flow 'into pervasive Defenderism'.[5] Elliott uses the example of William Caulfield, a Ballymoney flax-dresser, to demonstrate the process by which Catholic Defenders who had joined the United Irishmen during the mid-1790s reverted to Defenderism in the aftermath of the 1798 rebellion. She sees the low social status of Caulfield's recruits as an indication of their alienation from the middle-class leadership of the United Irishmen, holding that this 'pattern of class polarization' was repeated throughout the province. In Elliott's opinion, oaths from the post-1798 period show that the republican goals of 'aiding the French' and 'overturning the constitution' had indeed been adopted by the Defenders. On the other hand, she also feels that 'the rebellion had revived sectarianism with a vengeance', as is demonstrated by the fact that the Defenders became as concerned with taking the lives of loyalists as they were with overthrowing the government.[6]

It is in this common focus on sectarianism that the most significant oversight in the traditional interpretation can be found. For although Elliott claims that the revival of Defenderism is indeed demonstrative of class polarization, she fails to recognize that lower-class alienation was not an exclusively Catholic phenomenon. Correspondingly, there is a failure in the traditional interpretation to differentiate between the activities of the varying social strata within Protestant dissent. Elliott asserts that 'as dissenters withdrew from republicanism, the division between Protestant and Catholic became more rigid' and there was 'a corresponding flood into Orangeism'.[7] Thus, the Presbyterians are seen to have moved in a monolithic fashion from radical republicanism to reactionary loyalism in the space of a few brief months. In reality, the range of Presbyterian responses in the period following the rebellion were quite broad, and many lower-class dissenters shared the disillusionment of their Catholic neighbours with the United Irishmen's middle-class leadership.

The purpose of the first part of this book is to demonstrate that the old view requires significant modification. Specifically, there is strong evidence to suggest that republicanism remained strong in east Ulster after 1798. Moreover, it was Presbyterian radicals who were responsible for much of this continued resistance to the state.

Backgrounds

In order to understand the diverse roles played by Presbyterians in the aftermath of the rebellion of 1798, it is first necessary to examine the cultural geography of east Ulster in the preceding century. The dissenting population's political reactions to the events of the 1790s corresponded to settlement patterns, which varied regionally and often locally within individual counties. The closing decades of the eighteenth century had witnessed a period of widespread Presbyterian expansion into areas of traditional Catholic settlement in much of south Ulster and north Leinster. This migration bred sectarian disharmony on the local level, and it has been shown that Defenderism was established initially, and most permanently, in places where 'cultural frontiers' were created by this Presbyterian influx (particularly in south Armagh and south Down). Relatively recent losses of land and social status had alienated the descendants of the Catholic gentry, many of whom remained in the region. These dispossessed families remained influential with the general Catholic population and provided leadership to their lower-class co-religionists, who were themselves experiencing increasing economic competition from encroaching Presbyterian tenants at a time of rapid population growth. The most severe Defender disturbances took place in areas where the local Protestant gentry demonstrated an anti-Catholic bias by favouring lower-class Protestants both officially in their role as magistrates and, later, unofficially as sponsors of the Orange Order.[8]

In contrast to the areas of cultural frontier in south Ulster, the Presbyterian migration from Scotland to east Ulster was long term and was accomplished peacefully. As a result, little of the lingering resentment between Catholics and dissenters that existed elsewhere in the province occurred in Antrim and north Down.[9] Furthermore in these areas, overwhelming Presbyterian majorities and the relative distance from Catholic population centres helped to limit the emergence of the garrison mentality, which became so prevalent among Protestant populations elsewhere in Ireland during the 1780s and 1790s. Additionally, familial, cultural, and educational ties had carried the liberal ideals of the Scottish Enlightenment to Ulster during the eighteenth century, where they had their greatest influence on the Presbyterians of Antrim and Down.[10] At the same time, the absence of a strong Protestant 'ultra' loyalist faction and a liberal political environment appear to have facilitated cooperation between the sects in Antrim.[11] Other forces that helped to create the persistent militancy of the Presbyterians of east Ulster included the well-documented radical vein that ran through the body of the Presbyterian Church, which in turn combined with a legacy of resentment among dissenters over the second-class status that had been imposed on them (and codified in the Penal Laws of 1704) by the Anglican elite. Presbyterians were particularly incensed because they believed that they had saved Protestant Ireland from the Catholic threat of 1688–1690. Thus in the absence of significant local religious frictions, the dissenting population of much of east Ulster focused its political energy on its grievances against the Anglo-Irish ascendancy without being distracted by the sectarian concerns, which ultimately crippled the republican movement in much of the rest of Ulster. The above-described forces tended to act on all sections of the dissenting population of east Ulster in varying degrees. Yet important distinctions can be made in the motivations of the varying social strata of Protestant dissent. By the end of the eighteenth century, middle-class Presbyterian resentment was focused largely – in nineteenth-century liberal fashion – on the continued denial of political participation, which it found particularly galling in the face of its rapidly rising prosperity. The belief that English domination of the corrupt Irish parliament impeded economic development underlay the more theoretical aspects of the United Irishmen's

political thought, which was itself a combination of classical republicanism, Lockean contract theory and Painite popular sovereignty and natural
rights ideology.[12] Efforts by the middle-class founders of the United Irishmen to politicize the dissenting population of the countryside were facilitated greatly by the extremely high literacy rates of the Presbyterian lower
classes. Indeed, it has been argued that it was the indigenous radicalism of
east Ulster's weavers that was the most significant factor in the successful
politicization of the rural population of Antrim and Down.[13] Whether the
farmers and weavers of Antrim and Down were politicized by middle-class
emissaries from Belfast or radical ideology came from within, it worked on
a pre-existing hostility to the Anglo-Irish landholding class and the state
that supported it. It is here that the motivations of rural radicals diverged
significantly from those of their urban counterparts.

In the countryside differences in religion and ethnicity combined with
the egalitarian tendencies within the Presbyterian Church to critically
weaken the bonds of patronage and deference between dissenting tenant
and Anglican landlord. Additionally, conflicts between Presbyterian farmers
and weavers and the Anglo-Irish elite were not confined solely to rhetorical
questions of political status, for there were also outward manifestations of
physical violence, which can be attributed directly to social and economic
issues. By about 1750, rising population, commercialized agriculture and
rapidly expanding linen markets began to drive up the value of land in
Ulster. The coincidental expiration of a large number of leases in the 1760s
and 1770s led to an effort by landlords and middle-men to increase rents
and entry fines in order to take advantage of the rising land values. When
higher rents, rack renting, canting and occasional evictions coincided with a
severe economic downturn in the late 1760s, agrarian grievance manifested
itself in the large-scale Steelboy Movement of 1769–1773. The Steelboys
were a mostly Presbyterian alliance of cottier/weavers and farmers whose
activities were concentrated in Antrim, Down and the adjacent districts of
Derry, Tyrone and Armagh. Resistance consisted mostly of cattle houghing
and house burnings.[14]

In March 1772, the military descended on Antrim and Down in an effort
to suppress the discontent. Mass arrests followed and sixteen Steelboys
were killed in open battle with the army. The Steelboys themselves committed few acts of actual physical violence (only three deaths can be directly
linked to their operations), and popular support was shown by the government's inability to obtain convictions against Steelboys at numerous trials.
The government did succeed finally in obtaining twelve capital convictions
(ten of these in Antrim). At least seven executions were later carried out at
Carrickfergus, and although the number of deaths was low by the standards of the 1790s, their impact at the time should not be underestimated.
The executions were the first to have taken place in Antrim in ten years.
Five of the condemned were convicted for houghing near Ballymoney in
north Antrim. In 1795, Ballymoney was to found one of the first societies of

United Irishmen outside Belfast, and in 1798 its turnout during the rebellion was impressive. Lord Donegal expressed his concern over the impact of the trials on popular opinion: 'I would have wished a general confession had taken place, as it would have had a proper weight with the lower class who will be glad to have any reason for thinking them innocent and of course proclaiming they have died martyrs.'[15] The government had raised the ante on the level of violence and the lesson was not lost on the people. The flight of thousands, who feared being taken up for Steelboy activities, had an even greater impact on relations between the government and the Presbyterians of Antrim and Down. The heavy emigration of the early 1770s was due largely to economic factors, but countless others left as a result of government-sanctioned repression as 'whole villages' departed for Scotland and America.[16]

It was believed at the time that six to seven thousand families left out of fear of prosecution, and the government itself was deeply concerned about impact of this emigration on the economy. It is irrelevant that the role of the landlords and of government terror in this emigration was exaggerated. In the collective memory of the rural Presbyterians of east Ulster, the exodus of the 1770s was the result of the landlords' greed and government coercion, as can be seen in a Liberal–Unionist tract written long after the rebellion:

> [M]any things besides the French Revolution had worked to make the Ulster Presbyterians discontented. The Donegal evictions in the 1770s and the American War o' Independence were the most potent. In the 1770s, the landlords had turned out thousands o' Ulster tenants, who had for generations stood like a bulwark for them and England, to make room for others – usually papists – who wad pay higher rents, and the evicted tenants went to America w' fury raging in their hearts against the English rule that permitted the injustice ... Ay, there's nae doubt about it, the rebellion, as far as Ulster was concerned, was mair the effect o' the English betrayal o' the Scottish farmers than o' the French Revolution.[17]

The Anglo-Irish ascendancy and the British connection were held accountable for the social system, which had either driven people from the land through high levels of surplus extraction in the form of rent, tithes and taxes or acted as the agents of a terror that had forced thousands to flee for their lives. In fact, the persistence of rural lower-class Presbyterian resistance in the aftermath of the rebellion of 1798 can best be attributed to a vigorous hybrid of radical republican ideology, introduced by the Belfast middle classes during the 1790s, and less-focused but longer-term rural discontent. The United Irishmen tapped into pre-existing unrest and, along with guarantees of individual rights and participatory citizenship, they promised the elimination of tithes and the reduction of taxes and rent. The similarities between the agrarian Steelboys of the 1760s and the post-1798 Defender movement are quite striking. Contemporaries of the Steelboys stressed the pre-eminence of weavers in the movement. The Steelboys acted with military-like discipline, and north Antrim was particularly affected by the movement.[18] The most significant difference between the two groups was the Defenders' willingness to utilize physical violence. This, in turn, can be attributed directly to the government's creation of an environment in which capital force increasingly became the norm.

The immediate causes

Two central issues need to be explored in order to understand the persistence of lower-class Presbyterian resistance in the aftermath of the 1798 rebellion. Firstly, the causes of the deep-rooted Presbyterian animosity towards the Anglo-Irish ascendancy require examination. Secondly, the social fissure that occurred within the dissenting community and the interrelated breach between Belfast and the rural hinterlands of Antrim and Down bear investigation.

Social fault lines appeared in northern republicanism with the first middle-class defections from the United Irishmen in the spring of 1796, long before disillusionment with France or southern sectarianism can be cited as causative factors. Paradoxically, these initial withdrawals can be attributed to the success of the United Irishmen's efforts to expand the social base of the movement. The spectre of social revolution was raised (with the potential to overwhelm the relatively moderate political republicanism of the societies' middle-class founders) as the movement's ranks swelled with recruits from the lower orders. This fear continued to act upon much of the remaining middle-class leadership of the organization, and the resultant social tensions were compounded by the extreme caution displayed by the United Irishmen's military command in the face of the government's disarming campaign in the spring and summer of 1797. Arrests dating from the autumn of 1796 crippled the Belfast leadership while triggering further middle-class defections.[19]

The inactivity of the society's military commanders in the face of the severe repression of the spring and summer of 1797 bred tremendous resentment among the lower committees in the countryside. For, while the urban radicals may have faced arbitrary arrest, it was their counterparts in the countryside who faced the depredations of the military, Orange Order and yeomanry. A partial breakdown of central control ensued as unpopular orders from Belfast were increasingly ignored by disgruntled local committees (foreshadowing a process that was to become complete after the defeat of the rebellion of 1798).[20]

By the eve of the insurrection in May 1798, the revolutionary zeal of Belfast's middle class largely was dissipated. The combination of arrests and desertions decimated the provincial leadership and intimidated the survivors. When Leinster rose on 23 May, it appeared that the North might fail to act at all. On 29 May, already six days after the onset of hostilities in the South, the Ulster executive still refused to order a rising and was finally replaced.

Even then, the colonels of the Antrim military command refused to rise without French assistance, and the county commander resigned rather than lead a rebellion he felt was doomed to fail. In fact, it was not until a small cadre of frustrated extremists headed by Henry Joy McCracken, Henry Munro and Samuel Orr seized control, with the backing of much of the society's lower-class membership, that the final decision to rise was taken.[21] Antrim rose on 7 June 1798 and Down followed two days later. The rapidity of the defeat of the risings in Antrim and Down has been attributed to low turnout, which itself is seen as evidence of the decline of revolutionary ardour in the province due to the impact of government-sanctioned repression during the course of 1797 and the first months of 1798.[22]

Recently, Nancy J. Curtin has challenged this interpretation and has offered convincing evidence of a substantial mobilization in both counties, arguing: 'the numbers were there; it was leadership and opportunity that was wanting' and 'the persistence of rank-and-file militancy ... suggests that the organization was far more successful in producing revolutionary citizens than disciplined soldiers'.[23] It appears that the turnouts in Counties Antrim and Down must be examined in terms of class. It was the Belfast middle class, on which the foundation of the republican movement lay, that ultimately refused trial by combat. This timidity can be attributed to a variety of causes, such as the impact of Gen. Lake's disarming campaign, the fear generated by accounts of sectarian atrocities from the rebellion in the South, increasing distrust of France over its treatment of continental republican allies, and undeclared naval war with the United States. Yet an equal number of the better-off abandoned the cause because they felt there was no prospect of victory without French aid or, more pointedly, because they saw French troops as a necessary safeguard against the levelling tendencies of their own lower-class rank-and-file.[24]

It can be argued that outside of a radical core, the majority of the Belfast middle classes never intended to risk their lives or wealth in an open contest with the ascendancy and Britain. They did everything in their power to gain political participation through moral persuasion or the thinly veiled threat of military force dating from the volunteer movement of the 1780s. Even the movement's massive recruitment drive dating from 1794 can, at least partially, be viewed as an effort to overawe the government into timely concessions.[25] As Marianne Elliott describes it, when faced with the prospect of actual violence, 'the fat Belfast shopkeepers who had founded the United movement had shouldered their muskets to defend their property in 1798'.[26] The extent of the middle-class desertion and its impact on the republican cause was not lost on the people, and accounts of lower-class anger at this abandonment permeate government correspondence from the months following the suppression of the June rising.

Yet the forces that succeeded in driving much of the Belfast middle class from the republican ranks prior to June 1798 failed to have the same effect in the countryside. The provincial middling orders of manufacturers and large farmers did withdraw from active republicanism after the rebellion. But rural, lower-class Presbyterian resistance, often with the passive support of wealthier neighbours, continued. The departure of the middling ranks was reflected in the social composition of the post-rebellion leadership. James Hope, a key figure in the United Irish movement in the North, was himself a weaver, and when he brought the New Plan north in 1799, it was presented to several individuals of a similar social background. Those shown the New Plan included: Robert Henry (a schoolmaster), John Henderson (a wheelwright and United Colonel who commanded the rebel forces at Randalstown), and Robert Kirkpatrick (also a wheelwright) of Ballyclare. Robert Robinson from near Muckamore was a muslin manufacturer, while James Kerr from the Antrim town area and John Nevin of the parish of Ballyrashane in north Antrim were both farmers. Nevin, a United Captain who was extremely active from at least 1796, is the only man in this group who could be described as coming from a middling background, being a wealthy farmer with several sub-tenants.[27] The Rev. Hudson summed up the transformation that had occurred in the social composition of the republican leadership, stating, 'They are not officered as before [but] from the lower orders.'[28] A small hard-core cadre of middle-level leaders drawn largely from the ranks of the artisanate struggled to maintain some semblance of organization in the wake of the crushing defeat of 1798.

Beyond simply having less to lose in proprietary terms, what explains the sustained militancy of east Ulster's rural artisanate? The origins of eighteenth-century Presbyterian republicanism have been detailed closely in the historiography of the 1790s. Paradoxically, some of the same historians who have so efficiently charted the more than century-long development of Presbyterian radicalism are ready to see east Ulster's dissenters abandon their deep-rooted political tenants in the space of a few months during the summer of 1798. Rumours of sectarian outrage in the south supposedly led to the fear of Catholic majority superseding the Presbyterians' resentment towards the Anglican elite. The final element explaining the persistence of lower-class Presbyterian resistance is the escalating cycle of violence that dominated much of the last decade of the eighteenth century. During the rising itself, hundreds of Presbyterians were killed in open battle with government forces (the majority of these casualties occurring when defeated rebels were hunted down by loyalist cavalry in the gruesome pursuits that followed government victories throughout the rebellion).[29] In County Down, much of the town of Ballynahinch was burned after a battle, in which upwards of 400 rebels were slain. In Antrim, Randalstown and Templepatrick were put to the torch. At Ballymoney in the north of the county, the homes of anyone suspected of disloyalty were incinerated and the countryside for miles around was laid to waste. The town of Ballymena, where a committee of public safety had been set up during the rebel occupation, was plundered and a garrison was billeted on the population of the district for over a year after June 1798. Both the Catholic chapel and the

Presbyterian church were occupied by troops, and the ensuing desecrations added to the bitterness generated by having soldiers resident in almost every home.[30] In this environment, it is hardly surprising that the axis between Ballymoney and Ballymena (the regional centres of north and mid-Antrim respectively) witnessed the most enduring resistance in the North.

In the immediate wake of the rising, the prisons of east Ulster rapidly filled with defeated United Irishmen, and, as Thomas Pakenham states, 'It was the Presbyterian North that suffered most executions (according to official statistics, at any rate).'[31] Thirty-four people in the two counties were executed after trial. Countless others were summarily put to death upon capture.[32] Besides the summary executions, over eighty courts martial were held in Down alone. A large number of these men were encouraged by Lord Londonderry and Gen. Nugent, who feared the possibility that Cornwallis would grant clemency, to transport themselves to America.[33] Belfast failed to rise and, although there were numerous arrests there, it was in the countryside that, as A. T. Q. Stewart describes it, 'the hammer of justice fell on the men of no property, on the poor and unprivileged'.[34]

Notes

1   For the Defenders, see Thomas Bartlett, *The fall and rise of the Irish nation: The Catholic question, 1690–1830* (Savage, MD, 1992); Thomas Bartlett, 'Select documents XXXVIII: Defenders and defenderism in 1795', in *Irish historical studies* 24, no. 95 (May 1985), 373–94; L. M. Cullen, 'The political structures of the Defenders', in Hugh Gough and David Dickson (eds), *Ireland and the French Revolution* (Dublin, 1990), 117–38; Nancy J. Curtin, 'The transformation of the Society of the United Irishmen into a mass-based revolutionary organization, 1794–1796', in *Irish historical studies* 24, no. 96 (Nov. 1985), 486; Nancy J. Curtin, *The United Irishmen: Popular politics in Ulster and Dublin, 1791–1798* (Oxford, 1994); Marianne Elliott, 'The Defenders in Ulster', in David Dickson, Dáire Keogh and Kevin Whelan (eds), *The United Irishmen: Republicanism, radicalism and rebellion* (Dublin, 1993), 222–33; Marianne Elliott, *Partners in revolution: The United Irishmen and France* (New Haven, 1982); Tom Garvin, 'Defenders, Ribbonmen and others: Underground political networks in pre-famine Ireland', in *Past and present*, 96 (1982), 133–55; Jim Smyth, *The men of no property: Irish radicals and popular politics in the late eighteenth century* (New York, 1992).
2   For this traditional interpretation, see Elliott, 'Defenders in Ulster', 230–1; Elliott, *Partners*, 196–7, 238–9, 245–7; R. F. Foster, *Modern Ireland: 1600–1972* (London, 1988), 279–80, 285; Robert Kee, *The green flag, vol. I: The most distressful country* (London, 1972), 130–1; Thomas Pakenham, *The year of liberty: The history of the great Irish rebellion of 1798* (New York, 1969), 224, 346.
3   Foster, *Modern Ireland*, 279.
4   Ibid., 285.
5   Elliott, *Partners*, 244; Elliott, 'Defenders in Ulster', 230–1.
6   Elliott, *Partners*, 245–7; Elliott, 'Defenders in Ulster', 230–1.
7   Elliott, *Partners*, 245–6.

8   Elliott, 'Defenders in Ulster', 222–6; Smyth, *Men of no property*, 45–51.
9   Elliott, *Partners*, 20.
10 For the Scottish Enlightenment's influence on the Presbyterians of Antrim and Down, see Curtin, *The United Irishmen*, 17–18; Elliott, *Partners*, 20; Ian McBride, *Scripture politics: Ulster Presbyterians and Irish radicalism in the late eighteenth century* (Oxford, 1998); Ian McBride, 'William Drennan and the dissenting tradition', in Dickson *et al.* (eds), *United Irishmen*, 49–61; Smyth, *Men of no property*, 90.
11 For the impact of the political environment of Ulster on the development of the Defender movement, see Cullen, 'Political structures'.
12 For the sources of late eighteenth-century Presbyterian radicalism, see Curtin, *The United Irishmen*, 17–18; Ian McBride, 'The harp without the crown: Nationalism and republicanism in the 1790s', in an unpublished paper presented at the Folger Institute Seminar, 'Irish political thought in the eighteenth century', May/June 1998, 10–8; McBride, *Scripture politics*; Pieter Tesch, 'Presbyterian radicalism', in Dickson *et al.* (eds), *United Irishmen*, 33–48; Smyth, *Men of no property*, 88–91.
13 Peter Gibbon, 'The origins of the Orange order and the United Irishmen: A study in the sociology of revolution and counter-revolution', in *Economy and society* 1 (1972), 134–63.
14 James S. Donnelly, 'Hearts of oak, hearts of steel', in *Studia Hibernica*, no. 21 (1981), 44–58.
15 Quoted in ibid., 69.
16 Ibid., 63–72.
17 Andrew James, *Ninety-eight and sixty years after* (London, 1911), 84–5.
18 Donnelly, 'Hearts of oak', 7–73.
19 Elliott, *Partners*, 126–30; Curtin, *The United Irishmen*, 29, 78–80.
20 Elliott, *Partners*, 127–33; Curtin, *The United Irishmen*, 87–9.
21 Elliott, *Partners*, 204–6; Curtin, *The United Irishmen*, 265–8.
22 For the view that the turnouts in Antrim and Down were quite low, see Elliott, *Partners*, 204–6.
23 Curtin, *The United Irishmen*, 267–8.
24 Ibid., 88, 262–4.
25 Ibid., 29, 35.
26 Elliott, *Partners*, 238.
27 NAI RP 620/47/100, examination of Henry, County Antrim, 23 July 1799. For Nevin's background and role in the rebellion, see A. T. Q. Stewart, *The summer soldiers: The 1798 rebellion in Antrim and Down* (Belfast, 1995), 141–2, 249–50. For Henderson, see ibid., 75, 154–5.
28 NAI RP 620/ 7/73, The Rev. Edward Hudson, Ballymena, 6 April 1799.
29 For the Rebellion in the North, see Curtin, *The United Irishmen*, Chapter 10; Elliott, *Partners*, Chapter 6; Pakenham, *Year of liberty*, Chapter 3; Stewart, *Summer soldiers*.
30 Stewart, *Summer soldiers*, 144–63, 224–34; *Old Ballymena: A history of Ballymena during the 1798 rebellion* (Ballymena, 1938).
31 Pakenham, *Year of liberty*, 284.
32 Stewart, *Summer soldiers*, 234.
33 Thomas Bartlett, 'Clemency and compensation: The treatment of defeated rebels and suffering loyalists after the 1798 rebellion', in Jim Smyth (ed.), *Revolution, counter-revolution and union: Ireland in the 1790s* (Cambridge, 2000), 112–13.
34 Stewart, *Summer soldiers*, 234.

2

The first wave,
November 1798–June 1799

Support for the traditional view can apparently be discerned as early as August of 1798 when the surviving northern republicans failed to act on news of the French landing in Mayo, even after word of Lt Gen. Gerard Lake's defeat at Castlebar. This inactivity prompted John Pollock to write: 'I continue to be persuaded that this province is safe and completely cured of all disposition to insurrection.'[1] Yet by December, the Under Secretary, Edward Cooke, reported 'symptoms of returning turbulence' in a number of counties including Antrim and Down.[2] Similarly, the Lord Lieutenant, Cornwallis, expressed his deepening concern over affairs in the two counties in a series of letters to the Home Secretary.[3]

Accounts from both counties found the public mind increasingly disturbed; meetings were held and rumours widely circulated that the yeomanry would be disarmed and murdered prior to an insurrection scheduled for the New Year. More ominously, the disaffected felled timber, raided loyalists' homes for arms, and assassinated several persons who had given evidence against United Irishmen.[4] A number of loyalist accounts attributed the mounting violence to a Catholic prophecy that predicted a revolution by the end of 1798. Yet, this motivation was dismissed out of hand by Cornwallis, who observed that 'the predictions of an old Papist saint would not have much effect' on the largely Presbyterian population of east Ulster. Alternatively, the Viceroy was convinced that the disquiet in the North was due to an 'idea among the people that France w[ould] now make an effort', adding: 'that alone is the cause ... in Antrim and Down'.[5] Indeed, the rising disaffection in Ulster coincided with French naval preparations at Brest and the Texel during the winter of 1798–1799. This connection between continued resistance and the anticipation of French assistance shows that the republicans of east Ulster still endeavoured to pave the way for an invasion that would overturn the Irish state and sever the ties to Great Britain.[6]

Examples

On 19 November rebels burned the house of James Coleman near Doagh in south Antrim. Another band disarmed three Scottish soldiers who were travelling on the road from Ballymena to Derry on 8 December. At Tullyard in the north Down parish of Drumbo, rebels shot and wounded a weaver named Antwistle while he sat at his loom on the night of the seventeenth. This politically motivated crime was the result of Antwistle having given testimony against a United Irishman, who was hanged at Lisburn.[7] At Ballymena rebels cut the hamstrings of John Forsythe, a private in the 1st Royal Regiment of Foot, on the evening of Sunday, 30 December.[8]

By February 1799 what had been a trickle of depredations became a torrent. For example, near Antrim town on the night of the second, rebels attacked several loyalist homes. In one house they killed a man and 'dangerously wounded' a number of others.[9] Similarly at Killmurries near Portglenone, a party of upwards of forty well-armed men raided the house of an 'active' high constable (Mr Robinson), carrying off two muskets and a pistol. That same evening, the band assaulted six other homes. In one, they severely 'cut and stabbed' the owner, Luke Jebb. The group next struck the house of Mr McHenry, from whom they stole three muskets. Of these attacks *The Belfast News-Letter* reported, perhaps significantly, that the perpetrators 'took nothing but arms'.[10] As the month wore on, the level of violence continued to escalate. One group stripped Joseph Miller of his weapons near Kells, while at Ahoghill a party of well-dressed men removed seven guns and a number of swords from the home of a constable named McDonald. This band was remarkably bold in that its members made no effort to disguise their appearance.[11] Yet another party of armed men forcibly removed a blunderbuss and double-barrelled gun from the home of Edward Jones Agnew, esq. at Kilwaughter on the night of 21 February. Earlier that evening the group had forced its way into a schoolhouse, which served as an arms depot for the parish guard. They demanded weapons from the sentries and received four muskets for their efforts.[12]

In response to the escalading crisis, the Portglenone Yeoman Cavalry spent nine hours searching for suspects on 15 February. These efforts culminated in ten arrests; however, the local magistracy and yeomanry were utterly incapable of dealing with the crisis, and the regular army was relied on increasingly in an attempt to control the situation. For example, a party of the 22nd Light Dragoons captured two accused arms raiders, William Allen and John Clarke, near Kells Water on 22 February. On a more impressive scale, Lt Col. Green conducted a major sweep of the Ballymena area involving 400 men of the First Royal Foot. This nocturnal search netted 'several very suspicious persons'.[13]

Despite the best efforts of the local authorities, the attacks continued. In early March rebels burned several homes on the east Antrim coast belonging to members of the Glenarm Yeomanry, and loyalist members of that community complained of arms raids as an almost nightly occurrence.[14] On 8 March five men, their faces covered with green veils, raided Richmond Hall, the seat of Charles Rankin.[15] An extremely shocking episode took place at Crebilly, near Ballymena in the middle of the month, when a small party of rebels dragged a farmer and sub-constable, Andrew Swan, from his house, tied him to a tree and lashed him 500 times. Swan ultimately died from the wounds.[16]

The level of rebel activity was substantially lower in Down than in Antrim. Yet arms raids did occur and the northern part of the county was particularly troubled. For instance, in mid-March, at Lisburn and the surrounding districts, rebels were reported to be breaking into the houses of members of the yeomanry for the express purpose of disarming them prior to the anticipated French invasion. Moreover, correspondents claimed that the level of violence surpassed that which had preceded the rebellion.[17]

As the level violence and intimidation spiralled out of control, frantic loyalists took increasingly drastic steps to re-establish stability. In the east Antrim parishes of Larne, Carncastle, Kilwaughter, Raloo, Glynn, Broad Island, and Island Magee, local loyalists offered rewards of one hundred guineas for evidence leading to the conviction of arms raiders. Significantly, the underlying cause of this action was also the deep-rooted fear of renewed rebellion: '[W]e cannot avoid considering the daring attempts that have been lately made to get possession of arms in various parts of this county, connected with a villainous design to reduce the country to that calamitous situation from which it has lately so fortunately escaped.'[18] Similarly in Antrim, local subscribers at Antrim town provided funds to fortify the Market House as a 'safe refuge to the inhabitants in case of any future commotion'.[19]

As the security environment in east Ulster continued to unravel the central government increasingly became alarmed. In February 1799, Cornwallis found it necessary to order the regional military commander, Gen. Nugent, to 'act with vigour'.[20] The general was further instructed to place the disturbed areas of the northern district under the provisions of the Proclamation Act. Nugent duly summoned the Magistracy of County Antrim to a meeting at Carrickfergus on 11 March, at which the assembled justices 'unanimously agreed that the whole of County Antrim ... [was] in a state of disturbance'. More ominously, the magistrates requested that Cornwallis place the entire county under martial law. This petition was honoured the following day. Thus, nine months after the defeat of the rebellion the scale of active resistance in east Ulster again reached the point where the civil law no longer functioned.

Under the provisions of martial law the head of each household was required to place a list of all occupants on the door. The absence of any resident one hour after sunset, or an hour prior to sunrise, as well as the presence of any unlisted 'strangers', would expose the 'master' of the house to trial by court martial. Furthermore, the population was instructed to immediately turn in any unregistered firearms under the threat of a similar penalty. The authorities further offered rewards for information leading to the capture of those responsible for the wave of attacks. Special provisions recognized the central part played by blacksmiths and publicans in organizing and arming the disaffected. Members of these occupations who

had not already obtained licences were required to do so at the ensuing
county quarter sessions or face court martial. Moreover, Nugent reminded
the magistrates to pay close attention to the character of those applying for
such licences 'as without the greatest attention ... to this particular object,
the utmost exertions of government to restore peace and good order to the
country can be but of little avail'. Finally, any 'stranger or vagrant' was to be
arrested and examined closely by the local magistracy, and if no satisfactory
explanation for there presence was offered, they were to be handed over to
the military for sentence by a court martial.[21]

Despite the imposition of martial law, the nights continued to belong
to the rebels. In north Down on 2 April, the houses of several members of
the Castlereagh yeomanry were robbed of their arms.[22] At about the same
time, one of the most horrific episodes of 1799 occurred in the south Antrim
parish of Aghalee. There, 'perpetrators' set fire to four houses while the
residents were still inside. Three of the victims burned to death, and four
others were taken to the infirmary at Lisburn.[23] Less severely on the evening
of 12 April at Kells, 'rebels', their faces blackened, dragged six men from
their homes into the street, where they administered 'a most dreadful lash-
ing'.[24] Similarly on the sixteenth, an 'armed banditti' administered 'severe
whippings ... on different inhabitants' in the parishes of Dunaghy and Glen-
whirry in central Antrim. A short time later the same group flogged Henry
O'Hara, possibly to death, for having testified the previous June against
John Story for his part in the rebellion. Thus, at least in the short term, the
imposition of martial law failed to have the desired affect. If anything, the
disaffected only grew bolder. With remarkable nerve, armed men robbed
Cornet Burleigh, an officer of the 22nd Dragoons, of his sword and pistol at
high noon on 18 April, while he was travelling on the road between Connor
and Doagh. [25] Resistance to the rebels carried its own hazards, as two men
discovered in Donegore parish. The pair was 'very much wounded' when
resisting an attempted flogging on the night of 22 April.[26] As April drew
to its sanguinary close, east Ulster remained deeply disturbed. A new level
of barbarity was reached near the end of the month when 'a number of
wretches' hacked the tongue from the mouth of a Clough man in order to
'prevent his giving information'.[27]

Presbyterian Defenders

Clouding the picture of responsibility for post-1798 resistance is the overlapping membership of the United Irishmen and the Defenders, which dated
from the mid-1790s when Defender committees were absorbed into the
United Irish system with varying degrees of success. Moreover, the prob-
lems created by the decimation of the republican leadership of east Ulster
were compounded by the inactivity of its surviving members. The policies
adopted by the upper committees of the United Irishmen of patiently waiting
for French assistance, while preventing violent incidents, which could only

draw unwanted attention, were often disregarded on the local level. In the vacuum created by the breakdown of central control, Defender lodges with a tradition of independent action filled the void. Thus, a complex process appears to have been under way between 1798 and 1800. Defender lodges were reappearing, and by the middle of 1799 they dominated government intelligence reports of northern disaffection.[28]

However, a more subtle transformation can also be detected. Where United Irish units had ceased to function, it appears that radical Presbyterians were, in fact, being co-opted into the reconstituted Defender cells and that the sectarian ideology of these lodges was altered to accommodate new dissenting members. The Rev. Dr Cupples succinctly described this process in a report from Lisburn:

> a very considerable change seems to have taken place in the United system. The form of the obligation is altered and nearly approaches Defenderism, but is so modified as to accommodate such Protestants as prefer revolution ... to religious considerations. Persons of property and consequence are totally excluded from the present plan, because the failure of the former attempt is chiefly attributed to the timidity of that class. A line is therefore drawn between them and the people by whom the next attempt is exclusively to be made.[29]

Thus, an alternative view of the Presbyterian aftermath is suggested. In reality, the more militant of the Presbyterian artisans and weavers turned to Defenderism as a result of their disillusionment with the United Irishmen's middle-class leadership.[30] The disproportionate presence of weavers, in the examinations of those accused of swearing Defender oaths after 1798, is proof positive that the well-documented radicalism of Ulster's rural artisanate continued in the aftermath of the rebellion of 1798.[31] In fact – at least in the near term – it is more valid to describe post-1798 Defenderism in east Ulster as a class-based movement than as a sectarian one.

This process is clearly illustrated in a letter from Castlereagh to the Duke of Portland:

> Defenderism was introduced and it is principally under that organization, into which the most profligate of the dissenters have been prevailed on to enter, that whatever there is of treason in the North it is presently associated: they are destitute of leaders, and the people of substance, manufacturers, as well as farmers have withdrawn.[32]

To this, he might have added 'been arrested, transported or hanged'. The significance of this transformation should not be underestimated, for it not only demonstrates a continuing Presbyterian presence in post-1798 physical force resistance but also raises questions concerning the perceived sectarian bias of the Defenders. Instead of a uniform anti-Protestant ideology, Defender committees focused not on destroying 'heretics' but on overturning the government and assisting the French.[33] It is apparent that the Defenders in the two counties had been sufficiently politicized by the non-sectarian ideology of the 1790s to be able to accommodate Protestant membership. Further-more, precedents did exist: some Presbyterians in Antrim and Down had capitalized on the good will created by the United Irishmen's support of Catholic victims of the Armagh outrages of 1795 by joining the Defenders in an effort to further strengthen the bonds between the two radical move-ments.[34] Additionally, several young, Presbyterian United Irishmen from Templepatrick formed a Defender cell before the rebellion, having taken a modified version of the Defender oath.[35] Moreover, the evidence of a Pres-byterian presence, and perhaps even dominance, in post-1798 Defender cells in Antrim is overwhelming.

The reaction

The first Defender lodge to be destroyed effectively by the government was the Caulfield cell based in northwest Antrim. As early as 15 January the authorities had identified William Caulfield, a Ballymoney flaxdresser, as 'someone who ought to be apprehended and prosecuted'.[36] Caulfield's cell focused its efforts on swearing new members for the expressed purpose of 'assassinating' members of the yeomanry, and to 'assist the French in the event of a landing'.[37] By the end of January, six members of the group, including three deserters from the 84th Regiment, were in custody at Coleraine in east Derry. At least three of the men, including Caulfield, had demonstrated long-term radical proclivities; they had taken advantage of the amnesties offered by the government to the United Irishmen in 1797 and again after the rebellion in 1798. Thus, they faced being 'convicted a third time of having abused his majesties clemency by being most active emissar-ies in making Defenders'.[38] Caulfield, who was originally a defender, had become a United Irishmen by 1797. When, after the defeat of the rebellion, he came to the realization that the 'United Irishmen could not succeed', he reverted to the former movement and once again 'became desirous of making Defenders ... for the purpose of aiding the French in case they should land in this Kingdom, dethroning the King and overturning the Constitution'.[39] Caulfield was tried in April by court martial at Coleraine on charges of 'treasonable practices'. Gen. Nugent ordered the duly convicted Caulfield to be hanged, explaining that 'an example near Ballymoney [is] very neces-sary'.[40] Cornwallis confirmed the sentence on 17 April, and Caulfield was dead by the nineteenth.[41]

The general courts martial for Antrim convened at the Donegall Arms in Belfast on Saturday, 23 March. That day the crown presented its first case. The accused was James Hunter, who resided at Gallanagh near Glenarm on the east Antrim coast.[42] Hunter had been captured in arms at Ballyclare by elements of the Tay Fencibles on the evening of 12 March.[43] The military tribunal capitally convicted Hunter for 'treasonable practices', possession of illegal firearms and attempted murder. Yet as part of the Lord Lieutenant's effort to balance the 'necessary examples' with mercy, Lord Castlereagh mitigated the sentence to transportation for life.[44] In turn, this sentence, as was to become increasingly common in 1799, was commuted to service in the Prussian army. Hunter boarded the prison ship *Postlewaite* on 16 April. There he would sit, joined by an increasing number of fellow convicts, for four long months.[45]

Civil law never ceased to operate in east Ulster; rather it continued to complement the work of the military tribunals. In Antrim the county assizes first met at Carrickfergus on 19 March with Lord Kilwarden presiding. There, the court sentenced Henry Holywell to execution for his part in the murder of Robert Davidson during rebellion of 1798. This sentence was carried into effect on 25 March. As a final insult following the hanging, military surgeons dissected Holywell's body. Similarly in Down, the county assizes held at Downpatrick tried sixteen men in mid-March on charges related to 1798. These hearings resulted in twelve capital convictions, and at least three men, William McCaw, William Shaw and James Breeze, eventually died for their part in the rebellion.[46]

The court martial of David Woods held at Belfast in mid-April reveals much about activities of the post-1798 rebels.[47] Woods, described in the *Belfast News-Letter* as 'a smart looking young man', was accused of house burning and arms robbery. Samuel Cowie, a private in the Carrickfergus yeomanry, testified that Woods, who was armed with 'a brace of pistols' at the time, was one of two men who accosted him at the doorstep of his house and demanded his weapons. Cowie observed a larger party nearby and reported that Woods addressed his companion as 'Captain'. Under the circumstances Cowie wisely instructed his sister, who was inside the house at the time, to comply with Woods' demand. The following evening, the same group forcibly entered the home of Hugh Crymble, also a member of the Carrickfergus yeomanry. Crymble testified that Woods, upon gaining entrance to the home, 'took out money from his pocket' to pay for a window the group had broken, and 'they then departed'.[48] The significance of this simple act should not be underestimated for it proves that Woods considered himself to be acting under principled motives. Three further witnesses doomed Woods when they confirmed his participation in the burning of James Coleman's home, a capital offence, on the night of 19 November 1798. Woods, who knew Coleman, paid him a 'visit' accompanied by another man. While the little party was sitting by the fire smoking, Coleman's daughter observed a pair of pistols concealed under Woods' coat and warned her father. The terrified Coleman, who was already aware of a previous threat made on his life, managed to escape the house. Frustrated by their failure in what was most certainly an assassination attempt, Woods and his comrade burned the home.[49]

During his trial Woods declined the opportunity to 'to save his life' by giving evidence against his comrades and also refused to offer a defence.[50] In a final desperate act prior to his execution, Woods nearly effected an escape.

With the connivance of a guard, he rigged a rope and lowered himself to the ground outside his cell. Unfortunately, two passing dragoons foiled the attempt.[51] On Tuesday 23 April, following a procession that departed from Belfast at six in the morning, the authorities hanged Woods from a tree near Doagh in close proximity to the site of the Coleman house burning.[52] In the end, the affair offered stark comfort to local loyalists, for Woods refused a blindfold and demonstrated a calm bravery. Dr McCartney, a clerical magistrate, summed up the impact of the event on the local population: 'Evidences dare not come forward from the system of terror held, and from the conduct of Woods ... the party has been brought up to a contempt of death.'[53]

The military supported by local yeomanry units made several sweeps through Antrim in the second half of April, resulting in numerous arrests and the inevitable trials.[54] On 25 April, eleven armed men were captured near Doagh including two noted rebels, William Orr and Samuel Dickie. This group proved to be an element of the formidable Defender band headed by George Dickson.[55] Yet despite the arrests and courts martial, arms raids continued to be reported from nearly 'every part' of Antrim, the only exceptions being heavily garrisoned towns and the extensive estates of the Marquis of Hertford on the western periphery of the county, which had a largely Orange tenantry.[56]

Martial law did its heaviest work in May. Early that month after being found guilty of arms robbery, treason and rebellion, John Montgomery was 'ordered to serve the King of Prussia'. In Montgomery's case, many of these crimes had been committed during the rebellion.[57] Similarly, Robert McCleery was convicted for the murder of a loyalist prisoner, Robert Davidson, at Ballymena in 1798. Thus, it is evident that the authorities were using martial law to ensure convictions that might have been difficult to obtain in civil courts. McCleery, who was nearly sixty at the time, was taken for execution to the Moat at Ballymena, where two prisoners were forced to serve as his executioners. The pair hanged McCleery and severed his head, which was then displayed from the roof of the Market House.[58] Another particularly savage punishment was meted out to James Dowdall, a private in the 64th Infantry Regiment. The military judges sentenced Dowdall to a thousand lashes and transportation for life for his part in David Woods' escape attempt in April. Additionally, Dowdall was convicted for 'being drunk on his post' and for bribing another guard with 'drink'. Witnesses further testified that Dowdall was a close friend of Woods, having worked with him in a shop for two years, and stated that the accused would 'go to any length to serve him and would even go to hell to oblige him'. On the first day of May 1799, the sentence was carried out at Smithfield, where Dowdall 'received 500 lashes'. In a small act of mercy, the other 500 lashes were 'remitted'.[59]

From 27 April to 2 May, the court's attention was absorbed by the trial of John McCarragher from Dunbought, who stood accused of a myriad of political crimes. The list of accusations included arms robbery, flogging, administering Defender oaths and being in arms. One witness, Daniel McFadden, 'swore' that at twilight on the evening of 15 April, McCarragher, accompanied by a man named Hutchinson, administered the Defender oath to him outside his house. Additionally, a loyalist victim of a punishment whipping, Daniel Walker, described McCarragher's part in that event. McCarragher and another man dragged Walker from his bed, took him outside and forced him to 'stoop' while they administered 25 lashes. The motive for the attack was revealed when McCarragher and his companion stated that Walker's son (most probably a member of the yeomanry) had taken items from their friends after the battle of Ballinahinch. With a note of brutal irony, the court forced another victim, Hector McNeill, to testify against McCarragher by having him lashed a hundred times. Unsurprisingly, McNeill was then able to give the court martial the information it wanted. McNeill 'clearly' identified McCarragher as the man who had 'lashed him' in a punishment whipping.[60] Finally, two men, George Stone and George Wilson, who like McNeill obviously were deeply frightened at the prospect of giving evidence, failed to identify McCarragher as the man who had flogged them. Despite the coerced nature of the evidence, McCarragher was condemned to serve in the Prussian army.[61] Five other men were sent on board the *Postlewaite* on 5 May 'in order to serve his Prussian majesty'. These unfortunates had all had their court martial sentences commuted from death or arbitrarily been 'committed by magistrates under the insurrection act'.[62] Samuel Kelso, who had commanded the republican forces that took Clough in 1798 and who operated with McCarragher after the rising, was tried on 4 May for a full litany of crimes, including arms robbery, flogging, administering Defender oaths, being in arms, treason and rebellion. As in other cases, the court extracted the necessary 'evidence' from two men, John Gordon and William Smith, by ordering them to be flogged.[63] Kelso was duly sentenced to Prussian service.[64]

Perhaps the most important of the holdouts active in the winter and spring of 1799 was George Dickson of Crumlin, who had commanded the republican forces at Randalstown during the rebellion and went into hiding with Henry Joy McCracken in the wake of its crushing.[65] The 'strong, well-made' Dickson, who was about thirty in 1799, is a prime example of a United Irishman who elected to continue resisting actively as a Defender in the aftermath of 1798.[66] Moreover, Dickson appears to have played a leadership role in coordinating the efforts of the movement's semi-autonomous cells in the aftermath of 1798. At the very least, the authorities considered Dickson a major source of intimidation to loyalists.[67] In terms of religion, Dickson's adaptation of the *nom de guerre* the 'Northern Holt' in the winter 1798–1799 is highly suggestive of a Protestant or dissenting background as he obviously identified himself with the famous post-1798 Wicklow Protestant insurgent.[68]

William Orr of Creeve, who went by the alias Col. Green and wore a coat of that colour when he was 'out', served as Dickson's second in command. The Dickson band was directly implicated in a number of incidents including the disarming of a party of the Tays in 1798. Other episodes included arms raids on Agnew Castle and the homes of James Ferguson, esq., and Hugh Williamson, as well as numerous floggings.[69] The authorities captured of one of Dickson's men, a deserter from the royal artillery named James Mayes, who then gave information which led to the taking of eight other members of the band. At this point, Dickson offered to cease flogging loyalists and surrender in exchange for being allowed to transfer himself out of the country. Gen. Nugent instructed the local commander, Gen. Drummond, to accept this offer because of Dickson's 'great influence with the people'.[70] Yet before the deal could be finalized, members of the Toome yeomanry captured Dickson on 8 May. He was transferred promptly to Belfast and put on trial.[71]

Evidence revealed at Dickson's court martial on 14 May confirmed much about the disaffection that tore Antrim in the winter of 1798–1799. Dickson stood accused of 'treason and rebellion, robbing his majesty's soldiers of their arms when on duty, adding and assisting in administering unlawful oaths, flogging, and threatening to destroy the property of his majesty's loyal subjects, and plundering them of their arms'.[72] The testimony of James Marks, one of the witnesses against Dickson, is particularly revealing. Marks identified Dickson as the leader of a band of armed rebels that descended on the house of Andrew McDowell, where Marks was spending the night. The men dragged McDowell, a tailor, from his bed into the kitchen and bound his hands. Then, Dickson asked the tailor 'if he could dance … for he was a dancing instructor from France to teach a loyalist to dance'. The motive behind the assault became clear when members of the band stated that their 'accusation' against McDowell was the 'burning of houses'. Dickson proceeded to flog McDowell till he fainted. He then gave McDowell water and 'spoke lightly of his fainting'. Moreover, Dickson warned raucous members of the band not to break anything in the house and promised McDowell that he would 'pay him a guinea for every pane of glass' they destroyed. With that they left, cautioning that they would return and burn the house if testimony were given against them.[73]

At his court martial Dickson, like Woods, refused to inform and was described as 'very impudent' by Gen. Nugent.[74] The inevitable sentence of death by hanging was carried into effect the same day. One final horror awaited Dickson on the scaffold, for the rope from which he was suspended broke and the procedure had to be repeated. Again like Woods, he had refused a blindfold.[75] After the execution the *Belfast News-Letter* observed:

> This unfortunate man, it is said, was the intimate of Dickie, the leader of the Antrim Rebels, and it would appear had succeeded him in heading the few desperate wretches whom neither example nor mercy could reclaim, and whose depredations in this county of late gave great uneasiness to the well-affected inhabitants.[76]

William Orr, who was tried five days prior to Dickson, escaped with his life, although he was condemned to serve in the Prussian army. At Orr's court martial the primary witness for the prosecution explained that the 'prisoner repeatedly wanted [him] to become a defender'.[77]

The news of Dickson's capture and demise was of sufficient merit to warrant the attention of the upper levels of the Irish government, as a note from the Chief Secretary, Lord Castlereagh, confirms: '[A] rebel leader of the name Dickson, but known best by the title of the Northern Holt has been taken and executed at Belfast.' On the regional level, Gen. Nugent concluded that the elimination of Dickson, coupled with the 'example made of several others', meant that 'the County Antrim is nearly in as peaceable a state, as the other parts of his district'.[78]

Yet events would prove these assessments of returning passivity to be overly optimistic. On the night of 21 May, an assassin mortally wounded John Moore of Connor by firing a shot through the door of his house. Moore identified the man before he expired, and Gen. Drummond offered a 50-guinea reward.[79] An even more distressing episode took place on Monday morning, 24 May near Broughshane. A magistrate supported by the military conducted a raid on a house at Braid. His quarry was the members of a local Defender cell. Six armed men 'furnished with instruments for the purpose of whipping' were in fact discovered hiding within the home. Two of the men escaped, and the other four were taken to Broughshane and lodged in the house of the high constable, Mr Moore. A guard, consisting of the sub-constable (James O'Doran) and a soldier proved insufficient as the prisoners attempted to overpower their warders. In the ensuing scuffle, a musket discharge mortally wounded O'Doran, the father of eight children. The soldier, although stabbed several times with his own bayonet, managed to kill one of his assailants. Yet the remaining prisoners escaped, carrying away the body of their comrade. Moreover, with ominous implications for the loyalist community, no one in the town intervened during the affray, which occurred in broad daylight. Indeed, the magistrate, who had originally arrested the men, reported that the owner of the house where they were discovered ('a man in decent circumstances') insisted that 'there was not a creature there-in' except the members of his own family. The broad-based popular support reflected in these events, as well as the central role such sympathy played in the rebels' ability to survive, was summarized by a writer at the *Belfast News-Letter* in the following terms: '[P]eople who thus harbour such miscreants should be fully considered as the cause of all those direful and tragical events that have happened of late.'[80]

The courts martial slowly wound down, and the final cases were heard in late May. That month Samuel Martin Dickey, an important leader and former United Irish officer 'who had been taken in arms earlier that spring, was condemned to serve the King of Prussia'.[81] In a like manner, Hugh McVey, a member of the Dickson cell, was charged with shooting Benjamin Shelton and flogging. The more fortunate John McQuillen was acquitted of harbouring rebels and arms charges, while on less substantial evidence, the possession of a 'cartouche box', Robert Harper was sentenced to Prussian military service. [82]

Finally, for several days near the end of May, the court heard evidence against Robert McDonnell and John Eggleson for the murder of Andrew Swan.[83] Swan had been whipped brutally on 24 April by a party of rebels but lingered into May. Two local magistrates and Maj. Mannock, who interviewed Swan prior to his demise, gave a most damning testimony. One of these men, the clerical magistrate (the Rev. Richard Babbington), had administered 'the sacrament' to him. This latter fact establishes Swan as a member of the Anglican Church, furthering the argument that radical Presbyterians were targeting loyalist members of the established Church. Significantly, several members of the local community attempted to protect the accused by testifying on their behalf. For instance, Catherine, Mary and Wilson Armstrong all claimed that McDonnell had been in their home at the time of the attack, although they also seem to have contradicted each other in the specifics of their testimony. Similarly, members of Eggleson's own family attempted to provide him with an alibi, while William Dobbs, who was flogged on the same night as Swan, insisted that neither of the accused was present when he was whipped. But Maj. Mannock, who appears to have made great efforts to ensure that Swan was not implicating innocent men, sealed the case when he quoted the victim as follows:

> Yes McDonnell and Eggleson are the men who I mentioned in my examination. But oh! that Eggleson was much worse than McDonnell...Eggleson cried out, when I was a flogging, strike harder, cut him lower, hit him on the hips, it is no flogging at all.[84]

Unsurprisingly, both men were eventually convicted by the court. McDonnell was sentenced to serve in the Prussian army, while Eggleson was executed at the moat in Ballymena and his head displayed on the Market House.[85]

As late as 8 June, rebels burned two houses at Glenarm and flogged their owners.[86] Indeed, Gen. Nugent had observed a few days earlier: 'the spirit of discontent still exists in some counties of the North...the counties of Antrim, Down and Londonderry in which alone the people in rebellion last year are still in different degrees disturbed'.[87] Yet by the middle of the month, peace had been restored to most of the kingdom, and on 12 June the courts martial that had been sitting since March at the Donegall Arms were dissolved.[88] However, Cornwallis attributed the apparent placidity 'to the disappointment experienced by persons disaffected to the government in not obtaining the assistance from France which unquestionably they anxiously had expected on the intelligence of the sailing of the Brest fleet'.[89] Thus a full year after the defeat of the rebellion of 1798, east Ulster cannot be said to have embraced loyalism. Instead, persistent resistance had been suppressed by force, and disappointment over the failure of French assistance to arrive had restored a surface calm.

It is argued here that the myth of the Presbyterian withdrawal from active resistance in the immediate aftermath of 1798 is shattered by an examination of the events in the winter and spring of 1798–1799. Dozens, if not hundreds, of arms raids and floggings took place in 1799, and a number of men were assassinated, some of them literally being beaten to death. Alternatively, the authorities appear to have shown some hesitancy to utilize capital punishment, as only nine executions – six in Antrim and three in Down – can be thoroughly documented. This hesitancy is attributable to the restraining hand of Cornwallis, who personally reviewed every capital case. The government effectively did, however, eliminate fifty of the most dangerous offenders without creating martyrs by condemning them to service in the Prussian army. Perhaps, the most tragic sight witnessed in east Ulster during the long summer of 1799 was that of the prison ship *Postlewaite* slipping anchor from Belfast Lough. On board were forty-five Antrim men bound for Emden.[90]

Even the high summer was not utterly devoid of incidents. Someone shot and wounded a soldier of the Tays at Ballymena in mid-August, and the authorities found it necessary to circulate a 'Notice' which stated in full:

> As the people in general seem to have entirely forgotten that this country is still under *Martial Law*, it is found necessary to remind them of it; and to order that the regulations prescribed in General Nugent's Proclamation of 12th March; be most strictly adhered to.[91]

More importantly, a large number of Defenders, including key leaders like Thomas Archer, Robert Craig and Patrick Mitchell, had effectively gone to ground. The extremely deep-rooted nature of the disaffection that had taken hold of east Ulster in the 1790s would be reaffirmed in the first months of the new century.

The United Irishmen

Who then was responsible for the wave of violence that occurred in east Ulster during the winter of 1798–1799? As the traditional interpretation holds, a re-emergent Defenderism is detectable from January 1799. Yet responsibility for these depredations cannot be laid solely at the feet of the Defenders for there is evidence that some resistance continued on the local level under the banner of the United Irishmen through 1803 (particularly in northeast Down).[92] Additionally, the Ulster provincial leadership of the United Irishmen had not entirely ceased to function, and county committees occasionally met for some time after 1798. For example, a Provincial Committee met three times over a ten-day period in mid-September in response to the French landing in the west. This committee consisted of one member from each county in Ulster. At the first meeting an effort was made to re-establish the society's system of organization. The second focused on determining the willingness of the people to make another attempt. Gathering on the third occasion, the committee reviewed intelligence from agents who had travailed throughout the province, assessing the mood of the populace. Unsurprisingly, the counties that had failed to rise in June expressed a desire to do so after the French landed. In Antrim and Down the people had borne the full brunt of the state's wrath, and there was an extreme hesitancy to risk another trial of strength until the French showed signs of success.[93]

James Hope, the highly capable, Templepatrick muslin weaver, carried the New Plan of Organization to Antrim late in the winter of 1799, where it was shown to several of the surviving leaders in March. Indeed the evidence of the still formidable strength of the United Irishmen for some time after the rising is compelling. Thomas Watson of Belfast reported in February 1799 that he had nine regiments ready in Down.[94] In March, William Metcalf was confident that Down could rise in '24 hours'. A county committee consisting of delegates from seven baronial committees met that same month and adopted the New Plan of Organization. In April the government's sources described Down as 'the most forward of any county in Ireland'. Furthermore, it was estimated that Antrim, although 'not in so forward a state', had 8,000 men ready, even though they would only rise if Dublin were taken. Confirmation of Down's advanced state of preparation came in May when Samuel Dickey, an important leader of the Defenders and a former United Irish officer, was apprehended and revealed that County Down was 're-regimented and re-officered'.[95]

The United Irishmen appointed field officers at Templepatrick and the Grange near Toome.[96] A report from Antrim in April stated that the United Irishmen were 'ordered to be in readiness'. Spirits were maintained, and communications passed by the use of bonfires and curriers who travelled the counties on a weekly basis. Indeed, three local United Irish Directories still survived in Antrim, although only one remained fully active.[97] A Justice of the Peace, the Rev. Richard Babington, reported in May 1799 that a meeting of colonels had been held at Ballymena 'for [the] purpose of organizing County Antrim'. Five colonels from Down were in attendance, yet the republican leaders failed to establish the necessary links, and this appears to have been the last serious effort by the United Irishmen to reorganize the once formidable county.[98]

In Down, a meeting of the United Irish county committee took place at Dromore in the third week of July 1799, although it was not fully attended. A United Irishman who attended this gathering later explained to the informer James McGucken that they hoped to reorganize the county. Yet the delegates 'exclaimed much for the want of arms' and complained that Antrim was 'totally disarmed and disorganized', Furthermore, the committee had fully adopted the New Plan of Organization and 'resolved to suppress the robberies for arms and every outrage that might at all give the government any alarm or suspicion of their intentions'.[99] A remnant of this Down committee does appear to have convened as late as October 1799.[100]

The role played by McGucken, a Catholic Belfast attorney, must also be taken into account when assessing the inactivity of the United Irishmen in Ulster after 1798.[101] Despite the fact that he was self-serving and most certainly capable of telling his handlers whatever it took to keep the money flowing, McGucken, the United Irishmen's 'Attorney General' for Ulster, remained the most effective informer in Ireland. In addition, his status in the pre-rebellion organization led the new republican leaders, who were largely mid-level operatives who had survived the rising, to seek McGucken's advice on important matters.[102] In February 1799 McGucken met with Thomas Watson, William Metcalf, John Beatty and William Shaw, who were all leading United Irishmen in Down. These men informed McGucken that the people were 'busy preparing pikes' and that the anticipation of invasion was high, although there was no intention of rising until an accurate census of the disaffected could be taken. McGucken urged his handlers to make no effort to arrest these men as they remained an invaluable source of intelligence.[103] The County Down committee sent the above-mentioned Quinn to consult McGucken in late July 1799, specifically enquiring as to the likelihood of a French landing. He claimed that he had pointed 'out the treachery of the French and the little expectations now to be had'. In early October, McGucken conferred with William Minnis, a colonel from Ballynahinch. Minnis informed McGucken that the entire county looked to him for leadership. He also confirmed that the people were 'elated with [the] idea of an invasion'. Yet after speaking to McGucken, Minnis agreed with him 'as to the impossibility of succeeding without the French' and left vowing to prevent any activity that could lead to a 'partial rising'. At a similar meeting McGucken persuaded William Shaw of Warrington, who was in Belfast on mercantile business, to block 'every kind of disturbance until [the] French [should land]'. A short time later, McGucken met again with Beatty and Metcalf. Metcalf was determined to 'prevent every matter that may tend to disturb the county', for he believed that any attempted rising would 'be attended with unlimited massacre on the part of the government'. Beatty concurred, 'exclaiming he never would again turn out, unless an invasion [occurred]'. McGucken concluded this meeting with the understanding that the possibility of a revolt was remote. The following day Quinn called on McGucken and denied having encouraged rumours of impending invasion, stating that the only purpose of the county committee was to contact the radical leadership of Antrim and ascertain the republican strength of the province. Quinn explained that the republicans were incapable of acting by themselves on account of 'not having the means' or any organization, although he also felt 'they would readily do anything if they saw any probability of success'. Quinn further stated that he was determined to prevent further gatherings of the county committee, which he headed. By the end of the month, McGucken could report to his handlers that no meetings of the United Irishmen were taking place in either Antrim or Down.[104]

Even allowing for exaggerations on the part of the informer, it is obvious that McGucken was accurately describing the thinking of the surviving leadership of the United Irishmen in east Ulster. All now depended on the French, and there would not be another suicidal attempted rising without them. The attitude of the regional leadership mirrored the official policy of inactivity laid out by the National Directory in the New Plan of Organization. In east Ulster, as elsewhere, the United Irishmen had adopted a policy of dormancy.

Yet it would also be a mistake to assume that the inactivity and caution of the United Irishmen's leadership signified a rejection of republican ideology or a move to loyalism by the majority of the societies' rank-and-file. Instead, the prevalence of popular disaffection was repeatedly cited in reports received by Dublin Castle. In October 1799, McGucken also reported that 'the people no doubt are and always for some time will [be on the] look out for any matter that may offer an opportunity of taking an advantage', and the inactivity of the United Irishmen could be attributed directly to a 'want of leaders, arms and ammunition'. On the twenty-sixth, he conferred with a person from lower Antrim, who stated that the people were 'perfectly quiet, don't meet in committee, but would willingly do anything if ordered'. In Antrim, as in Down, the relative quiet was ascribed ultimately to 'the want of arms, ammunition and leaders of skill'. The informer had 'been among a number of former conspirators', including Walter Crawford, James Hyndman and William Stewart, and the news of French victories on the continent had 'elevated their spirits'. This supposedly convinced McGucken that 'the desire and inclination of revolt always remain[ed] with them'.[105]

Sectarianism

The failure of competent and astute observers to make any mention of a sectarian dimension in their accounts of the disturbed state of east Ulster is highly significant. What was often stressed was the predominance of the lower orders in continued disaffection. The loyalist W. A. Crosbie was quite aware of the need to focus on class and not religion when, in a letter to the Duke of Montrose, he denounced what he felt was Cornwallis' mild treatment of the disaffected:

> as [to] conciliating the minds of the lower Irish, Roman Catholics, or Presbyterians, I believe the attempt to be as foolish as the success is impractical. Whether we act with leniency or severity, their minds will be the same, but their disposition to act can only be curbed by punishment staring them in the face.[106]

The nature of Defender oaths from the period after the 1798 rising are proof of the political transformation which had occurred within many Defender lodges. A memorial from Coleraine in January 1799 states: 'the system of the United Irishmen has changed for that of defenderism. [They have been] binding themselves to the most horrid oath to dethrone the king... [and] assassinate all loyalists and assist the French in the event of landing'.[107] At a Defender meeting held in a field outside Ahoghill in late 1799, Archibald Campbell, a weaver who recently had emigrated from Scotland, was sworn 'for the purpose of collecting arms from those who had them ... [and] to destroy Orangemen and loyalists'.[108]

An important error in the traditional interpretation is the assumption that the desire represented in these oaths to strike at the Orangemen and yeomanry indicates the sectarian preoccupation of the post-1798 Defender movement and that hostility to loyalists had become the exclusive province of Roman Catholics. This view greatly underestimates the animosity which the repression of the 1790s had generated in the Presbyterian population of rural east Ulster. Widespread arrests began in the fall of 1796. In the spring of 1797, Lt Gen. Gerard Lake unleashed his forces on the province in a concerted effort to break the power of the republican alliance before it had the opportunity to act in conjunction with what was deemed by all parties to be an inevitable French invasion. By mid-1797 the government had adopted a policy of enlisting groups of Orangemen directly into the yeomanry. The Orange presence increased dramatically during the spring of 1798, when the government responded to the crisis environment of the period by enrolling thousands of Orangemen as supplementary yeomen.[109] This, in turn, made the identification between extreme loyalism and many yeomanry corps, or 'ultra' cliques within individual units, complete. Lake's disarming campaign of 1797–1798 was put into effect in the countryside by the military backed by the yeomanry. The massacres that followed rebel defeats during the northern rising were largely perpetrated by the yeomanry, whereas the white terror that lasted for months after the defeat of the rebel field armies can be directly attributed to extreme loyalism on the local level. It was Presbyterian United Irishmen who were the primary victims of this repression, both official and unofficial, in Antrim and Down.[110]

In fact, most post-1798 Defender oaths made no mention of religion and, in reality, an effort seems to have been made by the Defenders to appeal to the militant elements within the dissenting community. The United Irish strategy of passively awaiting French assistance and the relative moderation of their policies drove the more aggressively discontented Presbyterians into the arms not of the Orange Order but of Defenderism. This phenomenon is manifest in the evidence given by a long-time Presbyterian United Irish-man from Down, who stated under examination in August 1803: '[T]he Defender oath is vastly stronger than that of the United Irishmen. It is not an exclusive obligation as to religion, for many Presbyterians have taken it.'[111] Similarly, in communicating his fear of renewed plans for rebellion in Antrim, Mr Moore wrote, 'I believe the United Irishmen and Defenders [are] once more resolved on making another trial ... [and] that all those who were likely to be involved had taken the Defender oath.'[112] Moore made no distinction by sect, simply stating that those most likely to act had become Defenders. In May 1800, John Malcolmson was sworn as a Defender near Saintfield in central Down. His name (although attempting to distinguish sect by surname is an admittedly risky proposition) and, more importantly, his membership in the yeomanry, from which most Catholics had been purged by 1800, strongly suggest that he was a Presbyterian. The oath Malcolmson swore was simply 'to live [?] with his brethren and to obey the committee', again there being no mention of religion.[113] I am unable to find any genuine evidence of sectarian bias in these oaths until mid-1801, when at Milltown near Toome, Henry McGrogan was:

> led to a room where there was a Freemason's chair and produced a Roman Catholic prayer book and administered an oath...to overthrow the king and if ever possible he would put to death all Protestants ... [and] be true to the revolution in France.[114]

This oath was sworn at a late date and came from one of the only areas of County Antrim that had a predominantly Catholic population. It is, therefore, difficult to say whether it is at this point that sectarianism can be said to have triumphed finally in east Ulster or whether this particular case is an aberration. The term Protestant, as used in the Milltown oath, may well have referred to members of the Church of Ireland and not to Presbyterians, who were still more commonly known as Dissenters.

Presbyterians becoming reactionaries

Limitations also need to be placed on the traditional view of the 'flooding' of Dissenters to Orangeism. Although evidence of a Presbyterian movement into the Orange Order does exist, the motives behind it appear to have been quite varied and its extent greatly exaggerated. Responding to rumours that the Orange Order would rise with the United Irishmen in opposition to the proposed Union between Britain and Ireland, McGucken cautioned Edward Cooke against overestimating the scope of the *rapprochement* between republicans and the Order, stating that 'as to a reconciliation of the Orangemen and United Irishmen that I find can never take place here, the United Irishmen will never forgive them'.[115] This letter, written in March 1800 almost two years after the rebellion, further highlights the traditional interpretation's failure to recognize the depth of Presbyterian animosity towards loyalists on the local level. For many Presbyterians any migration into Orange lodges can best be viewed as an effort to shield themselves from the 'white terror', which followed the rebellion. As Thomas Bartlett notes, 'Prudence determined that a veil be cast over the exploits of those who espoused the republican cause; and the Orange Order beckoned.'[116] Additionally, just as many of the United Irishmen's recruits joined the Society prior to the rebellion as a result of coercive pressure or from the simple desire to be on the victorious side, a similar process is most likely to have served as a catalyst for the move to Orangeism in the months following the rising's defeat.[117]

In the same vein, the contention that by 1799 'the yeomanry had become

Protestantised and Orange' bears qualification because service in the yeomanry or militia was no more a guarantee of loyalty after 1798 than it had
been prior to the rebellion.[118] Intelligence received from Ballymena in April
1799 proves this point. Lt Ellis found 'some yeomanry corps disaffected'.
Significantly, he went on to state that the 'Presbyterians [were] as deep in
the plot as Catholics' and that the 'militia wouldn't stand true if the country
appear[ed] to be successful [in rising]'.[119] In fact, as late as March 1800, the
members of the Toome Yeomanry Corps found it necessary to take out an
advertisement in the *Belfast News-Letter* denying the validity of persistent
rumours that 'a number' of its men were Defenders.[120] In the repressive
environment which followed the spring of 1798, enrolment in the yeomanry
or Orange Order quite often masked a latent hostility to the government.

Yeomanry enlistments also raise several important, if problematic,
questions about the extent and timing of the Presbyterian withdrawal
from radical republicanism. Allan Blackstock shows that the Presbyterians
of Antrim and Down joined the yeomanry in two waves, initially in the
immediate aftermath of 1798 and secondly following the defeat of Emmet's
rebellion in 1803. Furthermore, while Blackstock allows that it would be
an 'oversimplification to claim all radical Presbyterians did ideological
somersaults in 1798 and joined the yeomanry and Orange Order', he argues
that when 'they did change, the yeomanry were the catalyst'. Indeed, Blackstock dates the initial phases of this process to the period immediately preceding the rebellion, citing the often-quoted letter from the Rev. Hudson
to his patron the Earl of Charlemont, which described an emerging fissure
between the Presbyterians and Catholics of Antrim.[121]

Ultimately, Blackstock's argument hinges on quantification. United Irish
membership returns for Antrim and Down at the movement's height in the
spring of 1797 show respective strengths of 22,716 and 26,153. The best
estimate of the United turnout in east Ulster during the rebellion in 1798 is
approximately 27,000.[122] Blackstock concurs with these figures, yet follows
the traditional interpretation of the risings' aftermath. He sees the yeomanry
'soaking up ex-radical Presbyterians'.[123] A fundamental flaw in this interpretation can be found in the yeomanry enrolment statistics that Blackstock
himself provides. In 1797, Antrim had 1,789 yeomen. By some point in
1799, this figure had risen to 2,872, an increase of 1,083. If, as Blackstock
compellingly argues, there was only a small Presbyterian membership in
the yeomanry of east Ulster prior to 1798 then, at most, slightly more than
1,000 dissenters can have made the transition from United Irishmen to
yeomen in the rebellion's immediate wake (disregarding the fact that a fair
number of these new enlistees were in all likelihood Anglicans, or Presbyterians, who had remained aloof from the republican movement). The
numbers for Down are similar, showing an increase of about 1,650, from
2,161 to 3,813. At first glance, these figures appear to be demonstrative of
a dramatic percentile increase in the yeomanry membership rates. Yet when
examined in an alternative light, a quite different picture emerges. Out of a

combined strength approaching 50,000 in 1797, slightly more than half the United Irishmen of east Ulster turned out in 1798. On the other hand, the yeomanry increased by a little more than 2,700 by 1799. Thus, even if all the new enlistees were drawn from the ranks of the more dedicated United men who actually participated in the rising, a highly dubious proposition, then at best ten per cent of the movement's core membership mutated from radical republicanism to active loyalism by 1799.[124] Alternatively, over 16,000 men remained in the society's military structure as late as the spring of 1799.[125] Thus, nearly a year after the crushing defeat of the rebellion of 1798, roughly six times as many Presbyterians remained members of the United Irishmen as had become, with whatever degree of sincerity, yeomen. In reality, the so-called 'soaking up' was more of a gentle evaporation.

Notes

1 TNA HO 100/81/377, Pollock to Wickham, 31 Aug. 1798. For Ulster's reaction to news of the French landing, also see ibid. 100/81/339, Pollock to Wickham, 26 Aug. 1798; ibid. 100/78/308, Gen Nugent to Gen Lake, Enniskillen, 30 Aug. 1798.
2 Cooke to Castlereagh, Dublin Castle, 20 Dec. 1798, C. Stewart (ed.), *Memoirs and correspondence of Viscount Castlereagh*, 4 vols (London, 1848–1849), vol. 2, 49–50.
3 TNA HO 100/79/276–80, Lord Cornwallis to the Duke of Portland, Dublin Castle, 21 Dec. 1798; ibid. 100/79/280–3, Cornwallis to Portland, 24 Dec. 1798; ibid. 100/85/1–3, Cornwallis to Portland, 2 Jan. 1799; 14 Feb. 1799, Stewart, *Memoirs Castlereagh*, vol. 2, 174.
4 TNA HO 100/79/276–8, Cornwallis to Portland, Dublin Castle, 21 Dec. 1798; NAI RP 620/41/98, Nugent to Cornwallis, 21 Dec. 1798; NAI, State of the Country Papers (hereafter SOC) 3249, Mr Skeffington to Cooke, Belfast, 18 Dec. 1798.
5 TNA HO 100/79/280–3, Cornwallis to Portland, Dublin Castle, 24 Dec 1798.
6 Ibid. 100/85/1–3, Cornwallis to Portland, 2 Jan. 1799; ibid. 100/85/259, Cornwallis to Portland, 23 Feb. 1799; ibid. 100/79/292, Cooke to Wickham, Dublin Castle, 29 Dec. 1798; ibid. 100/85/287, Cooke to Wickham, Dublin Castle, 28 Feb. 1799; Wickham to Castlereagh, Whitehall, 28 Feb. 1799, Stewart, *Memoirs Castlereagh*, vol. 2, 193.
7 *The Belfast News-Letter* (hereafter *BNL*), 21 Dec. 1798.
8 *BNL*, 8 Jan. 1799.
9 Ibid.; ibid., 22 Feb. 1799.
10 Ibid., 26 Feb. 1799.
11 Ibid.
12 Ibid.
13 Ibid.
14 NAI RP 620/46/79, Mr Moore to Castlereagh, 16 Mar. 1799; *BNL*, 15 Mar. 1799.
15 *BNL*, 12 Mar. 1799.
16 Ibid., 22 Mar. 1799; ibid., 4 May1799; ibid. 7 June 1799.
17 TNA HO 100/86/246–8, The Rev. Dr Cupples, Lisburn, 13 Mar. 1799.

18 Ibid., 1 Mar. 1799.
19 Ibid., 26 Feb. 1799.
20 TNA HO 100/85/287, Cooke to Wickham, Dublin Castle, 28 Feb. 1799.
21 *BNL*, 12 Mar. 1799; ibid., 15 Mar. 1799; TNA HO 100/93/140–1, Cornwallis to Portland, Dublin Castle, 11 Mar. 1799.
22 *BNL*, 5 Apr. 1799.
23 Ibid., 16 Apr. 1799.
24 NAI RP 620/46/136A, Hudson, Portglenone, 15 Apr. 1799; *BNL*, 16 Apr. 1799.
25 *BNL*, 19 Apr. 1799.
26 TNA HO 100/86/353, Nugent, Armagh, 26 Apr. 1799; *BNL*, 26 Apr. 1799.
27 *BNL*, 30 Apr. 1799.
28 TNA HO 100/89/47, Nugent, Armagh, 3 June 1799; NAI RP 620/46/79, Moore to Castlereagh, Ballydivity, 16 Mar. 1799; TNA HO 100/86/1–3, information given by Wright, May 1799.
29 NAI RP 620/7/73, Cupples, Lisburn, 19 Mar. 1799; TNA HO 100/86/246–8, Cupples, Lisburn, 19 Mar. 1799.
30 NAI RP 620/49/12, examination of Archibald Campbell, Weaver, County of Antrim, Sept. 1799, enclosed in Brig. Gen. Drummond, 12 Mar. 1800; ibid., examination of Henry O'Hara, 17 Feb. 1800; ibid., 620/58/79, examination of John Malcomson, County Down, enclosed in Mr Price to Castlereagh, 14 Aug. 1800.
31 For varying interpretations of the ideological and economic origins of rural Presbyterian radicalism, see Nancy J. Curtin, 'Ideology and materialism: Politicization and Ulster weavers in the 1790s', in Marilyn Cohen (ed.), *The warp of Ulster's past: Interdisciplinary perspectives on the Irish linen industry, 1700–1920* (New York, 1997), 111–38; Peter Gibbon, 'The origins of the Orange order and the United Irishmen: A study in the sociology of revolution and counter-revolution', in *Economy and society* 1 (1972) 135–63.
32 TNA HO 100/87/3, Castlereagh to Portland, 3 June 1799.
33 NAI RP 620/58/79, exam of Malcomson, County Down, enclosed in Price to Castlereagh, 14 Aug. 1800; ibid. 620/59/77, exam of Henry McGrogan, private in the Antrim Regiment of militia, Nov. 1801.
34 Curtin, 'Transformation of United Irishmen', 486.
35 T. Q. Stewart, *The summer soldiers: The 1798 rebellion in Antrim and Down* (Belfast, 1995), 74.
36 National Library Ireland (hereafter NLI), Kilmainham Papers (hereafter KP), MS 1207, Marsden to Lt Col Littlehales, Dublin Castle, 21 Jan. 1799.
37 NAI SOC 1018/15.
38 Ibid., 'Memorial of the town and magistrates and gentlemen of the town and neighborhood of Coleraine in Counties Londonderry and Antrim,' 28 Jan. 1799.
39 NAI RP 620/46/38, McNaughten to Castlereagh, 15 Feb. 1799; TNA HO 100/86/352, Nugent, Armagh, 22 Apr. 1799.
40 NLI KP MS 1207, 3, E. A. Naghton, esq. to Littlehales, 15 Apr. 1799.
41 Ibid. MS 1199, 44, proceeding of general court martial at Coleraine, Col Lord Murray presiding in Dublin Castle, Littlehales to Nugent, 17 Apr. 1799; *BNL*, 19 Apr. 1799.
42 *BNL*, 26 Mar. 1799.

43 Ibid., 15 Mar. 1799.
44 NLI KP MS 1199, 11, Maj. Gen. Nugent.
45 *BNL*, 16 Apr. 1799. The eleven other men were Gawn Watt, James McCaw, Alexander Finley, Henry Fleming, John Moffat, Hugh Devlin, David Bell, Benjamin Crocket, Thomas Dobson, William Ellison and Robert Robinson.
46 McCaw, Shaw, and Breeze were hanged at Downpatrick on Sat., 23 Mar. The executions of Hugh McMullan, James Collins, Andrew Marrow, James Marrow, Robert Glover, David McKelvy, and James Hewitt were postponed until 6 June and may well have been commuted to transportation. *BNL*, 22 Mar. 1799; ibid., 26 Mar. 1799; ibid., 2 Apr. 1799.
47 Ibid., 26 Apr. 1799.
48 Ibid., 26 Apr. 1799; NLI KP MS 1199, 351, proceedings of general courts martial, Belfast; *BNL*, 23 Apr. 1799; ibid., 23 Apr. 1799; ibid., 26 Apr. 1799.
49 Ibid., 26 Apr. 1799.
50 TNA HO 100/86/355–6, Dr McCartney, Antrim, 3 May 1799; NAI RP 620/7/73, McCartney, Antrim, 3 May 1799; NLI KP, MS 1199, 351, proceedings of general courts martial, Belfast; *BNL*, 26 Apr. 1799.
51 *BNL*, 26 Apr. 1799.
52 Ibid; ibid., 30 Apr. 1799.
53 TNA HO 100/86/355–6, McCartney, Antrim, 3 May 1799; NAI RP 620/7/73, McCartney, Antrim, 3 May 1799.
54 Ibid. 620/47/100, examination of Henry, County Antrim, 23 July 1799. For the prevalence of deserters in the resistance during the winter of 1798–1799, also see NAI SOC 1018/15, 'Memorial of the town and magistrates and gentlemen of the town and neighborhood of Coleraine in Counties Londonderry and Antrim,' 28 Jan. 1799; TNA HO 100/86/352, Nugent, Armagh, 22 Apr. 1799.
55 *BNL*, 30 Apr. 1799.
56 NAI RP 620/7/73, Nugent, County Antrim, 10 May 1799; TNA HO 100/93/140–1, Cornwallis to Portland, Dublin Castle, 11 Mar. 1799; ibid., 100/86/242–3, Castlereagh to Wickham, Dublin Castle, 2 Apr. 1799.
57 *BNL*, 7 May 1799.
58 Ibid.; ibid., 14 May 1799. The Antrim assizes had already convicted Henry Holywell and acquitted John McCleery in relation to the Davidson case(see *BNL*, 26 Mar. 1799).
59 Ibid. , 7 May 1799.
60 Ibid.
61 Ibid.
62 Ibid. The five were John Hutchinson, William Allen, Thomas Dick, Thomas White and Arthur Kenny.
63 Ibid.
64 Ibid., 31 May 1799.
65 Dickson also remained with Henry Joy McCracken after the defeat of the main rebel armies. For his role in the rebellion, see Charles Dickson, *Revolt in the North, Antrim and Down in 1798* (Dublin, 1960), 129, 130, 234 and Stewart, *Summer soldiers*, 103, 162–3.
66 For the physical description of Dickson, see *BNL*, 17 May 1799.
67 Ibid.
68 For reference to Dickson as the 'Northern Holt', see TNA HO 100/86/415–6, Castlereagh to Wickham, Dublin Castle, 22 May 1799, and NLI KP MS 1190, 353, Belfast, 14 May 1799.

69　*BNL*, 17 May 1799.
70　NAI RP 620/7/73, Nugent, County Antrim, 10 May 1799; TNA HO 100/88/340, Nugent, County Antrim, 10 May 1799.
71　Ibid., Nugent, County Antrim, 13 May 1799.
72　*BNL*, 17 May 1799.
73　Ibid.
74　TNA HO 100/88/340, Nugent, County Antrim, 13 May 1799. Dickson was convicted of 'robbing soldiers of their arms' on 14 May 1799. Cornwallis confirmed the sentence which was duly carried into effect; NLI KP MS1190, 353, Nugent, Belfast, 14 May 1799.
75　*BNL*, 17 May 1799.
76　Ibid.
77　Ibid.
78　TNA HO 100/86/415–16, Castlereagh to Wickham, Dublin Castle, 22 May 1799.
79　*BNL*, 24 May 1799; ibid., 7 June 1799.
80　Ibid., 31 May 1799.
81　Ibid.
82　Ibid.
83　Ibid.
84　Ibid., 7 June 1799.
85　Ibid., 18 June 1799.
86　Ibid., 14 June 1799.
87　TNA HO 100/89/47, Nugent, Armagh, 3 June 1799; ibid. 100/86/433–4, Castlereagh to Wickham, Phoenix Park, 26 May 1799. For these trials, see NLI KP MS 1201, 131–9, Marsden to Littlehales, Dublin Castle, proceedings of general courts martial at Belfast, 28 Jan. 1801.
88　Ibid., 14 June 1799.
89　TNA HO 100/89/41, Cornwallis to Portland, 12 June 1799.
90　*BNL*, 13 Aug. 1799.
91　Ibid.
92　NAI SOC 1018/15, 'Memorial of the town and magistrates and gentlemen of ... Coleraine', 28 Jan. 1799; NAI RP 620/49/11, McGucken, Belfast, 30 Mar. 1800; ibid. 620/80/89, Drummond, Belfast, 2 Mar. 1801; TNA HO 100/112/402–8, notes of secret information given to the Rev. Thomas Beatty, Vicar General and a magistrate of County Down, 17 Aug. 1803. On 19 Apr. 1800, the County Down assizes sentenced Patrick Savage to six months' imprisonment for attempting to swear James McCleland into the United Irishmen. *BNL*, 22 Apr. 1800.
93　NAI RP 620/40/133, 5 Oct. 1798.
94　Ibid. 620/7/74/6, McGucken, 2 Feb. 1799. For Watson, also see ibid. 620/7/74/16, McGucken, 3 Mar. 1799.
95　For estimates of United Irish strength, see TNA HO 100/86/355–6, McCartney, Antrim, 3 May 1799; NAI RP 620/7/73, McCartney, Antrim, 3 May 1799; ibid. 620/46/136A, Lt Ellis, Ballymena, enclosed in Hudson, Portglenone, 15 Apr. 1799. Metcalf was remarkably active and remained a primary, if inadvertent, source of intelligence for McGucken well into 1803. He served as a link for McGucken not only to the United Irishmen of County Down but to the Defenders as well. Metcalf was in fact heavily involved in Emmet's Rebellion in 1803; see Michael MacDonagh (ed.), *The Viceroy's post-bag: The correspond-*

*ence hitherto unpublished of the Earl of Hardwicke, the first Lord Lieutenant
after the union* (London, 1904), 274–7, 414–16. For his membership in the
Defender Movement, see NAI RP 620/7/74/18, McGucken, 14 Mar. 1799; ibid.
620/10/118/15, McGucken, Belfast, 3 July 1801.

96 Ibid. 620/7/73, McCartney, Antrim, 3 May 1799; TNA HO 100/86/355–6,
McCartney, Antrim, 3 May 1799.

97 NAI RP 620/ 7/73, Hudson, Ballymena, 6 Apr. 1799; TNA HO 100/86/27,
Hudson, Ballymena, 6 Apr. 1799.

98 Ibid. 100/86/27, McCartney, Antrim, 3 May 1799; ibid. 100/86/355–6,
McCartney, Antrim, 3 May 1799.

99 Ibid. 100/87/97, McGucken, Belfast, 30 July 1799.

100 NAI SOC 3363/2, McGucken, 12 Oct. 1799.

101 NAI RP 620/48/3, McGucken, Belfast, 4/5 Oct. 1799; NAI SOC 3363/1,
McGucken, 11 Oct. 1799; ibid. 3363/2, McGucken, 12 Oct. 1799.

102 For McGucken's status in the United Irishmen and effectiveness as an in former,
see Thomas Bartlett (ed.), *Revolutionary Dublin, 1795–1801: The letters of
Francis Higgins to Dublin Castle* (Dublin, 2003).

103 NAI RP 620/7/74/14, McGucken, Belfast, 28 Feb. 1799; ibid. 620/7/74/16,
McGucken, 3 Mar. 1799.

104 Ibid. 620/48/3, McGucken, Belfast, 4/5 Oct. 1799; ibid. 620/48/15, McGucken,
26 Oct. 1799; NAI SOC 3363/1, McGucken, 11 Oct. 1799; ibid. 3363/2,
McGucken, 12 Oct. 1799. Both John Beatty and Miniss had been members
of the County Down committee of United Irishmen prior to the rebellion, see
Dickson, *Revolt*, 159.

105 Ibid.

106 W. A. Crosbie to the Duke of Montrose, 25 Dec. 1798, *The manuscripts of J.
B. Fortescue, esq.* preserved at Dropmore, 4 vols (London, 1892–1894), vol. 4,
424.

107 NAI SOC 1018/15, 'Memorial of the town and magistrates and gentlemen … of
Coleraine,' 28 Jan. 1799; also see NAI RP 620/46/14, examination of Daniel
McFadden, Ballymoney labourer and examination of Daniel Curry of Pros-
pect Ballymoney, 15 Jan. 1799; ibid. 620/46/38, examination of McFadden and
Curry.

108 Ibid. 620/49/12, examination of Campbell of Ahoghill, Weaver, 10 Jan. 1800,
enclosed in Drummond, 12 Mar. 1800. Campbell was administered the Defender
oath by Thomas Caskey; a short time later Campbell attended a Defender meeting at Glebe. Also in attendance at this meeting were Thomas Caskey, William
Small, John Caskey, Alexander McDonnell and Robert Reaney (all Antrim
weavers).

109 Allan Blackstock, 'The social and political implications of the raising of the
yeomanry in Ulster: 1796–1798', in David Dickson, Dáire Keogh and Kevin
Whelan (eds), *The United Irishmen: Republicanism, radicalism and rebellion*
(Dublin, 1993), 242–3; Allan Blackstock, *An ascendancy army: The Irish yeomanry, 1796–1834* (Dublin, 1998), particularly 75–97.

110 For repression in the North both during and after the rebellion, see Nancy J.
Curtin, *The United Irishmen: Popular politics in Ulster and Dublin, 1791–1798*
(Oxford, 1994), 275–6; Marianne Elliott, *Partners in revolution: The United
Irishmen and France* (New Haven, 1982), 206, 237–8; Thomas Pakenham, *The
year of liberty: The history of the great Irish rebellion of 1798* (New York,
1969), 222, 228–31, 284; Stewart, *Summer soldiers*, 139, 145–7, 155–6, 216–

17, 223–64; Dickson, *Revolt*. For the yeomanry's role in the repression that preceded the rising, see Blackstock, *Ascendancy army*, 240–1.

111 TNA HO 100/112/407, notes of secret information given to Beatty, Vicar General and a magistrate of County Down, 17 Aug. 1803.

112 NAI RP 620/46/79, Moore to Castlereagh, 16 Mar. 1799.

113 Ibid. 620/58/79, examination of Malcomson, County Down, enclosed in Price to Castlereagh, 14 Aug. 1800.

114 Ibid. 620/59/77, examination of McGrogan, private in the Antrim Regiment of militia, Nov. 1801.

115 Ibid. 620/49/11, McGucken to Cooke, Belfast, 3 Mar. 1800; also see ibid., McGucken to Cooke, 9 Mar. 1800.

116 Thomas Bartlett, *The fall and rise of the Irish Nation: The Catholic question, 1690–1830* (Savage, MD, 1992), 239.

117 Curtin, *The United Irishmen*, 120–6, 277–9.

118 Foster, *Modern Ireland: 1600–1972* (London, 1988), 285.

119 NAI RP 620/46/136A, Ellis, Ballymena, enclosed in Hudson, Portglenone, 15 Apr. 1799.

120 *BNL*, 8 Apr. 1800.

121 Blackstock, *Ascendancy army*, 117, 136, 242, 274–5.

122 Curtin, *The United Irishmen*, 68–70, 277.

123 Blackstock, *Ascendancy army*, 242, 274.

124 Ibid., 117.

125 NAI RP 620/7/74/6, McGucken, 2 Feb. 1799. Also see, ibid. 620/7/74/116, McGucken, 3 Mar. 1799; TNA HO 100/86/355–6, McCartney, Antrim, 3 May 1799; NAI RP 620/7/73, McCartney, Antrim, 3 May 1799; ibid. 620/46/136A, Ellis, Ballymena, enclosed in Hudson, Portglenone, 15 Apr. 1799.

3

The second wave: active resistance, 1799–1800

The long winter nights of 1799–1800 witnessed the widespread return of flogging, arms raids and assassinations to rural east Ulster, proving the continued disaffection of a substantial element of the regions population.[1] In mid-December, Thomas Whinnery, the postmaster at Belfast, reported that in parts of Antrim 'loyal persons' were being assassinated 'almost daily', and he compared the conduct of the people to that which had preceded the rebellion in June 1798.[2] Whinnery was referring most certainly to the recent murders of James Love and Joseph Kelso. Armed men had dragged Love, a well-to-do farmer, from his home near Ballymena and shot him before the eyes of his father and sister on the night of 5 December. Kelso, a sergeant in the Carnmoney supplementary yeomanry, who was serving on attached duty with the Templepatrick yeomanry, was killed on the night of 12 December. This assassination was a politically tainted revenge killing carried out by the members of a Defender lodge in retaliation for the slaying of a man named William Brookmyers at the Roughfort Fair by another yeoman.[3] These deaths were not isolated incidents; the same night that Sgt Kelso was murdered, parties unknown shot a man named McKenna at Kells; while less lethally, an armed band forced its way into the house of John Harper, also at Kells, and removed a sword, pistol and gunpowder.[4]

The government took a number of steps in response to the escalating crisis. On the morning of Sunday 28 December several companies of regulars supported by units of the local yeomanry 'scoured' the south Antrim parish of Carnmoney in search of the men who had murdered Sgt Kelso. This sweep resulted in seven arrests.[5] Meanwhile, as the result of 'the frequency of the murders' in central Antrim, Capt. Hudson of the Portglenone Yeomanry recommended a thorough 'scouring' of the Ballymena area. Hudson, a hard line loyalist, had obtained intelligence revealing the location of a number of safe houses where the 'gangs which ha[d] lately infested this part of the country' sheltered at night. In response to Hudson's request, Gen. Drummond instructed the Tayshire regiment to conduct raids on suspected houses in the region. On New Year's Eve 1799 at three o'clock in the morning, the 'whole Tayshire' accompanied by guides drawn from the local yeomanry marched out of Ballymena. Prior to sunrise sections of two or three soldiers burst into the suspected homes, and a general search of the properties commenced at first light. In one of the cabins a yeomanry sergeant claimed to recognize an occupant as a member of a band that had knocked him to the ground and taken his sword. The soldiers then searched the home, dislodging some of the thatch from the roof in the process, which as the *Belfast News-Letter* related then 'unfortunately took fire and before it could be extinguished, consumed that and the adjoining cabin'. An 'accidental' house burning such as this can only have added to the existing tensions between the region's people and the military. Ultimately, the soldiers brought in thirteen prisoners as a result of the New Year's Eve raids. Several of these men were accused of harbouring rebels, one of flogging and another of having a stolen gun concealed in the thatch of his roof (this weapon, bearing the 'mark and number' of the regiment, had been taken from a party of the Tays' 'wayfared' on the road in December 1798).[6]

Beyond general searches, the primary step taken by the regional military command was to station small detachments of regulars in the towns of central Antrim. By early January 1800 elements of the Tayshire had been placed at Kells, Randalstown, Ahoghill, and Broughshane.[7] Yet despite these efforts, the security environment in Antrim, where 'robberies of arms ... attended with much ill usage; and murders [were] not infrequent' remained volatile.[8] In mid-January following a large and remarkably well-organized series of arms raids carried out by the Defenders in central Antrim, Gen. Drummond ordered the Tays to transfer their headquarters from Belfast to Ballymena. Moreover, the government deemed it prudent to dispatch reinforcements to the region. These, in the form of the Dunbartonshire fencible regiment, arrived from Cork in early March.[9]

As the security situation continued to unravel, Drummond conducted a thorough inspection of the district under his command and was dismayed to discover 'from the unvaried representations everywhere made by the gentlemen, magistrates and many farmers ... [that a] ... universal panic prevailed'. Furthermore, loyalists 'earnestly' implored him to protect them from 'the Banditti that infest[ed] them'. Many loyalists found it necessary to stay up throughout the night on watch. More ominously, others fled their homes entirely and sought refuge at military posts. Pro-government weavers removed the webs from their looms in a desperate attempt to save their livelihoods and carried them with them to garrisoned towns. In fact, the crisis was so severe that Drummond warned his superiors, 'it cannot continue long thus; they must abandon their farms and looms, lose their lives or join their tormentors – indeed their situation is truly pitiable'.[10]

From Ballymoney in north Antrim, Col. Munbe, commander of the Armagh militia, and Mr Hutchinson, a local magistrate, reported the existence of a 'conspiracy' throughout the area. In this instance, popular resistance took the form of an economic boycott, which targeted both local loyalists and the military. Indeed, the ability to effectively block the sale of potatoes, meal and general provisions 'to any loyal man or the army' on a regional basis is perhaps the clearest single indication of the extent of the prevailing disaffection in east Ulster in 1800. Furthermore, well-disposed people dared not testify against the rebels and risked 'assassination if they brought [foodstuffs] to the market or let the military have them'. Some loyalists went so far as to request that the military go through the pretence of confiscating the required goods so as not to draw the wrath of their neighbours.[11] Thus, politics and economy had become one, and loyalists and the government were at a disadvantage because of it. Finally, a meeting of the Grand Jury of County Antrim was held at Ballymena on 13 January, where the assembled magistrates reported: 'the dangerous banditti ... has forced many families to leave the country at great expense, to look for protection in such towns as are defended by the army'.[12] This exodus is perhaps the most important one of the untold story of the aftermath of 1798 in the north. It establishes with crystalline clarity the depth of the animosity felt by the rural majority towards the pro-government elements in their midst. In reality it is apparent that as late as 1800, loyalists, not former republicans, were the hunted minority in east Ulster. Musgrave and the government could not afford to tell this tale because the truth of the matter was that it was Presbyterians who were driving members of the established Church from the land. This, in turn, did not fit well with their efforts to build a post-rebellion Protestant consensus.

Indeed, the impact of the repression that dated from the fall of 1796 on east Ulster's Presbyterians should not be underestimated. The agents of this terror on the local level were most commonly an indistinguishable amalgam of Orangemen and the yeomanry. As Allan Blackstock notes in his comprehensive *An ascendancy army*, prior to the rebellion, 'the initial tardy enlistment and low volunteer-yeomanry continuity in Down and Antrim, areas of heavy Presbyterian settlement, points to the de-facto exclusion of dissenters [from the yeomanry] in eastern Ulster'.[13] At the same time, radical elements of the Presbyterian population worked to block enlistment from within. Moreover, this latter phenomenon persisted through at least 1800. For example, Hugh Beatty, a United officer during the 1798 rebellion, was 'taken up' at Ballymena in January 1800 for having 'made use of every means to discourage the enrolling of the yeomanry in this town'.[14] Additionally, the landlords who bore responsibility for raising the yeomanry corps wisely were reluctant to recruit from amongst their Presbyterian tenantry.[15] Therefore, in 1799 the number of yeomen in the two counties still grossly under-represented their respective populations. In Antrim, the ten corps that had been established by 1798 were concentrated on the southern and western peripheries of the county, closely corresponding to areas of Episcopalian settlement.[16] This phenomenon, in turn, raises important questions about the nature of sectarian animosity in east Ulster during the second half of the eighteenth century. In fact, it appears that the primary religious tension in much of the region was not between Catholic and Presbyterian but between members of the established Church and Dissenters. Until recently, the overt hostility between the two groups has been consistently underestimated or ignored by historians. These 'Scottish–English' divides continued into the nineteenth century. It hardly is coincidental that the sizable Hertford estates of southwest Down, with their predominantly Anglo-Irish tenantry, were a hot bed of Orangeism. Moreover in 1798, these estates provided approximately thirty per cent of County Antrim's yeomanry corps, making complete the correlation between extreme loyalism and membership in a number of individual yeomanry corps. Finally, the role played by several of these corps in the repression that both preceded and followed the rebellion can only have served to accentuate pre-existing animosities.[17]

Faced with a near total loss of control of areas outside of the towns, Gen. Drummond deemed it 'necessary to do something to raise the spirits of the loyalists and convince them, and the opposite party too, that government have not abandoned their friends'. Therefore, Drummond mobilized elements of the yeomanry and dispersed them throughout a number of smaller towns in central Antrim. Furthermore, he recommended that troops be dispatched to Kilrea, in heavily Presbyterian east Derry, explaining to his superiors that there was 'not a soldier from Coleraine to Toome on that side of the Bann'. He added:

> I have reason to think … that part of the County Derry is very badly disposed, many of the depredators from thence to join in Antrim, the whole when pursued, taking refuge in Derry. The region had never been disarmed; [and therefore,] it is now considered … to be a depot for … the disaffected.

In an effort to contain these cross-river movements, Drummond ordered fishing boats to be placed under guard along the length of the Bann.[18]

Lt Gen. William Gardiner, who bore responsibility for the entire northern military region, also found cause for 'much concern' over the state of affairs in Antrim. He agreed with his subordinate's plan to place the entire regional yeomanry on permanent duty, thereby 'securing the entire county at the same time'. This measure was required because, as Gardiner bluntly observed, 'There [wa]s scarcely sufficiency of troops to keep such an extent of country quiet, so long as a spirit of disaffection … prevail[ed]'.[19] The authorities played their final card on 23 January when, for the fourth time in as many years, Antrim was placed under martial law.[20] In the winter of 1800, the most disaffected county in Ireland was Antrim.

Responsibility and the Defender system

Cornwallis directly attributed the 'considerable mischief' occurring in east Ulster to 'a formidable banditti of the defenders'.[21] An example of the composition of a Defender cell came in late December 1799 when, 'in consequence of some strong information', a party of soldiers dispatched from Belfast brought in eight men from the parish of Carnmoney who were 'strongly suspected' in the (previously discussed) murder of Sgt Kelso.[22]

The individuals in question included Duncan McAlish (a calico glazier), Felix Reed and William Graham (servants of a Mr James Marshall), and James Smyth (Mr Marshall's nephew). Also arrested were John McCrum (a weaver), Samuel McCrum, Patrick Gilmore and Henry Fullerton. William Mitchell (a mason and slater), testified against the group, stating that McAlish, who had on a previous occasion attempted to swear him to the Defender oath, admitted, after having drunk 'a good deal', to his presence at the murder. Confirmation of Mitchell's statement was provided by a Mr William Graham, a partner in the House of Graham and Hunter.[23] Two Justices of the Peace, the Sovereign of Belfast John Brown, esq. and William Fox, esq., committed the eight men to prison on 11 March, because they 'did conspire and were privy to the murder of Mr. Joseph Kelso ... and [were] ... otherwise known to be of infamous wicked character'. This was done under the provisions of the Insurrection Act 'in hopes' of having them removed from the country. It is apparent that the intention was to have the group condemned to general service as they were examined by a staff surgeon and found fit for military duty.[24]

This case is illustrative of several key aspects of post-1798 resistance in east Ulster. First, it establishes the presence of an active Defender cell in close proximity to Belfast, proving that the movement was not confined solely to the north and middle of county Antrim. Moreover, the surnames of the committee's members clearly reflect a Protestant–Dissenter presence. Finally, all of the men, with the exception of James Smyth, were drawn from the artisan or labouring classes, the common denominator being social stratum, not sectarian affiliation.

Another snapshot of post-1798 Defenderism is provided by the example of a cell operating in north central Antrim. In the early summer of 1799, Robert Crawford, James Griffen and Francis Young flogged, cut and 'otherwise mistreated' Robert Alexander, the sub-constable at Cloughmills, who ultimately died from the wounds. These men remained safely in their homes near the Cloughwater until an informer gave them away in late January 1800. Clearly then the imposition of martial law in 1799 and the arrests and executions that followed failed in their primary objective, as many of the disaffected successfully melted back into the general population. Ultimately, Crawford was hanged near the scene of the outrage, while Griffen was executed in a location that was 'convenient to his former place of residence'. Young was shown mercy of a sort; the court sentenced him to 500 lashes and transportation for life.[25]

There is sufficient evidence to establish the existence of a central committee of the County Antrim Defenders operating from Ballymena, although the evidence does not permit a determination of the exact role it played. Yet this committee clearly had a part in coordinating activity, maintaining communications and supplying munitions to Defender lodges throughout the region. The best account of this body comes from the information given by a Defender captain, Samuel Hume, who was captured early in 1800. Hume had been an important United Irishman during the rebellion, and he joined the Defenders in the aftermath. After his capture, he provided the authorities with invaluable intelligence as to the structure and leadership of the movement throughout Antrim. Along with correctly identifying a number of messengers, captains and higher-ranking officers, Hume named meeting places and pointed to those responsible for individual acts of resistance. Among other things, Hume described how the Defenders used the home of John Moore, a Ballymena innkeeper, as a meeting place for the county committee. The committee held its meetings on Saturdays, utilizing the distractions created by market day to mask their activities and account for the presence in town of men from outside the immediate area.[26]

It is possible to identify two men as the leaders of the Antrim Defenders. Hume stated unequivocally that Dr Patrick was 'Colonel of defenders' and that James Thompson, a Ballymena apothecary, was 'an officer of superior rank to captain of defenders'.[27] Confirmation of the pair's status came from McGucken, who pointed to his 'friends', Drs Patrick and Thompson of Ballymena, as the 'the two chief leaders' of the Defenders in Antrim. McGucken had both men to be arrested in March 1800 and strongly recommended that they not be released under 'any other terms but immigrating to America'.[28] The Dr Patrick referred to by McGucken was in fact the Presbyterian obstetrician John Patrick, who had served as a member of the committee of public safety set up in Ballymena by the United Irishmen during the rebellion.[29] Patrick survived the government's purge of 1800. Despite being described as a 'convict', which 'referred to serious offenders, who received a sentence of either death or transportation', his name later appears on a list of 'the elders on record as holding office in the congregation [Ballymena Presbyterian] in or soon after 1812'.[30] James Thompson, a Ballymena apothecary, apparently avoided conviction in 1800, although his disappearance from the records may indicate that he did ultimately agree to transport himself from the country.

The hard-core field commanders are identified more readily. These men included Patrick Mitchell, a former weaver originally from Tyrone who used the aliases of Donnelly and the Black Cock, although he was most commonly styled 'General Mitchell'.[31] A former United Irishmen, Mitchell was by 1799 a member of the Defenders' central committee for Antrim, which met at Ballymena, and he also served as a fundraiser and emissary for that body. Throughout 1798–1801, Mitchell worked tirelessly to maintain communications between Defender cells in Antrim, as he had done earlier with regional United Irish committees. He is also known to have travelled to Dublin in 1799 as a delegate from the North, returning with instructions to disarm the yeomanry 'for rebellious purposes'.[32]

Working in conjunction with other former United Irishmen, such as Thomas Archer, William Craig, John Moore and Samuel Hume, Mitchell played a central role in planning and coordinating the numerous arms raids carried out during the winter of 1799–1800. Indeed, local authorities pointed to Mitchell as the 'planner and chief commander of all the robbing parties of arms', while Gen. Drummond confirmed in 1801 that he 'was the head of, or at least deeply concerned in the disturbances last winter [1799–1800]'.[33] Further confirmation of Mitchell's status in the movement came in testimony given at the extensive courts martial held at Ballymena during the winter and spring of 1800, where many of the condemned men identified him as the 'means of bringing them to so disgraceful an end'.[34] In spite of this, as late as May 1800 Patrick Mitchell was still travelling Antrim in an effort to recruit Defenders.

Mitchell was believed to have fled Antrim in the early summer of 1800, although he reappeared in the spring of 1801, when he was implicated heavily in a new wave of robberies and house burnings. In reality, it appears that he had 'been skulking' about in the region for the entire period. The ability of this desperately wanted man, first identified by the authorities in February 1799, to go to ground in central Antrim for such extended periods of time strongly suggests the long-term survival of a regional system. Mitchell was finally taken in the winter of 1801 and confined in Ballymena, whence Col. Anstruther recommended that he be removed to the Provost prison in Dublin.[35]

Another important rebel leader was William 'General' Craig, who worked closely with Mitchell from at least early 1799.[36] Craig participated in a number of arms raids in the winter of 1798–1799, and, like so many other members of the movement, he successfully evaporated into the countryside of Antrim during the high summer and early autumn of 1799. He reappeared in government reports later that year, when he was identified further as a Defender colonel.[37] In the most dramatic episode of post-1798 resistance in east Ulster, Craig served as the field commander for a highly coordinated and exceedingly daring series of arms raids planned by Mitchell. On 19 December, Mitchell and John Moore 'sent summonses to a number of Defenders … ordering them to meet' at Craig's home near Clough Mills. The following night the men duly assembled at the house for 'the purpose of disarming a number of the yeomanry'. Craig wisely postponed the raid that evening because of a snowfall, which would have enabled the inevitable pursuers to track them.[38] On the evening of 13 January 1800, the plan finally was put into action. That night the Defenders struck a number of yeomen's homes in succession. In the process they killed one of the part-time soldiers and severely beat several others. The ultimate prize was the fourteen muskets they carried away with them into the darkness.[39] The scale of this operation, combined with the degree of coordination required to carry out the raid, is demonstrative of the strength and relative sophistication of the Defender system in central Antrim as late as the spring of 1800.[40] Moreover, the rebels proved to be remarkably discerning in targeting the notoriously extremist Rasharkin yeomanry corps. This unit was drawn from the heavily Anglican districts on the western periphery of County Antrim, and when coupled with the fact that the Rasharkin was a supplementary corps, there is a very strong likelihood that its members were Orangemen.[41] In any case, the members of the Rasharkin Corps continued to play an important part in the suppression of Defenderism through 1800.

The raids of 13 January triggered a formidable response from the government. These efforts were facilitated greatly by the capture of a Defender captain, Samuel Hume, near Clough Mills on the day after the attack. Hume had played a leadership role in the raids, and, unfortunately for the outstanding rebels, he gave substantial evidence in order to save his life.[42] Most damningly, Hume identified Craig as the commander of the operation. Although Hume later recanted part of his evidence, the overall quality of his intelligence proved to be quite high as it led to the recovery of the stolen weapons, which had been greased and concealed in a bog between Ballymoney and Craig's house, and the arrest of several of those involved.[43] Craig himself was eventually apprehended by members of the Rasharkin Corps in late May 1800 and conveyed to Ballymena for trial a short time later.[44] With obvious pleasure, Brigade Maj. Munbe, commander of the Antrim yeomanry, reported Craig's capture to Gen. Drummond on 26 May stating: 'from recent robberies in that neighbourhood and other circumstances ... the sooner he is tried the better for the country as he was much respected and esteemed by his party here [Ballymena]'.[45] At Ballymena on 4 July 1800, the military court found William Craig guilty of 'being a rebel, acting in furtherance of the rebellion' and, in direct reference to his role in the raid on the Rasharkin, 'commanding a party as colonel of said party on or about the thirteenth day of January 1800 in the robbery of yeoman of their arms for rebellious purposes'. The Defender colonel was sentenced to be 'hanged by the neck until he is dead at the place of common execution near Ballymena, and his body to be buried under the gallows'. This sentence was confirmed by the Lord Lieutenant, as was common procedure, on 10 July and was promptly carried into effect.[46]

Thomas Archer

The most notorious example of a post-1798 Presbyterian Defender cell is the one headed by Thomas Archer, a former apprentice shoemaker and member of the Antrim militia.[47] Archer deserted prior to the rebellion and joined the United Irishmen, serving prominently with the republicans at the Battle of Ballymena in 1798.[48] Contemporary accounts described him as five feet six with a dark complexion, black hair and grey eyes, further noting that he had suffered some facial scarring as a result of smallpox.

The authorities first identified Archer in the summer of 1799, when his name appeared on a list of deserters involved in arms raids and floggings.[49] In all likelihood, Archer served in the band commanded by George Dickson, alias General Holt, which was active during the autumn and winter of 1798–1799. This supposition is based on the fact that Archer himself was referred to repeatedly as General Holt in testimony given during courts martial in 1800; he may well have adopted the *nom de guerre* in order to capitalize on Dickson's popularity with the people.[50] In any event, Archer, like so many others, successfully escaped the roundup that occurred during the winter of 1799 and emerged as the leader of a separate body by the autumn of 1799. These diehards rapidly developed a reputation for ferocity as floggers and arms raiders and were deeply dreaded by loyalists in the central Antrim region.[51] In a colourful summary of the group's activities, the *Belfast News-Letter* reported:

> the principal objects of their vengeance appear to be either those who have been unfortunate enough to have personal disputes with any of the gang; or such as were *notorious* for having deserted the good cause of rebellion. Woe to the man who coming under these descriptions, is unhappy enough to fall into their hands; they generally give such persons five minutes to prepare, and then deliberately blow out their brains! We have been credibly informed that *Archer* has had the audacity in open day to stand singly, on the high road, and armed with two large pistols, *examined* the passengers returning from market, to see if any of his proscribed list were to be found. There have been several unhappy victims to their diabolical vengeance.[52]

Yet, despite Archer's notoriety, there are only limited verifiable accounts of the band's actions, beyond the generic stories that they 'pillaged, flogged, carded and outraged the loyalists ... with the most astounding impunity'.[53]

The most severe documented example of violence on the part of Archer is the previously mentioned murder of James Love, a well-to-do farmer living at Kildowney with whom Archer had had a previous violent encounter. On the night of 15 December Archer, accompanied by six members of his gang, entered Love's home, dragged him outside and, following a brief scuffle, shot him with a pistol before the eyes of his family.[54] Yet Love was also an ardent loyalist, which made him 'both politically and personally obnoxious' to Archer, and the murder may more aptly be described as an assassination. A similar event occurred on the night of 6 January 1800, when members of the band fired several shots into the home of Henry O'Hara, a Crumlin farmer, wounding both O'Hara and his father (the latter in the head).[55] In light of these events the *News-Letter* reported a short time later:

> It appears that a desperate gang of villains about ten in number, chiefly deserters, are the authors of the whole mischief ... [A]t the head of the clan is the noted Archer and a fellow named Dunn: these desperados make no hesitation to commit the most barbarous and unprovoked murders.[56]

The problem for the historian is that the accounts of Archer come from the Tory press, loyalist gentry and magistrates, or officers of the regular army and yeomanry, all of whom were charged with bringing him to heal. Nonetheless, a close reading of the extant sources makes it is possible to partially penetrate the black legend that built up around Archer and tease out alternative interpretations to some of the key questions raised by his activities. Indeed, it is argued here that an examination of the Archer band offers important insights into the nature of popular resistance in east Ulster following 1798.

Undoubtedly, the core issue raised by the Archer band pertains to its relationship with the general population of the region. More specifically, why was Archer able to remain at large for almost two years after the defeat of the northern rising, and what does that ability tell us about the attitudes of the people? Intimidation undeniably played its part in this ability, and Archer's utter ruthlessness is well-documented:

> [Because] his hiding places were well known ... to a considerable number of the government adherents, none dared to give the information necessary for his arrest, as failure in the attempt was sure to be followed by speedy and violent death to the informer. [57]

Yet, it is also apparent that another equally important phenomenon was simultaneously at work. In reality, the group 'swam' in a sympathetic sea. The *Belfast News-Letter* pointed to this alternative when it queried, 'Strange it is that eight or ten men should be able to keep a whole district of country in alarm and terror, [especially when] it is probable, that if the country people would be active in giving information of their retreats to the military, the whole party might soon be secured'.[58] An indication of the level of active support present in the region came in the first days of 1800 when thirteen men from the Ballymena area were brought in 'several of whom [were] accused of having allowed the gangs which ha[d] infested this part of the country of remaining in their houses without giving informa-tion of it'.[59] Weeks later in early 1800, a member of the Toome yeomanry named McCauley was arrested for harbouring members of Archer's band. McCauley was later convicted of the charges, and the fact that he was both 'a man of some property and a member of the Toome Yeomanry' is perhaps the best indication of the broad range of popular sympathy that permitted outstanding rebels to remain at large for so long.[60] Finally, when the Bally-mena district was disturbed by 'numerous bands' in the winter of 1801, Col. Anstruther declared: 'the country people either from fear or affection shelter them. They are the same people who harboured Archer'.[61]

Another issue is that pertaining to acts of common criminality. Here the evidence is quite clear. There is simply no evidence that Archer engaged in activities motivated by personal gain. Even the staunchly loyalist *News-Letter* acknowledged in 1800 that the band's 'depredations seem[ed] almost confined to the collection of arms'. Moreover, the paper had no trouble distinguishing between what it saw as politically motivated activities such as arms raids, and those driven by simple avarice: 'there have been some depre-dations committed in the parish of Killead, but these were confined to plun-der alone'.[62] In fact, most accounts point to a political orientation, however loosely defined. Henry O'Hara, the victim of one of Archer's attacks, con-cluded simply that the band's focus was to do 'all in their power to make the people rise in rebellion'.[63] In a more colourful rendition, *Old Ballymena* describes Archer's motives as follows:

> numerous Orange Associations ... were established in this county, and their members, wherever they could be found assailable, were selected as special objects of Archer's violence. The sight of 'God save the King' upon the door of an Orange lodge-room always drove him into the wildest and most dangerous paroxysms of excitement.[64]

Despite the colloquial language, it is obvious that, at least in popular memory, Archer was driven not by personal gain but by a visceral antipathy to loyalism.

Perhaps the clearest indication of a political orientation on the part of the band can be found in the group's integration into a broader regional Defender system. The evidence for this incorporation is derived from a variety of sources and is therefore quite persuasive. First, the group's status as defenders was confirmed at trials held in January and February 1800. For example, a military court charged James Caskey, a known member of the Archer band, with 'administering an unlawful oath, called the Defenders oath, acting in the furtherance of rebellion, by being a member of a society called Defenders'.[65] In a like fashion, on 8 March 1800 the court tried Thomas Stewart, another well-documented band member, for 'applying to a good and faithful subject ... to become a Defender, and associating with Thomas Archer – alias General Holt, in arms, in furtherance of the rebellion'.[66]

More importantly, the group appears to have operated at times under the direction of the field commander of the Antrim Defenders, Patrick Mitchell. Members of Archer's band repeatedly testified at Ballymena and described 'this fellow [Mitchell] for being the means of bringing them to so disgraceful an end'.[67] Furthermore, when Mitchell was finally taken in 1801, George Hutchinson, an influential regional magistrate directly linked him to Archer: 'I have every reason to think he [Mitchell] was an associate of Archer.'[68]

The most telling example of the Archer band's integration into a regional system is its participation in the disarming of the Rasharkin corps in January 1800. This event was planned by Mitchell and carried into effect by the Defender colonel, William Craig. Two days after the attacks Gen. Drummond wrote: 'firelocks to the number of fourteen were taken by Archer's gang from the supplementary of the Rasharkin Yeomen ... one man shot and ... several people severely beaten'.[69] In a similar vein, the *Belfast News-Letter* confirmed in a larger article about the Archer band: 'there have been several unhappy victims to their diabolical vengeance ... one or two of the Rasharkin and Finvoy Yeomanry are said to have lost their lives in bravely attempting to resist being robbed of their arms'.[70] The significance of these simple realities should not be underestimated, for they place an active Presbyterian Defender cell at the epicentre of the most Protestant county of Ireland as late as 1800, thereby turning the historiographical interpretation of post-1798 east Ulster on its head.

The declaration of martial law on 23 January put tremendous pressure on the disaffected in Antrim. By early February the military had captured the majority of the Archer band's members, effectively shattering the group. The *News-Letter* noted with obvious pleasure: 'I have the satisfaction of acquainting you that the knot of ruffians, who so lately infested the neighbourhood of Ballymena, is in a manner completely broken up.'[71] The paper identified the captured men as McCorrly, Dunn, Ryan, Sheall, Nixon and Dr Linn, and correctly commented on the 'awful fate' that was in store for them. Yet Archer remained at large.[72] One of the men, John Ryan, had surrendered to Col. Anstruther, who persuaded him to rejoin the group 'for the purpose of betraying their haunts'. Ever-cautious Archer seized and threatened to kill Ryan upon his rejoining the band. The turncoat managed to escape when Archer, being 'overpowered by liquor', fell asleep. Ryan promptly returned with a party of soldiers, but they arrived 'minutes after that miscreant [Archer] had removed'.[73] After the event, Gen. Drummond calmly wrote, 'I am sorry to say Archer is not yet taken, though still in this parish [Ballymena] and has lately committed several daring and atrocious acts.'[74] Ryan, on the other hand, despite his service to the government, was convicted of being a rebel and sentenced to death.[75]

The authorities wasted no time in making examples of the members of the band. On Saturday 22 February, just past three in the afternoon, Ryan and John 'Major' Dunne, Archer's second in command, were taken to the moat outside Ballymena and 'launched into oblivion'. After the execution, Dunne's body was gibbeted briefly, and subsequently both men were buried under the gallows.[76] A military tribunal had condemned Dunne for, amongst other things, 'being in arms and one of the gang of rebels associated for rebellious purposes ... serving under the command of a rebel general ... Archer'.[77] Other members of the band followed in quick succession. The court sentenced James Caskey and 'Doctor' William Linn to death after trials held on the 17 and 18 February.[78] Caskey died at Ahoghill on Monday 3 March. The 'celebrated' Dr Linn, who had earned his nickname by having worked briefly as, or for, a Ballymena surgeon/apothecary, was held over for execution at Randalstown on the fourth.[79]

Another of Archer's associates, the aforementioned Kildowney shoemaker Thomas Stewart, was condemned by the court on 8 March to hang at Dundermotbridge for, amongst other things, attempting to swear 'a good and faithful subject' to the Defender oath.[80] The only member of the band to escape capital conviction was the yeoman Charles McAuley, who may well have given evidence against other members of the group. McAuley, although convicted for his part in the assault on the home of the Rev. Dr Henry, was merely sentenced to jail until he could raise the funds for a seven-year bond to insure his future good behaviour.[81] The court sentenced Matthew Boyd from Kells to death for being a rebel, arms robbery and 'administering unlawful oaths [all while] acting under the command of Thomas Archer ... in furtherance of the rebellion'.[82] Boyd was the final member of Archer's band to die, being executed on the moat at Ballymena on 17 May.[83]

The most famous of the members of the Archer band is Roger 'Roddy' McCorley. This notoriety was born via the medium two popular folk ballads, which made a legend of the young Presbyterian miller's son from the west Antrim parish of Duneane.[84] The earlier, anonymous, ballad was written shortly after the rebellion and survived in the oral tradition for nearly 200 years before being transcribed in the mid-twentieth century. Significantly, it identifies McCorley as both a Presbyterian and a Defender. The second, and far more popular, song was composed by Ethna Carbery in the 1890s for the centenary of the 1798 rising. [85]

In reality, very little is known about McCorley. It seems highly likely that he was a United Irishman who participated in the battle for Antrim town in June 1798. What is certain is the fact that he remained 'out' for nearly two years following the rebellion. During this time he joined Archer's band and was converted, or reverted, to Defenderism, for which he was ultimately hanged on Friday 28 February 1800.[86] The well-armed McCorley was captured in late January near Ahoghill after a lengthy chase by elements of the aforementioned Rasharkin yeomanry under the command of George Bristow, esq.[87] Given the fact that the members of this corps were still actively pursuing the men responsible for raiding their homes earlier in the month, it is quite likely that McCorley had played a part in the attacks. The military court that heard his case condemned McCorley 'to be hanged at Toomebridge for his great atrocities'. Like Archer, the government so reviled McCorley that Castlereagh's order confirming the execution bore the caveat 'we are further pleased to direct that after his body is executed ... it may be given over to the surgeon of the Tay Fencibles for dissection'.[88] The *Belfast News-Letter* offered its readers a cautionary description of McCorley's execution:

> a most awful procession took place here, namely, the escorting of Roger McCorley ... to the place of execution, Toome Bridge, the unfortunate man having been breed in that neighbourhood. As a warning to others it is proper to observe that the whole course of his life was devoted to disorderly proceedings of every kind; for many years past, scarcely a Quarter Sessions occurred, but what the name of Roger McCorley appeared in a variety of criminal cases! His body was given up to dissection and after words [*sic*] buried under the gallows.[89]

Archer himself finally was captured on Monday 3 March after a presumed friend, Jemmy O'Brien, sold him to the government. The rebel was hiding in O'Brien's home in the townland of Galgorm Park, adjacent to the Star Bog, when the turncoat got word to Capt. Dickey of Archer's whereabouts. The captain, whom Archer later claimed he had the opportunity to kill on several occasions but chose not to, led a mixed party of the Portglenone cavalry, Tay fencibles and his own Ballymena yeomanry to O'Brien's that evening.

As the soldiers approached the cabin, O'Brien's son, who was unaware of the plot, alerted Archer at the last moment. Making a dash for the bog, he managed to conceal himself in a water-filled hole for several hours until a hunting dog accompanying one of the yeomen gave away his position. In a final act of defiance, Archer attempted to discharge his blunderbuss at the soldiers, but O'Brien had prudently wet his powder. The yeomen bayoneted Archer several times and then carried their severely wounded prisoner back to Ballymena. An elated editor briefly summed up the impact of the Archer's arrest for local loyalists: 'Thus, happily, a dangerous banditti are completely broke up, and, I trust we may now look for tranquillity being restored to this distracted country'.[90]

Two days following his capture, a court martial found Archer guilty of murder and 'being a rebel in arms in the furtherance of the rebellion [and] ... many other acts of cruelty'. His reputation was such that the officers of the court deemed it necessary to make an example of his body. Thus, after execution, Thomas Archer's corpse was dissected by surgeons of the Tays. His remains were then exposed in a gibbet on 'the Moat' (a hill) outside Ballymena for a period of months. They were visible for miles around and in clear sight of his parents' home.[91] In an act that can only be viewed as reverential, local youths eventually removed Archer's bones from their cage and buried them in the corner of a Protestant churchyard.[92]

The purge

Perhaps the best indication of the scale of the disaffection that gripped Antrim two years after the great rebellion are the extraordinary efforts required to be taken by the government to break its hold. 'A great number of prisoners ... of very bad character were being held' as the result of the widespread sweeps conducted in late January and early February. On 10 February, the government convened a general court martial at Ballymena, which over the ensuing months proved to be the most deadly in Ireland during the year 1800.[93] The trials continued until 17 May, and the military court heard over 100 cases. Charges included rebellion, arms robbery, disarming yeomen, flogging and administering Defender oaths, and forty-three men were convicted for these crimes. Another five individuals were sentenced for 'being men of wicked principles, not having the fear of God before their eyes, and being moved and seduced by the devil', or more simply perjury. One man was tried for making 'rebellious and treasonable expressions, [for example,] Tis to the wrath of God to have a king ... and that hell might receive the souls of all loyalists, and arraign them at the bar of damnation'.[94]

The ferocity of the sentences meted out at Ballymena in the winter of 1800 can only be understood in the light of the fear that popular resistance had generated in the hearts of local loyalists. An example of their sanguinary demands came in the 23 March issue of the *News-Letter* in which an editor found it necessary to defend the Lord Lieutenant against accusations of excessive leniency: 'thirteen of these wretches had been executed this week in the co. Antrim? Was the accusation against the Noble Marquis that he did not shed blood enough?'[95] In the end, the government executed seventeen of the men convicted at Ballymena. To ensure the broadest audience for these 'examples', the death sentences were carried out at a number of locations in the northern half of county Antrim, including Ballymena, Ballymoney, Cloughmills, Clough, Dundermot Bridge, Connor and Toome Bridge. A further fifteen men were transported for life to Botany Bay, two after having been lashed a mind-boggling 500 times. Three individuals were transported for lesser periods of seven or five years, while twenty-three others agreed to transport themselves out of the country rather than risk trial. Eight men were condemned to serve in the army.[96] The recent work of Michael Durey on courts martial allows us to put the Ballymena trials in a national perspective and the results are startling. Throughout Ireland in the year 1800, courts martial passed fifty-seven death sentences, forty of which were ultimately confirmed by the Viceroy. Seventeen of the latter, or nearly half, occurred in Antrim.[97]

It is also important to note that, despite the imposition of martial law, civil courts continued to function. Therefore, any attempt to quantify the scale of the government's crackdown must also take these cases into account. At the Antrim assizes held at Carrickfergus in April 1800, the court heard the case of William McIlnea, who was being tried for a political murder committed the previous July. McIlnea, a blacksmith, was convicted of using one of the tools of his trade to disembowel a man named McKelvey as they walked on the road in the twilight. The motive behind this brutal crime was McIlnea's 'suspicion' that McKelvey was an informer. Found guilty, McIlnea was executed on 19 April. In a long-winded letter to the editor an anonymous author offered a loyalist perspective on the root causes of the crime:

> Such is the justly merited fate which sooner or later must arrest the followers of such cursed practices; practices evidently the result of those diabolical principles, so industriously circulated, and instilled into the minds of thousands in this island. When we see to what a pitch of depravity ... those fatal principles of Infidelity and Deism, coupled with Jacobinism and Rebellion ... it appears that this nefarious system carries its proud influence beyond the reach of human laws, by teaching men to deny revealed religion.[98]

It is important to note that there is no mention of sectarianism in this tirade.

The Antrim assizes continued to try to execute political prisoners throughout August. At a trial held on the eighth, the jury convicted a school teacher (John Cox), of high treason for 'acting as a leader' during the rebellion. Judges then sentenced Cox to be hanged and quartered on 1 September; the delay between sentencing and execution would allow Dublin Castle to review the case.[99] Civil justices condemned four other men to death that month for participating in arms raids in the previous spring. Among these individuals are two identifiable defenders, Hector McNeill and Daniel McFadden.[100]

Ultimately, the arrest, court martial and execution of most of the Defender movement's leaders during the winter and spring of 1800, coupled with a strong military presence, had largely broken the movement's back, yet the system had 'taken a deep root', and the participation of better-off farmers continued to cause Cornwallis some concern.[101] It was not until April that Littlehales could report that the 'examples recently made in County Antrim' had restored tranquillity and checked 'the rebellious spirit of Defenderism'.[102]

The motives

The violence of the winter 1799–1800 cannot be attributed to sectarianism. There is no mention whatsoever of a religious component in contemporary accounts of the events of the period, nor was the simple desire for vengeance the primary motive of the rebels, although it undoubtedly played a part. Instead, evidence that emerged at northern court-martials repeatedly established 'that an essential part of the plans and conspiracies of the Defenders ... [wa]s to keep alive ... the opinion of assistance from France'. Moreover, these machinations widely were successful as intelligence 'from every quarter' confirmed that 'the idea of a powerful cooperation of foreign aid [wa]s now exceedingly prevalent and the hopes of the disaffected of a French invasion [we]re revived'.[103]

Finally, several aspects of the resistance that disturbed east Ulster between late 1798 and 1801 lend credence to the argument that the Presbyterians of Antrim and Down did not abandon the republican cause with unseemly haste. Most simply, the epicentre of post-1798 resistance was mid-Antrim, an area that had an overwhelming Presbyterian majority. That it was found necessary to rely on the military to quell these disturbances in Antrim is a further indication that the Presbyterians of the county had not rushed into the yeomanry and Orange Order. If the Presbyterian farmers and weavers had become overwhelmingly – or at least sincerely – Orange, these depredations could have easily been dealt with on the local level. Weight of numbers would have ensured that the Defenders were hunted down. The survival of the Defender movement was always based on its ability to melt away into the general population. In the case of central and north Antrim, this by necessity required at the very least the passive support of rural Presbyterians. Men like Archer, Craig and Mitchell stayed out for two years with no word of their whereabouts reaching the authorities.

Notes

1 NAI RP 620/48/26, McGucken to Pollock, Belfast, 13 Dec. 1799; ibid. 620/48/39, McGucken to Cooke, 23 Dec. 1799; see also ibid. 620/49/9, Drummond to Littlehales, Belfast, 15 Jan. 1800.

2 NAI RP 620/48/28, Thomas Whinnery to John Lees, Belfast, 14 Dec. 1799.
3 *BNL*, 13 Dec. 1799; ibid., 7 Jan. 1800.
4 Ibid., 7 Jan. 1800.
5 Ibid., 13 Dec. 1799.
6 NAI RP 620/49/2, Drummond to Gen. Gardiner, Belfast, 4 Jan. 1800; ibid., Maj. Thompson to Drummond, Ballymena, 1 Jan. 1800; *BNL*, 4 Jan. 1800.
7 Ibid., 7 Jan. 1800.
8 NAI RP 620/49/9, Drummond to Gardiner, Belfast, 15 Jan. 1800.
9 *BNL*, 7 Jan. 1800; ibid., 21 Jan. 1800; ibid., 18 Mar. 1800.
10 NAI RP 620/49/9, Drummond to Gardiner, Belfast, 15 Jan. 1800.
11 Ibid.
12 Ibid.
13 Allan Blackstock, *An ascendancy army: The Irish yeomanry, 1796–1834* (Dublin, 1998), 129.
14 NAI RP 620/49/1, Capt Thompson to Drummond, Ballymena, Jan. 1800; ibid. 620/49/2, examination of Samuel Johnson against Hugh Beatty, 2 Jan. 1800; ibid., Gardiner to Littlehales, Drumilly, 6 Jan. 1800.
15 Blackstock, *Ascendancy army*, 80, 129, 215–16; Ian McBride, *Scripture politics: Ulster Presbyterians and Irish radicalism in the late eighteenth century* (Oxford, 1998), 190.
16 Blackstock, *Ascendancy army*, 64, 79–86, 216, 240; McBride, *Scripture politics*, 187–89.
17 For Anglican–Presbyterian hostility in the second half of the eighteenth century, see McBride, *Scripture politics*, 187–90. For an example of similar Scottish–English conflict in northwest Ulster, see Breandán Mac Suibhne, 'Up not out: Why did north-west Ulster not rise in 1798?', in Cathal Póirtéir (ed.), *The great Irish rebellion of 1798* (Dublin, 1998), 83–100. For the inter-relationship between the Orange Order, Anglicanism and the yeomanry on the Hertford estates, see Blackstock, *Ascendancy army*, 64, 90, 216, and 240.
18 NAI RP 620/49/5, Gardiner to Littlehales, Drumilly, 18 Jan. 1800; ibid. 620/49/8, Drummond to Gardiner, Belfast, 15 Jan. 1800.
19 Ibid. 620/49/5, Gardiner to Littlehales, Drumilly, 18 Jan. 1800.
20 Ibid., Gardiner to Littlehales, 23 Jan. 1800. These reinforcements eventually included the Dunbartonshire fencibles under Lt Col, Scott, who arrived in Antrim town in mid-March to replace the Tays who had moved earlier to Ballymena, *BNL*, 18 Mar. 1800; also see, ibid., 7 Jan 1800. For Drummond's move to Ballymoney, see *BNL*, 28 Jan. 1800.
21 TNA HO 100/93/188–9, Cornwallis to Portland, Dublin Castle, 17 Mar. 1800.
22 NAI RP 620/49/12, Drummond to Littlehales, Belfast, 12 Mar. 1800.
23 Ibid. 620/49/11, examination of William Mitchell of the Parish of Carnmoney, mason and slater, Belfast, 22 Feb. 1800; ibid. 620/49/12, John Brown, esq., Sovereign of Belfast, Belfast, 1 Mar. 1800, *BNL*, 31 Dec. 1799.
24 NAI RP 620/49/11, Brown and William Fox, esq., two Justices of the Peace, Belfast, 11 Mar. 1800; NLI KP, MSS 1197, 1198, 1200; NAI RP 620/49/12, Drummond to Littlehales, Belfast, 12 Mar. 1800. An appeal was made to allow Smyth to 'instantly transport himself for life' by Mr William Graham, to whom Smyth was apprenticed, and Mr John Fulton, his uncle. The Sovereign supported this application citing Smyth's youth; he was sixteen at the time, although the influence of those interceding on his behalf undoubtedly played a greater part in the decision.

25 NAI RP 620/49/19, information of Samuel Hume, Ballymoney, 26 May 1800; NLI KP MS 1200, 385–87, general court martial at Ballymena, 9 Apr. 1800, enclosed in ibid., MSS 1197, 1198, 44–5, Marsden to Drummond, Dublin Castle, 16 Apr. 1799.

26 NAI RP 620/49/19, information of Hume, Ballymoney, sworn 26 Jan. 1800 before George Hutchinson, esq. and Maj. Munbe; ibid. 620/49/17, Drummond to Littlehales, Belfast 24 Apr. 1800; ibid. 620/49/16, McGucken to Cooke, Belfast, 28 Mar. 1800. Members of the Ballymena Defender committee named by Hume were still in custody in May when Gen. Drummond complained, 'Indeed as our own guardroom is too crowded, I much wish to get rid of them [another group], as well as the Defenders ... that sat in committee at Ballymena.' ibid. 620/49/18, Drummond to Littlehales, Belfast, 6 May 1800.

27 Ibid. 620/49/19, information of Hume, Ballymoney, 26 Jan. 1800.

28 NAI SOC 3397, McGucken, Belfast, 16 Apr. 1800; NAI RP 620/49/16, McGucken to Cooke, Belfast, 28 Mar. 1800.

29 For Patrick's role in the rebellion, see A. T. Q. Stewart, *The summer soldiers: The 1798 rebellion in Antrim and Down* (Belfast, 1995), 129, and 132. Another informant revealed in May 1800 that Dr James Thomson 'of Ballymena, [an] apothecary', was 'an officer of superior rank to captain' and that Dr Patrick 'is a Colonel of Defenders', see NAI RP 620/49/19, information of Hume, Ballymoney, 26 Jan. 1800.

30 NAI Prisoners' Petition Cases, 559, petition of John Patrick, 2 Apr. 1800; the definition of the legal status of 'convicts' is that of the National Archives Ireland; *Old Ballymena*, 101.

31 NAI RP 620/49/89, Col. Anstruther to Drummond, Ballymena, Feb. 1801.

32 NAI RP 620/49/19, information of Hume, Ballymoney, 26 Jan.1800; ibid. 620/49/89, Anstruther to Drummond, Ballymena, Feb. 1801; ibid., Drummond to Littlehales, Belfast, 2 Mar. 1801; ibid., Hutchinson to Drummond, Ballymoney, 26 Feb. 1800.

33 Ibid., Anstruther to Drummond, Ballymena, Feb. 1801; ibid., Hutchinson to Drummond, Ballymoney, 26 Feb. 1800; ibid., Drummond to Littlehales, Belfast, 2 Mar. 1801.

34 Ibid. 620/49/19, Hutchinson to Drummond, Ballymoney, 26 Feb. 1801.

35 Ibid., information of Hume, Ballymoney, 26 May 1800; ibid. 620/49/89, Drummond to Littlehales, Belfast, 2 Mar. 1801; ibid., Hutchinson to Drummond, Ballymoney, 26 Feb. 1801; ibid., Anstruther to Hutchinson, Ballymena; ibid., examination of William [Whilie?], County Antrim, 4 Mar. 1799.

36 Ibid., Anstruther to Drummond, Ballymena, 26 Feb. 1801.

37 NLI KP MS 1201, 24–5, proceedings of general court martial at Ballymena, 4 July 1800, _____ to Drummond, Dublin Castle, 10 July 1800.

38 For Craig's role in these raids, see NAI RP 620/49/19, information of Hume, Ballymoney, 26 Jan. 1800 and NLI KP MS 1201, 24–5, proceedings of general court martial at Ballymena, 4 July 1800, _____ to Drummond, Dublin Castle, 10 July 1800. For Archer's connection to Mitchell, see NAI RP 620/49/89, Hutchinson to Drummond, Ballymoney, 26 Feb. 1801.

39 Ibid. 620/49/9, Drummond to Gardiner, 15 Jan.1800; *BNL*, 21 Jan. 1800.

40 For Craig's role in these raids, see NAI RP 620/49/19, information of Hume, Ballymoney, 26 Jan. 1800, and NLI KP MS 1201, 24–5, proceedings of general court martial at Ballymena, 4 July 1800, _____ to Drummond, Dublin Castle, 10 July 1800. For Archer's connection to Mitchell, see NAI RP 620/49/89, Hutchinson to Drummond, Ballymoney, 26 Feb. 1801.

41 For the link between supplementary yeomanry units and the Orange Order, see Blackstock, *Ascendancy army,* 92–7.

42 At least two men, Alexander Stewart and William Scullion, who had been arrested with Hume, were executed for their part in the raids. For Stewart, see NLI KP MS 1197; for Scullion, see *BNL,* 31 Jan. 1800 and NLI KP MS 1200, 349–50, Marsden to Drummond, Dublin Castle, 12 Apr. 1800. For Hume, see ibid., 411–13, proceedings of general court martial at Ballymena, 22 Apr. 1800, enclosed in Marsden to Drummond, Dublin Castle, 26 Apr. 1800; NAI RP 620/49/17, Drummond to Littlehales, Belfast, 24 Apr. 1800; *BNL,* 31 Jan. 1800. The paper states that Hume 'was one of the rebel leaders, who during insurrection ... commanded a party of insurgents ... ' It also describes him as a Defender at the present time. For Hume, also see Ruán O'Donnell, *Robert Emmet and the rising of 1803* (Dublin, 2003).

43 *BNL,* 25 Feb. 1800; NAI RP 620/49/19, information of Hume, Ballymoney, sworn 26 Jan. 1800 before Hutchinson and Munbe; for the quality of Hume's information, see ibid. 620/49/17, Drummond to Littlehales, Belfast, 24 Apr. 1800.

44 Ibid. 620/49/19, Drummond to Littlehales, Belfast, 29 May 1800; ibid., Munbe, Ballymoney, 26 May 1800.

45 Ibid.

46 NLI KP MS 1201, 24–5, proceedings of general court martial at Ballymena, 4 July 1800, Marsden to Drummond, Dublin Castle, 10 July 1800; ibid. MS 1197, no page number, minutes of court's martial, 10 July 1800.

47 Archer and eight other members of the band were Presbyterians. For the religious composition of Archer's band see, 'Ceremony to remember United Irishmen held in Ballymena'. *RTE News,* 2 Dec. 2002. 13 July 2006. www.rte.ie/news/2000/1202/ceremony.html.

48 Stewart, *Summer soldiers,* 166; *Old Ballymena: A history of Ballymena during the 1798 rebellion* (Ballymena, 1938), 51.

49 For the description of Archer, see *BNL,* 7 Feb. 1800. Alternatively in *Old Ballymena,* 51, Archer is described as of 'very dark complexion ... stout, vigorous, determined, [and] distinguished by a species of wild and savage bravery'. NAI RP 620/47/100, examination of Henry, County Antrim, 23 July 1799.

50 Trial of Thomas Archer, alias Gen. Holt, Ballymena, 5 Mar. 1800, Anstruther presiding, enclosed in NLI KP MS 1200, 285–7, Castlereagh to Drummond, 7 Mar. 1800; ibid. MS 1197.

51 *Old Ballymena,* 51–3.

52 *BNL,* 21 Jan. 1800.

53 *Old Ballymena,* 51.

54 *BNL,* 13 Dec. 1799; *Old Ballymena,* 52.

55 NAI RP 620/49/12, examination of O'Hara, County Antrim, 17 Feb. 1800; trials of John Dunne and John Ryan, Ballymena, 12–15 Feb. 1800, enclosed in NLI KP MS 1200, 253–5, Dublin Castle to Drummond, 17 Feb 1800.

56 *BNL,* 4 Feb 1800.

57 *Old Ballymena,* 51.

58 *BNL,* 21 Jan. 1800.

59 NAI RP 620/49/2, Thompson to Drummond, Ballymena, 1 Jan. 1800.

60 *BNL,* 7 Feb. 1800; General court martial at Ballymena, 5 May 1800, enclosed in NLI KP MS 1200), 430–1, Castlereagh to Drummond, Dublin Castle, 9 May 1800; ibid. MS 1197, no page number, minutes of court's martial, 1800.

61 NAI RP 620/49/89, Anstruther to Hutchinson, Ballymena, 26 Feb. 1801. For

a meeting of an upper-level committee held in the early summer of 1801 with the objective of reorganizing Down in order to disarm the yeomanry prior to an anticipated invasion, see ibid. 620/10/118/15, McGucken, Belfast, 3 July 1801.

62 *BNL*, 21 Jan. 1800.
63 NAI RP 620/49/12, examination of O'Hara, County Antrim, 17 Feb. 1800.
64 *Old Ballymena*, 52.
65 General courts martial held at Ballymena on 17 and 18 Feb. 1800, enclosed in NLI KP MS 1200, 257–8, Castlereagh to Drummond, Dublin Castle, 23 Feb. 1800. For Caskey's membership in Archer's band, also see *BNL*, 4 Mar. 1800.
66 General courts martial held at Ballymena on 8 Mar. 1800, enclosed in NLI KP MS 1200, 351–2, _____ to Drummond, Dublin Castle, 12 Apr. 1800. For Stewart's membership in Archer's band, also see *BNL*, 4 Mar. 1800.
67 NAI RP 620/49/89, Hutchinson to Drummond, Ballymoney, 26 Feb. 1801.
68 Ibid.
69 Ibid. 620/49/9, Drummond to Gardiner, Belfast, 15 Jan. 1800.
70 *BNL*, 21 Jan. 1800.
71 Ibid., 4 Feb. 1800.
72 Ibid.
73 NAI RP 620/49/9, Drummond to Littlehales, Ballymena, 21 Feb. 1800.
74 Ibid.
75 NLI KP MS 1200, 253–5, Dublin Castle to Drummond, 17 Feb 1800.
76 *BNL*, 25 Feb.1800; trials of Dunne and Ryan, Ballymena, 12–15 Feb. 1800, enclosed in NLI KP MS 1200, 257–8, Castlereagh to Drummond, Dublin Castle, 23 Feb 1800; also see ibid. MS 1197.
77 Trials of James Caskey and William Linn, Ballymena, 17 and 18 Feb. 1800, enclosed in ibid. MS 1200, 253–5, Dublin Castle to Drummond, 23 Feb. 1800.
78 Trials of Dunne and Ryan, Ballymena, 12–15 Feb. 1800, enclosed in ibid., 257–8, Castlereagh to Drummond, Dublin Castle, 23 Feb 1800.
79 *BNL*, 4 March 1800.
80 General court martial at Ballymena, 15 Feb. 1800, enclosed in ibid., 258–62, Castlereagh to Drummond, Dublin Castle, 23 Feb. 1800; ibid., 256, Littlehales to Drummond, Dublin Castle, 24 Feb. 1800; ibid., MS 1197, no page number, minutes of court's martial, 1800.
81 General court martial at Ballymena, 5 May 1800, enclosed in ibid. MS 1200, 430–1, Castlereagh to Drummond, Dublin Castle, 9 May 1800; ibid. MS 1197, no page number, minutes of court's martial, 1800.
82 General court martial at Ballymena, 15 Feb. 1800, enclosed in ibid. MS 1200, 258–62, Castlereagh to Drummond, Dublin Castle, 23 Feb.1800; ibid. MS 1197, minutes of court's martial, 1800. Other members of the band included Frances Loughridge, Patrick Devlin and Charles McAuley (see respectively *Old Ballymena*, 52; NAI RP 620/49/12, examination of O'Hara, Ballymena, 17 Feb. 1800; general court martial at Ballymena, 15, 17, 21 Feb. 1800, enclosed in NLI KP MS 1200, 258–62, Castlereagh to Drummond, Dublin Castle, 23 Feb. 1800).
83 *BNL*, 23 May 1800.
84 For McCorley's religious background see, Stewart, *Summer soldiers*, 156.
85 In 1948, the National Graves' Association placed a memorial to McCorley at Toome Bridge, see Peter Collins, 'The contest of memory: The continuing impact of 1798 commemoration', in *Éire–Ireland* 34, no. 2, 1999, 44–6. In

2004, Sinn Fein proposed naming a newly constructed bridge over the Bann after McCorley. This offer was nearly accepted by north Antrim loyalists of the PUP who recognized the McCorley as part of their own heritage. The effort ultimately failed. There also exists a staunchly republican Roddy McCorley Society with its headquarters in west Belfast, which was founded in 1972. For McCorley's place in the ballad tradition of County Antrim, see Tom Munnelly, '1798 and the ballad makers', in Cathal Póirtéir (ed.), *The great Irish rebellion of 1798* (Dublin, 1998), 160–70; also see, Stewart, *Summer soldiers*, 156. Stewart, drawing from the ballad tradition, dates McCorley's execution to Good Friday, 1799. The change of the execution's date to Good Friday was probably made in the interest of dramatic effect. There is, in fact, no record of a court martial or execution taking place on or about that date. Since 1961 versions of Carbery's 'Ballad of Roddy McCorley' have been recorded by the Clancy Brothers, the Kingston Trio, Roger McGuinn and Shane MacGowan, amongst others.

86 For McCorley's membership in the Archer Band, see *BNL*, 4 Feb. 1800; ibid. 4 Mar. 1800.
87 Ibid., 4 Feb. 1800.
88 NLI KP MS 1200, 262–3, Castlereagh to Drummond, Dublin Castle, 23 Feb. 1800; ibid. MS 1201, 99, Francis Patterson, esq., Attorney General, 12 June 1800; *BNL*, 4 Mar. 1800.
89 *BNL*, 4 Mar. 1800.
90 *BNL*, 7 Mar. 1800; *Old Ballymena*, 53–4.
91 *Old Ballymena*, 55–6; trial of Archer, alias Holt, Ballymena, 5 Mar. 1800, Col. Anstruther presiding, enclosed in NLI KP MS 1200, 285–7, Castlereagh to Drummond, 7 Mar. 1800. Another indication of Archer's significance in the eyes of the government was Castlereagh's prompt confirmation, only two days after conviction, of the sentence of death.
92 *BNL*, 11 Mar. 1800; *Old Ballymena*, 56.
93 TNA HO 100/93/188–9, Cornwallis to Portland, Dublin Castle, 17 Mar. 1800; NAI RP 620/49/9, Drummond to Littlehales, Ballymena, 21 Feb. 1800.
94 NLI KP MSS 1197, 1198, 1200.
95 *BNL*, 21 Mar. 1800.
96 For the Ballymena courts martial, see NLI KP MSS 1197, 1200, 1201. Also see, Helen Landreth, *The pursuit of Robert Emmet* (New York, 1948), 166–7. Landreth fails to give dates and citations, while locating Ballymena in County Down.
97 Michael Durey, 'Marquess Cornwallis and the fate of the Irish rebel prisoners in the aftermath of the 1798 rebellion', in Jim Smyth (ed.), *Revolution, counter-revolution and union: Ireland in the 1790s* (Cambridge, 2000), 134.
98 *BNL*, 22 Apr. 1800.
99 Ibid., 8 Aug. 1800.
100 Ibid.
101 TNA HO 100/93/188–9, Cornwallis to Portland, Dublin Castle, 17 Mar. 1800.
102 Ibid. 100/93/259–64, Littlehales to Cooke, Dublin Castle, 5 Apr. 1800.
103 NAI RP 620/49/9, Munbe, Ballymoney, 26 May 1800.

4

1801–1804

Freemasons

Despite the lull in active resistance brought about by the cessation of hostilities between Britain and France in 1802 much of Ulster continued to be disturbed partially by what the authorities typically referred to as riots. These affrays took the form of faction fights at fairs and markets between parties of Orangemen and groups that were commonly described as Freemasons. Contemporaries differed in their assessment of the causes of these fights and further disagreed over the question of the social, political and religious composition of the Masons. For instance, William Richardson, a clerical magistrate at Moy in County Tyrone, believed that the riots were entirely political in nature and that the sectarianism evidenced in parts of Ulster over the past few years had been put aside. In fact, Richardson felt that the 'tail of the United Irish' had rallied in the Masonic lodges. Moreover, he was concerned deeply about the spread of Masonry and the overt hostility it demonstrated towards the Orange Order.[1]

These so-called riots were particularly frequent in the Ahoghill area of west-central Antrim in the second half of 1802, where they were most often described as conflicts between yeomen and United Irishmen. In one incident, the 'United men' were accused of being the aggressors, and twenty of their members were brought up on charges. Similar accounts came from County Down, where 'the people were said to bear the strong hand over the yeomen' at fairs and markets. At the Christmas fair of 1802 at Saintfield in Down, money was offered for the 'head of an Orangeman'.[2]

Perhaps the most serious of the riots occurred in east Derry in the spring of 1802. The area had long been disturbed by what the regional military commander called prevalent 'religious contests'. Masons gathered in large groups at regional fairs and markets, and at the Garragh Fair on 24 May they violently beat some 'yeomen and Orangemen'. At the Kilrea Fair on 7 June, a more serious conflict took place between some yeomen from Antrim and a party of Masons from Vow Ferry. The ensuing 'battle' resulted in two deaths, both Masons, and sixteen wounded. Six Orangemen were tried later at the Londonderry assizes for their part in the incident. The court sentenced the yeomen to six months of imprisonment and fined them five marks apiece.[3] The Loyalist *Coleraine Constitution* described the affair as follows:

> About six o'clock in the evening after the greatest part of the people were supposed to have gone home, a large mob, calling themselves Freemasons and headed by the master of the Vow Lodge, assembled in a very

tumultuous manner, armed with large sticks and quarter poles and calling
out any Orangemen and Protestants. The Orangemen (who had all gone
home except seventeen) took every affront without their least injury and
after been severely beaten they took refuge in a house where they secured
themselves as well as they could, but the mob attacked them there also and
broke the windows with large stones. At last the Orangemen were obliged
to have recourse to what arms they had – at first only powder, which served
only to make the mob more furious. They were then obliged in their own
defence to fire ball, which soon dispersed them but not until two men were
killed and several badly wounded. Two of the rioters have since been taken
and sent to Derry and several have fled.[4]

Yet important distinctions emerged from official correspondence. A local
magistrate, James Paterson, described the assailants as 'Catholic Masons of
the lowest class with whom some profligate Protestants ha[d] mixed', who
had a common 'dislike [of] yeomen and Orangemen'. In other words, the
'mob' was motivated not by religious bigotry but by a common animosity
to the Orange Order and yeomanry. The presence of 'profligate Protestants'
in the Masonic party lends credence to the view that these contests had a
political and not religious foundation.[5]

Indeed, the Kilrea district was the only part of Derry to have risen,
albeit briefly and ineffectually, in June 1798. Furthermore, the targets of
these assaults at the fairs and markets were Orangemen and yeomen, and
not Protestants generically. This reality is established by the presence of
Protestants in the mobs themselves. The frequently used term 'profligate
Protestants' appears to have been a loyalist euphemism for lower-class Presbyterians. Importantly, no mention of sectarianism was made in accounts
of similar riots occurring in other areas of Ulster. Finally, the ability of such
groups to overwhelm fairly sizable parties of Orangemen at public events
in the heavily Presbyterian districts of northwest Antrim and east Derry
strongly implies popular dissenter support for the Masonic–United Irish
alliance and continued resentment towards loyalists.[6]

1801–1803: Emmet's rebellion in the north

The dormancy in active resistance brought about by the peace between
Britain and France did not signify the total abandonment of the radical
cause by the Presbyterians of Antrim and Down. Yet at the same time, it
is undeniable that republican ranks had thinned substantially, and there
was an extreme hesitancy to risk any form of open confrontation without
French aid. Compounding these difficulties were religious tensions within
the radical remnant and an increasing distrust of the motives of Napoleonic
France. Nonetheless at the onset of 1803, Defenderism was still considered
'very general' in Antrim, and members of the movement were said to be
'always anxious for a renewal of war'. Indeed, 'scattered' local societies
continued to operate in both counties, although meetings were infrequent

and the level of activity quite limited. What was described as a divisional committee, comprised of some members of the old County Down committee, convened at Saintfield on Christmas Day 1802. This ultimately successful effort put a stop to the activities of a weaver named Holt (quite likely an alias), who 'had been lately active in forming societies to plunder and assassinate'. However, this example seems to have been the exception rather than the rule, and county committees no longer functioned in either Antrim or Down. The paralysis imposed by the cessation of hostilities appears to have nearly completed the long-term process of the breakdown of centralized control within not only the United system but Defenderism as well.[7]

The outbreak of war in May 1803 rekindled the anticipation of French assistance among surviving northern rebels, and numerous gatherings of the disaffected were reported in the months that followed. In June, the Rev. Cupples received a communication informing him of the many meetings being held and requesting that he 'warn the loyal in his neighbourhood of the increase of the Defenders'.[8] William Minnis, a United leader from Saintfield, informed McGucken in early June that his part of the country was 'anxiously waiting for invasion' and that, although they had not lately held meetings, 'the spirit yet continues to a great extent'. According to the inspector of the Antrim yeomanry, the Ballymena region was 'particularly ill off' owing to the 'want of an active magistrate', and a 'general meeting of the United Irishmen' attended by an emissary thought to have recently returned from France took place there in July.[9]

Yet, despite Thomas Russell's efforts, the North failed to rise in support of Robert Emmet's rebellion. However, limited reactions to Russell's endeavours did occur in both Antrim and Down. The day after the defeat of the Dublin rising, the military commander at Belfast, Gen. Colin Campbell, summarized the movements triggered by Russell's overtures to the disaffected of east Ulster, stating: 'the country is not in so safe a state as might be wished'. 'Armed parties' had been sighted in many areas of Antrim. On the night of the 23 June, a sergeant in the Antrim militia reported from Shanecastle that he had seen 'numbers of people' moving towards Ballymena. At Carnmoney, where Russell's proclamation was posted on a meetinghouse door, 'the people ... had been in motion all night' in preparation for an attack on Belfast that never materialized. Crumlin men were also 'at drill', and a soldier claimed he had been stopped by an armed party near Larne, where 'he saw 400–500 men at exercise'.[10] McGucken's younger brother (who had 'great influence with the Defenders') was out with the 'Malone Boys' on the night of 23 June. In fact, the relative inactivity of the region can most accurately be attributed to a want of arms, and the belief that any rising attempted without massive foreign assistance was doomed to failure. As McGucken informed Marsden on 25 July, 'The people in general seem all at a loss. Although in many parts anxious for a rising, yet they can't see how it is to be effected, having no system amongst them. Arms they have, but few.'[11] Simply put, caution, not loyalty, lay behind the unwillingness of the Presbyterians to risk everything in another unequal contest with the ascendancy.

In August 1803, an informant claimed that Russell had 'succeeded greatly in organizing a large part of County Down', particularly the parishes in the Downpatrick area. He continued that the rebels planned to 'attack ... as the nights [were growing] longer [and] no quarter [was to be given] to Yeomen or Orangemen'.[12] Nor were these accounts of the disturbed state of east Ulster confined solely to the pens of overly alarmed local gentry and magistrates. The commander of the northern district, Lt Gen. Campbell, wrote to the military secretary in Dublin, 'All the counties in the district are perfectly quiet, except Down and Antrim, in which [there are] reports [of] strong symptoms of disaffection.'[13]

While many contemporaries viewed the failure of the Presbyterians to respond in any meaningful way to Russell's endeavours as an indication of the dissenting population's return to loyalty, several observers ascribed the relative quiet of the Presbyterians to factors other than a newfound fondness for the state. Sir George Hill, an east Derry landholder, forwarded intelligence he had obtained 'from old Presbyterian rebels', on whom he felt he could rely, to the Under Secretary Marsden. Hill discovered that 'there [was] still however in Antrim a bad spirit amongst some few of the Presbyterians'. The Dissenters would 'not however stir, at least in concert with the Catholics nor unless a successful invasion took place'.[14] In Hill's mind, it was not loyalty that held the Presbyterians back in 1803. It was sectarian distrust and, more pointedly, an unwillingness to act without French assistance. Like Hill, the Rev. Cupples thought that the Presbyterians had withdrawn due to a growing fear of their former Catholic allies.

> The dissenters of all denominations are impressed with the persuasion that the present is a Popish conspiracy, and menaces extirpation and ruin to Protestantism. Those [Presbyterians] who were deeply engaged in the last rebellion and most anxious to make a common cause with Catholics have now the greatest dread and suspicion of them.[15]

Cupples based his supposition on the fact that 150 Protestants at Ballynahinch in central Down had left the yeomanry rather than serve with Catholics. He concluded from this act: '[I]f Protestants in Ballynahinch [who were] very republican, act thus, we may safely infer a fortiori that they [sectarian animosities] prevail elsewhere.'[16] Information given in mid-August 1803 by a Presbyterian United Irishman from Down revealed that the United Irishmen were now 'confined' to northeastern districts of that county and the immediate environs of Belfast. He went on to explain that the few Protestants (members of the Church of Ireland) and Presbyterians who were still 'engaged in the conspiracy style[d] themselves United Irishmen [while] the papists [we]re defenders'. The informer anticipated that the Presbyterians and Catholics would 'fall out immediately if successful – as their objects in framing a new constitution now must be totally different'.

Furthermore, the relationship between dissenters and Catholics was not the only sectarian strain affecting the republican remnant, for the 'Protestants of the established Church [were] not at all trusted – except a few Deistical leaders'.[17] The informer stated that a breakdown along sectarian lines was inevitable in the aftermath of a successful revolution; by implication the process of religious polarization was not yet complete in mid-August 1803. This examination also provides evidence of a (albeit greatly diminished) Presbyterian/United Irish presence in east Ulster republicanism even in the aftermath of Emmet's rebellion.

Ranking members of the administration tended to stress the role played by distrust of, and disillusionment with, Napoleon for the Presbyterian withdrawal. William Wickham, the Chief Secretary, saw the potential utility to the regime of this impression. In a letter written to John King in November 1803, Wickham stated, 'The loyalty of the North is very much due to the persuasion of the Presbyterians that Napoleon is not a republican, but tho' it has no better foundations it might not be rejected and [is] very usable.'[18] In a communication written to Lord Hawkesbury a year after Emmet's rebellion, Hardwicke, the Viceroy, expressed the opinion that the northern yeomanry could be safely drawn upon for service elsewhere in Ireland. Hardwicke directly attributed the loyalty of the North, or at least that of the middling classes from which the yeomanry was predominantly drawn, to the perception 'that the conduct of France ... produced a very important change ... amongst the greater portion of those who ha[d] property to lose ... yet this change [was] nowhere so apparent or complete as in the province of Ulster'.[19]

Conclusions

Despite these frequent observations that sectarian animosity and/or disillusionment with France had finally succeeded in driving the Presbyterians from the republican fold by 1803, radical undercurrents still flowed beneath the surface in parts of east Ulster. The same informer who cited the prevalence of sectarian tensions within County Down's dwindling republican movement also felt that if the United Irishmen were to 'find the smallest prospect of success', they would 'instantly attack the military posts'.[20] More significantly, Gen. Campbell, who had by far the greatest access to intelligence and was in the best position to gauge the overall political climate of the northeast, reported to the Chief Secretary at the end of August 1803 that the northern district had been quiet throughout the month 'in as much as no acts of violence ha[d] occurred'. Yet, Campbell had no doubt that 'the spirit of insurrection' was 'still afloat', especially 'towards Saintfield and the mountains of Ballynahinch' in County Down and 'in the County Antrim north of this place [Belfast]'. Campbell continued, 'The inhabitants are very much in the moor, and frequently from home during the night, meetings for seditious purposes certainly take place.' Sixty-two men were in custody at

Belfast and the 'general belief' was that thousands of pikes had been concealed. Campbell concluded, 'The quiet of these counties depends solely in
the establishment of strong [military] posts.'[21]

What then can account for the near total withdrawal of Presbyterians
from proactive physical force resistance by 1803, if not by 1798 or even
1800, as is argued in the traditional interpretation? Kevin Whelan has
attributed this gradual erosion to loyalist efforts to depict the secular rising
in the South as a sectarian blood bath. Loyalist polemicists began a concerted effort in May 1798 to create a split between Catholic and Presbyterian United Irishmen, even prior to the outbreak of rebellion in the North in
June. Government-sponsored newspapers joined in shortly thereafter, and
this agenda continued in the years that followed, culminating in the publication in 1801 of Richard Musgrave's *Memoirs of the different rebellions
in Ireland*. The primary purpose of Musgrave's work, according to Whelan,
was 'to reattach Presbyterians to the fragmented Protestant consensus'.
Exaggerations of Defender–United Irish disharmony during the Ulster rising
were added to the pre-existing accounts of Catholic outrages in the South
in continuing attempts to break the radical religious alliance in Antrim and
Down. These efforts succeeded in driving a flood of United men into the
arms of the Orange Order. Whelan concludes that the most important factor
in severing the Catholic-dissenter tie was the revival of anti-Popery triggered by Napoleon's signing of the Concordat with the Pope in 1801, which
seemed to confirm the alarmists' worst fears of a Catholic conspiracy.[22]

I would like to offer a modified interpretation of the causes and progress
of the Presbyterian withdrawal from radical republicanism. First, it is obvious that some northern dissenters did leave the United society before, during
or shortly after the rebellion of 1798, as the traditional interpretation holds.
This flight can be linked to a fear of both loyalist forces and Catholic neighbours. The middle class was represented most prominently in this exodus, as
Gen. Nugent made clear in May 1799: '[U]nless the French should land a formidable force, no thought of insurrection would be made in the minds ... of
those who have anything to lose.'[23] However, this withdrawal of the middle
class did not signify the total departure of Presbyterians from northern
republicanism; the more militant members of the artisan class continued
to be active well into the new century. Ultimately between 1801 and 1803,
this Presbyterian remnant also withdrew or, more accurately, was reduced
to a state of inactivity due to a combination of loyalist propaganda, revived
anti-Popery and disillusionment with Napoleonic France over the signing
of a peace treaty with England. A secret report of the informer McGucken,
dated Belfast, 21 October 1801 states:

> Signing the preliminaries of peace ... came at a good time as the people were
> about to form committees expecting an invasion. [N]othing [was better] for
> the stability of government [than peace which] has completely disgusted
> my old friends and they now speak of emigrating to America ... the people
> are also disgusted at France.[24]

This, in turn, was the last straw for Presbyterian physical force republicanism in the North. The near total absence of reports of activity by either Defenders or United Irishmen in 1802 confirms the fact that any real hope for a successful revolution had died on the treaty table.[25] Finally, I have found strong evidence that the inactivity of the years following 1801 did not necessarily signify a return to loyalty by the majority of the Presbyterians of Antrim and Down, at least of the lower orders. The key, instead, was a rational decision not to risk destruction in the face of the preponderant military strength of the state without assistance from France.[26]

Afterwards

Indeed, well into 1804, there is evidence of continued disaffection. In the summer of that year, William Taylor obtained information from a Carrickfergus stone mason that 'the Defender business' was 'carrying on rapidly in and about Ballymoney and all that part' and he feared 'a nightly assassination to be attempted'.[27] The autumn of 1804 found Mr. Skeffington, a long-time Belfast magistrate, arguing quite persuasively that, although he believed there was no 'systematic plan of treason ... in the counties of Antrim and Down', he did 'not agree with the generality of gentlemen' of the region, who held the opinion 'that a return to sentiments of loyalty [wa]s very general in those counties'. Instead, Skeffington still saw the necessity of making distinctions between classes, not sects, in qualifying east Ulster's 'return to loyalty'. He allowed: '[M]any of the higher classes are now sensible of their former folly.' Yet, he feared, 'the great bulk of the people are as much inclined to be led astray ... as ever'.[28]

Certainly we must look to O'Connell and the emergence of Catholic nationalism in the 1820s as a significant motive force in the Presbyterian withdrawal from the radical fold.[29] However, recent work by Kirby Miller offers a fuller explanation. Following an apparent lull between 1803 and the termination of the Napoleonic Wars, acts of overt social resistance on the part of working-class dissenters reappeared in 1816. In turn, the final transformation to unionism came about not as the result of sectarianism but as a result of 'hegemonic' socio-economic, political, and religious pressure from their social superiors. Moreover, a massive, largely politically motivated, lower-class Presbyterian emigration removed thousands of the disaffected from the region. As Miller notes: '[F]rom the early 1800s to mid-century the letters written by Ulster Presbyterians who emigrated to the United States often exuded alienation ... as they perceived or at least portrayed themselves as economic and even political refugees from an inequitable and repressive society.' He concludes that 'the taming of Ulster's Protestant lower classes would be a prolonged, uneasy and even transatlantic development'.[30]

Simply put then, lower-class Presbyterian radicalism did not disappear in the aftermath of 1798; rather, it went underground in 1802 or 1803 only to re-emerge in the 1810s. Perhaps, most pointedly, it can be argued that many or most of the former Presbyterian United Irishmen never became loyalists. In reality, they either remained a sullen presence in east Ulster or ultimately left Ireland (or more accurately were driven out) in a lengthy process that lasted decades. It was the next generation that only fitfully embraced unionism, dating from the second half of the 1820s.

Notes

1   William Richardson, Moy, 2 May 1803, Michael MacDonagh (ed.), *The Viceroy's post-bag: The correspondence hitherto unpublished of the Earl of Hardwicke, the first Lord Lieutenant after the union* (London, 1904), 264–5.
2   NAI SOC 1025/1, [?] McGucken to Pollock, Belfast, 3 Jan. 1803.
3   NAI RP 620/62/12, William Gardiner to Marsden, Armagh, 16 June 1802; ibid., W. Gardiner to Pollock, 15 June 1802; James Paterson, County Derry, enclosed in ibid.; James H. McIlfatrick, *Sprigs around the pumptown* (Coleraine, 1996), 21.
4   The Coleraine Constitution, June 1802, quoted in McIlfatrick, *Sprigs*, 21.
5   NAI RP 620/62/12, J. Paterson, County Derry.
6   As Kevin Whelan notes, Ahoghill was an 'intensely Presbyterian' centre. Kevin Whelan, *The tree of liberty: Radicalism, Catholicism and the construction of Irish identity* (Cork, 1996), 67.
7   NAI SOC 1025/1/[?], McGucken to Pollock, Belfast, 3 Jan. 1803.
8   NAI RP 620/66/32, John Howe to Edmund McNaghten, 11 Sept. 1803.
9   Ibid. 620/65/95, Maj. Robert Innis [?], 13 July 1803; ibid., Matheson to Innis, 8 July 1803.
10 Ibid. 620/64/128, Brig. Gen. Colin Campbell to Littlehales, Belfast, 24 July 1803.
11 McGucken to Marsden, Belfast, 25 July 1803 in MacDonagh, *Viceroy's Post-bag*, 415.
12 TNA HO 100/112/402, notes of secret information given to Beatty, Vicar General and Magistrate of County Down, Garvaghy, 17 Aug. 1803.
13 NAI SOC 1024/2, Lt Gen. Campbell to Littlehales, Armagh, 1 Aug. 1803.
14 NAI RP 620/65/73, Sir George Hill to Marsden, Coleraine, 28 July 1803.
15 Ibid. 620/11/158, Cupples to Archer, inspector general of prisons, Lisburn, 14 Sept. 1803.
16 Ibid.
17 TNA HO 100/112/402–8, notes of secret information given to Beatty, Vicar General and Magistrate of County Down, Garvaghy, 17 Aug. 1803.
18 Ibid. 100/114/205, Wickham to King, Dublin Castle, 19 Nov. 1803.
19 Ibid. 100/121/14–16, Earl Hardwicke to Lord Hawkesbury, Dublin Castle, 20 July 1804.
20 Ibid. 100/112/407–8, notes of secret information given to Beatty, Vicar General and Magistrate of County Down, Garvaghy, 17 Aug. 1803.
21 NAI SOC 1024/4, Campbell to Wickham, Belfast, 31 Aug. 1803.
22 Whelan, *Tree of liberty*, 130, 133–8, 153–5.
23 NAI RP 620/7/73, Nugent, County Antrim, 10 May 1799.
24 Ibid. 620/10/118/18, McGucken, Belfast, 21 Oct. 1801. For renewed organizational efforts by the disaffected prior to the peace accord, also see TNA HO

100/106/264, Drummond, Belfast, 7 Sept. 1801.

25 For the peaceful state of the North during 1802, see Gen. W. Gardiner's report from May stating: 'that from each division of the Northern District the reports are uniformly of industry and tranquility', NAI RP 620/49/141, W. Gardiner to Marsden, Armagh, 1 May 1802.
26 Ibid. 620/65/73, Hill to Marsden, 17 Mar. 1803; NAI SOC 1024/4, Campbell, Belfast, 31 Aug. 1803; ibid. 1028/19, extract of letter from Skeffington, Belfast, 10 Oct. 1804.
27 Ibid. 1028/4, William Taylor to Lees, Carrickfergus, 20 Aug. 1804.
28 Ibid.
29 Marianne Elliott, *The Catholics of Ulster: A history* (New York, 2001), 271–2; Ian McBride, Scripture politics: Ulster Presbyterians and Irish radicalism in the late eighteenth century (Oxford, 1998), 223–5. As McBride states, 'In the political sphere, then, Catholic emancipation can be identified as the point of no return for Ulster Presbyterians.'
30 Ibid. 1028/19, extract of a letter from Skeffington, Belfast, 10 Oct. 1804. In fact, post-1798 Defenderism survived on a localized basis until the early 1810s when a more centralized regional system re-emerged. Tom Garvin has shown that 'in the extreme northeast' the new Defenderism 'actually inherited some Protestant leadership for a few years after 1815'. Tom Garvin, 'Defenders, Ribbonmen and others: Underground political networks in pre-famine Ireland', in *Past and present* 96 (1982), 144–5. Kirby A. Miller, 'Forging the "Protestant way of life": Class conflict and the origins of unionist hegemony in early nineteenth-century Ulster', in David A. Wilson and Mark G. Spencer (eds), *Ulster Presbyterians in the Atlantic world: Religion, politics and identity* (Dublin, 2006), 128–65.

Part II
South Munster, Galway and Mayo

5

South Munster

Socio-economic backgrounds

With some 60,000 souls, Cork city was the vibrant heart of the highly
commercialized south Munster region. The second city of Ireland had successfully established itself as a key port for provisions in the north Atlantic
trade network. The driving force behind this process of commercialization was a combination of improving landlords and an interwoven stratum of merchants, shippers and agricultural middlemen. Consecutively, the
rapid expansion of market capitalism created strong internal trade links
between Cork city and the surrounding agricultural districts of Counties
Cork, Waterford and Kerry, which increasingly focused their production to
meet the needs of the Atlantic provisions trade. An important result of commercialization, particularly in the highly fertile tillage districts of north and
east Cork, was the tripartite division of rural society into a predominantly
Protestant upper class gentry of landowners, a largely Catholic middling
order of farmers and cattlemen, and an overwhelmingly Catholic lower
stratum of cottiers and labourers.[1] Significantly, it is exactly this type of
advanced economic region, centred on a cosmopolitan city, which is associated with the emergence of radical republicanism in Ireland in the 1790s.
Indeed, the United Irishmen of Belfast and Dublin have been shown to have
utilized pre-existing trade networks and connections to disseminate their
radical ideology amongst the rural populations of the surrounding counties.
Moreover, urban activists knew their audiences well, and along with participatory democracy, they promised the alleviation of key economic grievances
such as rents and tithes.[2] The potent United Irish organization of Cork city
appears to have followed a similar trajectory in the 1790s.

Religious tension was a salient feature of life in south Munster during
much of the eighteenth century. A relatively large number of English settlers
had established themselves in the region during seventeenth century, and
correspondingly, Protestant gentry and clergy were thick on the ground.
This settlement pattern was prevalent particularly in the fertile and densely
populated tillage districts of northern and eastern County Cork. Moreover,
influential elements of the planter elite exhibited a profound anti-Catholic
bias, which had manifested itself in a number of ugly sectarian-motivated
incidents in Munster during the course of the eighteenth century.[3]

The rapid expansion of market capitalism during the second half of the
eighteenth century, combined with demographic pressure in the form of
rapid population growth, dramatically increased the cost of living in south
Munster for those who could least afford it.[4] Cottiers and labourers thus

found themselves increasingly trapped between rising rents and falling wages, in a classic example of the economists' price scissors. The rural poor responded to the disruption of their traditional socio-economic world with collective agrarian action in the form of the secret societies. Originating with the Whiteboys in 1761, these redresser movements attempted to block the enclosure of common land and to moderate the level of the exactions made by landlords, clergy and middlemen in the form of rent and tithes.[5] Founded in County Cork in 1785, the better-organized Rightboys made the mitigation of tithes their primary objective.[6] An act of parliament had exempted pasture land from tithes in 1735, and from that point on the burden fell exclusively on tillage lands. Furthermore, Anglican clerics who had previously demonstrated a willingness to negotiate rates below the legally sanctioned ten per cent increasingly sought to capitalize on the economic opportunities created by commercialization. Although Protestant ministers were often hesitant to raise tithe rates directly themselves, they were far more willing to sell collection rights to middlemen – 'tithe farmers' – who then ruthlessly squeezed the people in order to make the greatest return possible on their investment.[7] Finally, tithes were an issue, unlike wages or conacre rents, which could unite all the social strata of Catholic society.

Radical backgrounds

The evidence of a substantial, long-term, republican presence in Cork is compelling. In 1790, Denis Driscol began publication of the increasingly radical *Cork Gazette*, which was to have a remarkably long run through the autumn of 1797. The *Gazette* was the only newspaper in Ireland to openly support Paine's deistical religious opinions, and between 1794 and 1795 Driscol printed several editions of *The age of reason* in the city.[8] These prints were disseminated widely throughout the region. As the notorious informer, Leonard McNally, a Cork native, reported in 1795: 'Paine's works are in everyone's hands and in everyone's mouth. Large editions have been printed off by O'Driscol ... and sent over the country; they have got into the schools and are the constant subjects of conversations with the youth.'[9] Indeed, it is apparent that Cork's rightful place is alongside Dublin and Belfast as a source of radical published radical material in the 1790s. The sustained popular disaffection exhibited by the surrounding region can only begin to be understood in this light. In a discussion of the role played by schoolmasters in the dissemination of radical ideology during the 1790s, Kevin Whelan cites the example of the Cork teacher, John Hurley, who was involved in anti-tithe activities during 1794:

> He had several of the country people subscribed for a newspaper. He used to read the French debates and other seditious publications to the multitude ... Hence the parishioners became politicians, talked of liberty and equality and appointed a day to plant the Tree of Liberty.[10]

The formal presence of the United Irishmen in south Munster dates from 1793, when the society's first club was founded in Cork city by the Kinsale attorney, William Webb.[11] More intense efforts by the United Irishmen to organize Munster were initiated in late 1796 and inevitably focused on Cork. In November of that year, Arthur O'Connor travelled home to attend a meeting of the Cork United Irishmen, which had been called by his brother Roger who was an important member of the local society. This visit appears to have been part of a larger endeavour by the national executive to complete the organization of the provinces prior to the arrival of the Bantry Bay expedition.[12] In the spring of 1797 the United Irishmen further enhanced their organizational efforts, and by the autumn they had successfully established a broad-based regional structure centred on Cork city.[13] The movement had particular success swearing members in the suburbs and Liberties of the city as well as in the heavily commercialized parishes of northern and eastern County Cork stretching eastwards into Waterford. With the arrest of Roger O'Connor in the spring of 1797, the key leadership role in the city's United Irish movement and recruiting drive was played by the socially radical Cork woollen draper, John Sweeny.[14] Building on pre-existing socio-religious tensions, the republican emissary's enrolment efforts were greatly facilitated by the immediate political and economic climate. Accounts of the government's ruthless attempts to crush the potent republican movement of Ulster, coupled with stories of atrocities perpetrated by the province's Orangemen, created a furor amongst the Catholics in the south.[15] As Gen. Dalrymple, the commander of the garrison at Cork frankly explained, 'Accounts of northern atrocities "greatly enraged" the people.'[16]

Further aiding the United Irishmen's recruitment drive was a war-induced, economic downturn in 1797, which was deftly exploited by the society's propagandists. A Cork land agent described this phenomenon as follows: '[T]he taking off the bounty on land carriage [flour] to Dublin and the late duty on salt have been a great means of perverting the minds of the lower order.'[17] That autumn Cork United Irishmen were engaged in an economic boycott against members of the local yeomanry, thereby combining social and economic grievance with political activism.[18] Indeed, by the end of the year 1797, south Munster had a sizable, well-organized and highly motivated cellular United Irish military structure in place.[19]

One other aspect of south Munster republicanism sets it apart from the movement elsewhere in Ireland. To a far greater extent than its Leinster counterpart, the Cork society focused its efforts on politicizing the rural poor by distributing propaganda that fed on pre-existing socio-economic grievances. Thus from an early date the United Irishmen of the region successfully merged pre-existing agrarian concerns, such as tithes, with new radical concepts like natural rights and universal manhood suffrage.[20] This had important implications for the future.

The failure to rise in 1798

Why then did south Munster fail to rise in 1798, despite the existence of a substantial militarized republican movement centred on Cork city? To begin with, the United Irishmen of Munster had been led to believe by the movement's national leadership that no rising would occur prior to June. In any eventuality, the republicans of Cork had never intended to rise in the absence of a French landing.[21] Additionally, the provincial society had effectively been decapitated by the arrest of John Sweeny on March 28 and the nearly simultaneous trial, release and move to England of Roger O'Connor. The Dublin-based Sheares brothers attempted to fill the void, but their presence in the capital, coupled with their preoccupation with events at the national level and ultimate arrest just prior to the rising, robbed Cork's United Irishmen of leaders at the critical moment.[22]

Perhaps of greatest importance, as the result proximity and prevailing wind patterns, the authorities identified Munster and, more specifically, Cork harbour as the logical target of a French invasion. As a result, the entire south Munster region became flooded with troops. Compounding the problem was a severe economic downturn dating from the autumn of 1797, which added the fear of agrarian rebellion to the already traumatized local magistracy. In turn, these justifiably alarmed local loyalists demanded, and received, reinforcements to the already substantial military presence.[23] The radicals of Cork thus were confronted by an overwhelming display of strength by the state. Moreover, much of the county was disarmed vigorously in the weeks prior to the rebellion.[24] Finally, it must be remembered that the twin hearts of Irish republicanism in the 1790s, Belfast and Dublin, both failed to act at the critical moment. Although Dublin's United Irishmen did attempt to rise, they were pre-empted at the last hour by a rapid governmental mobilization and prudently retired to their homes. In Belfast, the United Irishmen of the republican movement's birthplace opted against an open contest with that city's powerful garrison. Given its relative isolation – for unlike Belfast and Dublin, Cork could not rely on the support of the surrounding counties – it is unrealistic to fault the city's radicals for having risked no more than their eastern urban counterparts.

In summing up the political status of south Munster during these key years, Dickson affirms:

> a robust revolutionary movement had developed a military capability in the course of 1797; the pivot was the Cork City organization ... It is irrefutable that across at least half of Munster there was a high level of popular disaffection evident by the early months of 1798 ... [and] we have seen that the circulation of printed propaganda from Cork and Dublin was most impressive and not by any means confined to the urban Anglophone world[25]

Pointedly then, the region failed to rise in May 1798, not because of an absence of popular enthusiasm, but because of the success of the government's pre-emptive, disarming campaign that spring, a heavy regional military presence and the loss of vital leaders on the eve of the rebellion. Essential questions remain: what became of this once formidable republican structure in the aftermath of the rebellion? Perhaps more importantly, what happened to the politicized popular disaffection so evident by 1798?

A continued republican presence

There is strong extant evidence that Cork's United Irishmen maintained a presence in south Munster at least until July 1803. A number of key issues are raised by the persistence of the region's republicans. Specifically, how widespread was the movement and what was the relationship between the Munster republicans and the reconstituted United Irish leadership in the capital? Finally, the south of Ireland was struck by successive waves of agrarian agitation between 1798 and 1803, and both the authorities and the United Irishmen were convinced that this disaffection could be readily channelled into active support for the overthrow of the government. What then, if any, was the relationship between the rural agitators and republicans?

In March 1799, Robert Harding forwarded intelligence from Cork to Dublin Castle, which confirmed that the republican flame still flickered in the city. Harding reported that Timothy Conway travelled to Dublin in late February or early March 1799 'on bad business', while the Rev. William Stawell had recently returned from a similar mission. Both men were former proprietors of the United Irish-funded newspaper, the *Harp of Erin*, and strongly suspected of being members of the Cork sub-directory, prior to the rebellion.[26] The veracity of this information was borne out in the weeks that followed. James McGucken, the highly reliable informer, confirmed that Stawell had been summoned to Dublin in order to carry the society's New Plan of Organization back to Cork.[27] Furthermore, Lord Castlereagh received a letter in April from Mr Judkin, who was 'secretly employed', which identified Conway as 'one of the directory at Cork'.[28] McGucken, later that month, included Councillor Dennis 'from Cork' on a list of known United leaders he felt ought to be arrested. Dennis was also identified as a member of the earlier sub-directory.[29] Thus, it safely can be concluded that the United Irishmen strove to retain some semblance of a regional structure in Cork at least through the spring of 1799.

Agrarianism in the aftermath of 1798

Disaffection of a different nature also appeared in County Cork in 1798 when a wave of agrarian agitation struck Munster with surprising ferocity in the aftermath of the rebellion. Superficially, the disaffection that centred on the counties of Limerick, Cork and Tipperary (although there were incidents throughout the province) seemed to be the latest manifestation of the long-term phenomenon of 'Whiteboyism'. This generic term denotes the activities of the agrarian secret societies that first appeared in the south of Ireland in the early 1760s.[30]

The Whiteboys are depicted most commonly as reactive with a primary focus on the redress of local grievance; and, in reality, the post-1798 movement in County Cork continued to address the traditional concerns of tithes and rents.[31] Yet it is evident that a fundamental transformation had occurred by the winter of 1798–1799. Prior to the 1790s the agrarian secret societies exhibited an extreme hesitancy to utilize capital force. As Thomas Bartlett notes: 'These essentially conservative protests were not, by eighteenth-century standards, particularly violent ... there was much intimidation and threatening behaviour, but significantly death was rarely inflicted by the protesters.'[32] But in the aftermath of 1798, agrarian activists in County Cork demonstrated a remarkable willingness to employ extreme levels of physical violence. Perhaps more importantly, for a period of years following 1798, the secret societies supported the overthrow of the socio-political system via the medium of a French invasion, a decidedly pro-active motivation.

Post-rebellion disaffection was evident in County Cork as early as September 1798 when the authorities arrested two blacksmiths 'caught' manufacturing pikes near Oysterhaven. A short time later unknown individuals cut down thirty ash trees for use as pike handles. On 14 September a relatively minor incident occurred that foreshadowed the strikingly brutal events that were to become commonplace in the months that followed. That night intruders cut off, or 'cropt', the ears of six horses belonging to a man who resided on the northern outskirts of Cork city. The motivation ascribed to the crime was the fact that the individual in question had 'taken his tithes'.[33] In other words, the animals' owner was a tithe farmer, one of the despised middlemen capitalists who purchased, or rented, the right to collect tithes from ministers in response to the opportunities offered by the emerging market economy during the second half of the eighteenth century. These men of business were inevitably more efficient and ruthless than the clergy in extracting maximum rates and as a result were often bitterly resented. It hardly is surprising that tithe farmers had been one of the primary targets of the earlier Whiteboy and Rightboy redresser movements in Cork.[34]

In fact, what can most accurately be described as an overt tithe war raged in County Cork throughout the winter of 1798–1799. This simple reality was obvious by January 1799, when members of the Cork establishment described the impact the anti-tithe agitation was having locally. That month Mr Longfield reported from Cork city that 'in the eastern part of this county ... not a tithe farmer or proctor dare[d] show his head'.[35] Similarly from north Cork, a Mr Freeman wrote, 'Notices threatening death to all dealers in tithes, should they proceed to decree any person, have been universally posted ... at every chapel from Churchtown to Millstreet.' Most significantly, the anti-tithe agitation was coordinated as 'emissaries' were known to be crisscrossing the county, holding 'nightly' meetings.[36] Undeniably by February, the situation had degenerated to the point where it drew the attention of the Lord Lieutenant, Cornwallis, who bluntly informed the Duke of Portland: 'In County Cork the usual resistance to the payment of tithes continues accompanied by the cruel persecution of those employed in collecting them.'[37]

Specific outrages included the murder 'in a most barbarous and savage manner' of a tithe farmer and his assistant at a house only six miles from Cork city on the night of Saturday 19 January. The victim, a farmer named Timothy McCarthy, paid the ultimate penalty for having rented the tithes of the parish of Carrigrohanebeg. Similarly at Glanworth in north Cork, a band of so-called 'rebels' met nightly in 'great force'. This group contained a sizable mounted element, which permitted them to operate over a large area. Members of the band attempted to murder a Mr Hanlon at Castletownroche and, although the primary target escaped, his under-bailiff was beaten 'almost to death'. A particularly brutal attack took place in Rathcormack, where a number of men forced their way into the home of the Rev. Mr Blackwood, an Anglican cleric. In addition to destroying Blackwood's tithe records, the likely objective of their visit, the intruders also butchered his processor, a member of the Elgin fencibles, who had the misfortune to be in the house at the time. After killing the soldier they 'cut the body in small pieces'. In a like fashion, although with less sanguinary results, marauders entered the residence of the Rev. Campion and destroyed tithe notes valued at £200; they also grievously injured two of the minister's servants.[38] Near the end of January, another process server was decapitated near Kildorrery, while several others were severely beaten.[39] Indeed, the level of violence evident in the anti-tithe campaign of the winter of 1798–1799 compares quite unfavourably with that of its most recent antecedent, the widespread Rightboy movement of the 1780s. The Rightboys, who similarly focused much of their attention on the issue of tithes, were responsible for as few as four deaths during the six years they were active in County Cork between 1785 and 1791.[40]

What then explains the willingness of post-1798 agrarian movements in south Munster to utilize extreme physical violence? As illustrated above, the post-1798 agrarian secret societies in south Munster demonstrated a surprising willingness to utilize extreme violence. It is argued here that the most satisfactory explanation for this striking development is the brutalization of Irish society in the 1790s. The ideologically driven war with revolutionary France and the rise of radical republicanism in Ireland engendered tremendous fear in Irish loyalists and the government, who responded with increasingly savage repression. The litany of atrocity between 1793 and 1798 is well known. The military shot down some 250 people during the militia riots of 1793; hundreds, if not thousands, of Defenders were killed or sent to the fleet between 1794 and 1798; the Orange Order drove between 5,000 and 7,000 Catholics from their homes in mid-Ulster during 1795–1796; the bloodbath of the great rebellion of 1798 resulted in somewhere between 20,000 and 30,000 deaths in a few short months. Simply put, the state tacitly sanctioned the creation of an environment in which capital force was the norm.

In addition to the three dozen executions that took place in Cork in 1798, the neighbouring counties of Limerick and Tipperary offered the people of Cork proximate examples of loyalist and government-sponsored terror. Over a three-week period in June 1798, seventy-six men were tried by court martial at Limerick on charges related to the rebellion. Seven of these individuals were executed, and twenty-two others transported. In Tipperary, the rabid high sheriff Thomas Judkin Fitzgerald waged a vicious flogging campaign prior to the rebellion against United Irishmen, both real and imagined.[41]

Moreover, officially sanctioned terror in the form of courts martial persisted. For example, a massive wave of agrarian agitation in the west was brutally suppressed during the winter and spring of 1799. At Galway over seventy-three cases were heard, which resulted in eighteen capital convictions and a like number of transportations. Similar trials were held at Ballinarobe and Castlebar in Mayo, leading to at least twenty-two death sentences. In 1800, as a result of Defender activity, a major court martial was convened at Ballymena in County Antrim, where seventeen capital convictions were ultimately carried into effect. Indeed, as late as December 1803 in Counties Tipperary and Waterford, areas largely untouched by the political turmoil of the 1790s, Special Commissions sentenced seventeen men to hang. In reference to these latter cases, Thomas Prendergast observed, 'His inquiries into the causes and effects of the outrages' that had led to the trials had 'nothing of a political tendency'. Instead, 'their objects were to drive from the neighbourhood strange workmen ... or to interfere with the letting of farms'. Prendergast concluded, 'The present disturbances, frightful as they are, are nothing more than a revival of the old Whiteboy spirit that [for] fifty years past has at different and frequent periods prevailed.'[42] That a fundamental transformation had occurred is confirmed graphically by the fact that only about fifty deaths, including government-sanctioned executions, can be attributed to the combined disturbances of the Whiteboys, Rightboys, Oakboys and Steelboys between 1760 and 1790.[43]

Another striking divergence in post-1798 agrarianism in County Cork is revealed in a manifesto posted at Glanworth in January 1799. The motivational forces that drove the earlier secret societies are aptly summarized by Jim Smyth as follows: 'None of these movements challenged the system of land ownership, or sought to abolish rents or tithes. Rather they agitated for a reduction of those exactions to levels sanctioned by custom as fair.'[44] Alternatively, the Glanworth manifesto demanded the outright abolition of tithes rather than their mitigation. It further forbade 'any man to pay or take' tithes.[45] Nor was this document an isolated aberration, for evidence revealed at the courts martial assembled to deal with the agrarian crisis in

March 1799 established that the 'people ... by their oath [we]re bound to pay no taxes or tithes, and to assemble when called'.[46]

The significance of this transformation should not be underestimated. By endeavouring to eliminate tithes in their entirety, the secret societies called into question the legitimacy of a central facet of the Protestant ascendancy – the right of the established Church to levy taxes on the Catholic majority. Thus, an extremely important evolution is revealed. The Whiteboys during the 1760s never questioned the entitlement of the established Church to collect tithes. However, mercenary middlemen tithe farmers who charged rates above the customary, if not technically legal, level were targeted as violators of the moral economy.[47] Similarly, the Rightboys did not directly challenge the Protestant minister's ownership and collection rights. Although in addition to tithe farmers the Rightboys also often attacked proctors who, for a price, did the collecting for the actual owners.[48] Yet during the formative decade of the 1790s, efforts to limit tithes to customary levels were supplanted by endeavours to eliminate them in their entirety. Hence, the very legitimacy of the established Church was called into question.

The motivating force behind this transformation was the Society of the United Irishmen, which had made its most dramatic inroads in the highly commercialized tillage districts of east Cork during 1797. It is hardly coincidental that these same parishes were the ones most affected by the anti-tithe agitation of 1798–1799. Along with participatory democracy, the United Irishmen promised to abolish the taxes and tithes.[49] By injecting the Enlightenment and Thomas Paine into the picture the United Irishmen pointed to the irrationality and simple unfairness of a system where the often desperately poor majority supported the Church of a far better off minority.

The evidence of this process is substantial. In a meeting at Cloyne in October 1797, the Cork United Irish leader John Sweeny addressed an assembled body. He knew his audience well for he focused his speech on the issue of tithes.[50] Most importantly, he pointed to the need to eliminate the 'state-sponsored church', exhorting the people 'not to pay [tithes] ... and to due all in our power to obstruct the sd. Tythe being paid'.[51] The tithe war of 1798–1799 is proof positive that the lesson was taken to heart. Thus, at least for a time, the radical republicanism of the United Irishmen intersected with the redress of agrarian grievance. The end result was a highly focused hybrid – the 'educated Whiteboy'.[52]

Perhaps of even greater importance, the success of the anti-tithe agitation – and it was highly successful, indeed at least in the short term – strongly suggests that large numbers of people expected to avoid the penalties traditionally associated with non-payment. In turn, the only plausible explanation for this assumption is a widespread popular belief that a French invasion would soon overturn the Protestant ascendancy and disestablish the Church that sustained it.

Evidence for the broad-based anticipation of foreign assistance is substantial. William Kirby, a magistrate who lived at Tallow on the western extremity of County Waterford, expressed 'great concern' over the 'unpleasant state of the country' in a letter to Lord Castlereagh written in mid-January 1799. Although his home district was 'tolerably quiet', the neighbouring east Cork Barony of Kinnatalloon was 'in a dreadful state of disturbance' as 'scarcely a night [passed] without a robbery attended with savage cruelty'. Kirby identified the responsible parties as a 'well-armed' band operating from the village of Conna, headed by a deserter from the Clare militia named Michael Bryan, and gave the following most ominous warning: 'They look forward with confidential hope to the arrival of a French force on the southern coast ... [and] when that ... occurs they will rise in a mass.'[53] Similarly, Mr Harding believed the 'repeated acts of outrage' were a means of 'preparing the minds of the lower orders' for participation in a rising planned in conjunction with a French landing.[54] In the Blarney area, the people talked 'openly of rising', while the disaffected felled trees within two miles of the Liberties of Cork city for use as pike handles. Furthermore, a county committee was believed to hold meetings in the house of a farmer named Buckley at Whitechurch, where a provincial committee had met 'often' during the preceding winter.

Of greatest concern to local loyalists were the persistent rumours of an imminent rising, although all sources of intelligence acknowledged that this would not take place in the absence of a French invasion.[55] In fact for several years following 1799, the ebb and flow of agrarian agitation in Cork closely mirrored the degree of anticipation of invasion, and it was not until the French defeat at Trafalgar in 1805 that this connection was permanently severed.

Throughout the winter of 1798–1799 agrarian depredations continued to plague the property owners in County Cork. Near Blarney in early March, 'rebels' burned three houses, two at Grenagh and one belonging to a tithe proctor at Knockilly. On the night of 18 March, a man named Creedon, who lived in the Liberties of Cork city, had six cattle destroyed as punishment for having rented land out from under a family named Connell.[56] The approach of spring was accompanied by increasingly shrill cries from local loyalists for decisive action by the government, as one gentleman asserted: 'We must outrage the constitution ... by acts of severity [before] we can preserve it.' In response the military scoured the countryside, taking up the members of three separate agrarian cells totalling some thirty men.[57] More significantly, the commander of the southern military district, the exceedingly brutal Gen. Gerard Lake, placed the counties of Limerick, Tipperary and Cork under martial law.[58]

As arbitrary military justice rapidly supplanted civil law in County Cork, 'judges determined not to try rebels and the Grand Juries of the city and county ... left them to be tried by courts martial'.[59] By 23 March, Lake felt the imposition of military law was having the desired effect:

The country is quiet and every report from the different parts of the district gives reason to hope that tranquillity will soon be restored, as the dread which the people have of courts martial will keep them quiet till the French come.[60]

Similarly, Gen. Myers, commanding the garrison at Cork city, confidently informed his superiors on the twenty-sixth that he had arrested twenty men for houghing cattle, thereby putting an end to the 'mischief'.[61]

Yet the courts martial also revealed some rather unsettling facts to the authorities. The difficulty the government experienced in obtaining testimony against the accused was demonstrative of widespread popular support for the secret societies. Moreover, Gen. Lake found '[the] people universally sworn throughout the district', confirming the broad-based participatory nature of post-1798 agrarianism in Munster.[62]

Despite the establishment of summary military justice in March, outrages, albeit on a diminished scale, continued to disturb Cork. The most shocking episode was the assassination at Macroom in April of Robert Hutchinson, a magistrate and prominent member of the regional gentry. Fifteen well-armed assailants graphically demonstrated the degree to which the deferential conventions of the moral economy had collapsed in the county by the winter of 1799 when one of them thrust a pike through Hutchinson's heart on the staircase of his home.[63] Dozens of arrests ensued, including that of the apparent ring leader John Duggan, alias Captain Thunderbolt. The resultant trials by court martial of John Duggan, Callaghan McCarthy and Owen Scanlan, and of Daniel Reen, who had been Hutchinson's steward for twenty-four years, revealed a number of striking features pertaining to the event. Firstly, the members of the party considered themselves 'sworn United Irishmen'. Furthermore, the band appeared to be part of a wider conspiracy that had scouted the homes of a number of 'respectable magistrates and gentlemen', which were targeted for assassination.[64] On 14 May the authorities executed John Duggan, Callaghan McCarthy, Owen Scanlan, Timothy Buckley and Dennis Duggan for their roles in Hutchinson's murder. After hanging, their heads were cut off and displayed as an awful example on Macroom's bridewell.[65] Other members of the group responsible for Hutchinson's death, including the actual assassin, Charles McCarthy and his brother Owen, were captured in Kerry in late June.[66]

Cornwallis was troubled sufficiently by the events in Munster to order an investigation into the state of affairs of the entire southern military district. The man assigned to this duty, Gen. Clarke, duly travelled through much of the southwest of Ireland during April and May. In his report to the Viceroy, Clarke identified the complex nature of the agitation and was also harshly critical of local landlords, comparing them quite unfavourably to their counterparts in England:

> It appears from the evidence given at most of the Court's Martial that the lower order (particularly the murders of the late Mr. Hutchinson) have determined to murder every gentleman in the country evidently with a view to drive them from their homes and divide their estates, or at least

to intimidate them, so that they may rent the land at their own price; The great sources of these diabolical principles seem to spring from the dislike to tithes ... The Middle Man is likewise a great grievance as from his inordinate rapacity in letting his land to the cottager who is unable to pay his rent and support his family with any kind of comfort owing to the rate of labour which is regulated by the landlord. I am sorry to add that gentlemen do not in general treat their inferiors with the kindness and humanity people of that station of life experience from the higher orders in England.[67]

Yet having allowed for the agrarian focus of the discontent, Clarke summarized that he had 'every reason to believe that the disposition of the people [wa]s not good ... they [we]re ready to rise should the French land in this country'.[68]

In the end, some sense of the scale and ultimately successful nature of the anti-tithe campaign of 1798–1799 can be gleaned from a 'report on the outrages committed in the Diocese of Cloyne'. The author, the Anglican Bishop of Cloyne, explained the impact of the movement as follows: 'Very few will attempt to serve processes for tithes, the proctors in general have given up their books and arrears for 1798–1799 unpaid, while [the] clergy [are] reduced to distress.'[69] In fact as late as 1802, tithe holders in County Cork were attempting to recoup the revenues lost in 1798–1799. Although parliament passed a Compensation Act 'for the benefit of clergy whose tithes were withheld in 1798–1799', the difficulties involved in their actual collection remained formidable. Indeed, Richard Orpen, high sheriff of County Cork, prudently resisted requests from tithe owners in the east Muskerry parishes of Inishcarra and Aghabulloge to provide small cavalry detachments as escorts for collectors, arguing that 'in order to put into effectual force the provisions of this act, which is a service highly obnoxious ... it would require in this extensive county no small military force ... to aid civilian power'.[70]

Daniel Cullinan and the reorganization of the United Irishmen: political events of 1803

The summer of 1799 found much of Ireland calm for the first time in several years. This state of placidity was tied directly by numerous observers to popular disappointment over the failure of the French to invade. Yet by autumn of the year, reports of widespread disaffection were once again flowing into Dublin Castle. For instance, in September a member of the Meath militia stationed in Cork city revealed a plot, which he claimed had succeeded in subverting 'several soldiers'. Gen. Myers promptly conducted an investigation and discovered 'that a system of tampering with the troops [wa]s again at work'.[71] Shortly after Christmas, Lord Longueville cautioned: '[O]ur people are badly disposed. We cannot eradicate rebellion and murder from their daily thoughts.' More ominously he added, 'If some thousands of Frenchmen land here, they [the people] will all join them, [and therefore] the rebellion has not been subdued.'[72] Longueville complained weeks later: '[Although] our weather is very bad [it is the] dispositions of our natives [that] give us more melancholy foreboding.'[73] In late December 1799, Longueville again gave warning in the same terms. Nor in his eyes was the discontent exhibited that winter undirected for, revealingly, he discerned in it the hand of the 'French General Clarke and his aide de camp Mr. Bradshaw'. The pair was thought to be near Cork harbour seeking passage to France 'from whence they [we]re to communicate intelligence', preparing 'the people here to rise to assist a French invasion'.[74]

In reality, the ubiquitous 'General Clarke' was Daniel Cullinan, the middle-aged son of a Cashel blacksmith.[75] Cullinan, about forty years old in 1800, was described as tall and dark with a facial scar extending from his left nostril to his lip. Additionally, he is known to have attended an Irish seminary in France; and considering his age, there is a strong likelihood that he was resident in France during the formative revolutionary period. Yet whatever the source of his radical orientation by 1798, and probably earlier, Cullinan was an active member of the Society of the United Irishmen. Indeed, his experience on the continent, level of education and language skills made Cullinan an obvious candidate for assignment to France, and in early 1798 the movement dispatched him as an emissary to the Directory.[76] As Chief Secretary William Wickham later confirmed, Cullinan 'was very deeply implicated in the Rebellion of 1798'.[77]

Between the defeat of the rebellion and his capture late in 1803, Daniel Cullinan remained vigorous in his dedication to the republican cause. During this five-year period he traversed the country, utilizing a bewildering array of disguises and aliases, the most common of which was 'General Clarke'. This *nom-de-guerre* most certainly was taken from Gen. Henri Clarke, a second-generation Frenchman of Irish decent who played a key role in coordinating French invasion plans with the United Irishmen in Paris.[78] The real Gen. Clarke's status as a republican descendant of the Wild Geese made Cullinan's choice of alias an inspired one. For in popular perception, particularly in south Munster, the utilization of such an identity fused older Jacobite traditions with radical republicanism.

The first extant record of Clarke's presence in Ireland reached Dublin Castle in August 1798, from Harding, who wrote, 'General Clarke in the French service is in some part of this country.' The dispatch also contained intelligence of an impending rising in Cork and Kerry. Perhaps significantly, the appearance of Clarke in Munster directly coincided with the French invasion of Mayo.[79] In any event, following the crushing defeat of the Franco-Irish army in September, 'General Clarke' disappears from the records for over a year. In fact, it was not until August 1799 that Gen. Charles informed his superiors that he was 'on the lookout' for a person who had recently arrived from France 'under the name of Clarke ... in the neighbourhood of Kilkenny'.[80]

The reorganization of the Society of the United Irishmen

Efforts by the United Irishmen to reorganize provincial networks clearly were under way by the spring of 1800. As Ruán O'Donnell notes in his important *Aftermath*, by March 1800, 'a cadre of United Irish emissaries were engaged in an attempt to rebuild the organization in Leinster', and 'similar meetings and activities were reported ... particularly in Munster'. [81] These efforts followed the New Plan of Organization, which sought to avoid the major flaws of the old system, namely the prevalence of informers and the tendency of local committees to act independently of central control. Therefore, communications were to be carried by word of mouth, thus avoiding the use of the written documents that had so often fallen into the hands of the government in the past. [82]

The reorganization of the movement on the provincial level was entrusted to a small cadre of highly competent activists, including the chimerical 'General Clarke'. Cullinan moved tirelessly throughout the country, working to re-establish networks and disseminate the New Plan. [83] During the late summer of 1800, he was in Ulster 'for the purpose of organizing the province', where the ever-vigilant McGucken viewed a copy of the plan in Belfast on 20 September and described it as 'very ingeniously drawn ... and very inflammatory'. [84] In January 1801, 'General Clarke' was in Donegal, where it was reported that 'his plan of organization [was] getting on fast'. [85] Later in the year, Cullinan and Hope journeyed to Leinster, where they attempted to establish contact with the noted Wicklow guerrilla leader Michael Dwyer, who was still holding out in the mountains. Although ultimately unsuccessful, this effort appears to have been an attempt to coordinate the activities of Dwyer's band with those of Cullinan's own followers in the Munster. [86]

The news of French victories on the continent in the spring of 1801 renewed the hope of foreign intervention amongst the disaffected across Ireland. This fact was reflected by an increase in the level of radical activity in Munster. [87] For instance, a 'committee' meeting was held in Cork city in May, where the assembled delegates asserted that 'the French w[ould] certainly invade in June or July'. Similarly, the system was said to be 'advancing in east Cork', where a sizable body gathered near Castlelyons. This latter conclave ostensibly met on 'ordinary business', but importantly, 'the conversation ran upon the folly of their giving up what they should very shortly want, their pikes'. [88]

Significantly, Cullinan returned to the province early that summer; his reappearance dovetailing neatly with accounts of the French triumphs in Europe. Although he had changed his alias, Cullinan's presence in the region was detected by the local authorities in mid-July. Gen. Myers sent a dispatch to Dublin in July, reporting: 'A man named Murphy, the famous priest in the Wexford Rebellion, [who was in fact long dead] had been in Cork for several days'. Moreover, the man had previously been in Limerick, 'where he was stirring up trouble'. Myers concluded, 'The man in question is certainly the person who goes by the name of General Clarke.'[89]

Cullinan conducted two well-attended meetings in Cork that July, the objective of which was the 'reorganization and readiness to support a French invasion'. Those in attendance were cautioned against carrying out arms raids as they 'only dr[e]w the attention of the government'.[90] The rationale behind this policy was laid clearly out in the United Irishmen's New Plan of Organization:

> This plunder of arms was always the cause of counties being proclaimed that fruitful source of every crime. [A]ssassination having become frequent, we must disassociate from it, killing the Yeoman or Magistrate wouldn't change the system which is the root and provides justification for repression.[91]

The New Plan was based on the following assumption: '[T]he mass of the population of Ireland are panting for emancipation [and] they will most freely follow at any period the Republican talent ... whenever they call them forth to act.'[92] Thus, the leadership believed that it was unnecessary and dangerous to allow local committees to continue to operate autonomously.

A number of vital facts about the effectiveness of post-1798 United Irish networks are revealed by the activities of Daniel Cullinan. First, Cullinan's ability to move, apparently at will, throughout the province despite the best efforts of the local authorities and the sizable reward of £500 strongly suggests that a network of sympathizers and safe houses was in place. Similarly, his capacity to support himself for extended periods of time in disparate regions of the country while constantly shifting abodes clearly demonstrates that he was funded from a centralized source. Furthermore, the organization had the ability to coordinate the distribution of such resources. Most importantly, Cullinan's role as provincial organizer under the auspices of the United Irish executive in Dublin, as established by accounts from a variety of credible sources, confirms the survival of a centralized republican structure. Finally, the often hazy quality of the government's intelligence on Cullinan is itself demonstrative of the success of the United Irish movement's efforts to maintain secrecy in the aftermath of 1798.

Indeed, it was not until August 1801 that Thomas Judkin Fitzgerald, the rabidly loyalist high sheriff of Tipperary, correctly identified 'General Clarke' as 'Cullinan, son to a farrier in Cashel'.[93] A report from Gen. Myers that same month noted that Cullinan, again using the alias Father Murphy, had recently been to Kinsale on the southern coast of Cork as well as Glin in Kerry. With obvious consternation, the general attributed his inability to capture Cullinan to the rapidity with which he shifted locations and declared of the rebel: '[He is] more dangerous than any [man] I have yet heard of ... a bloodthirsty villain of most dangerous talents ... he has no objection to become a martyr'.[94] By September, the ever-elusive General Clarke had returned to Limerick, where a letter thought to have been written in his hand was intercepted and turned over to Fitzgerald. Further intelligence obtained by the sheriff revealed that the population of the region anticipated a French landing, although he believed that with a concerted effort on the part of the authorities, the 'farmers of substance ... would join the government and separate from the lower order'.[95]

Munster and Emmet's rebellion

With the signing of the preliminaries of peace between Britain and France in the autumn of 1801, the window of opportunity opened by French military triumphs in the spring of that year slammed shut. Correspondingly, the absence of reports of activity, either agrarian or more overtly political, confirms the fact that the disaffected were keenly aware of the international situation. Yet by the early autumn of 1802, it was obvious to the United Irish exiles in France that the Treaty of Amiens would not hold. In October of that year, Robert Emmet was dispatched to Ireland to prepare the country for a rising in conjunction with the French invasion, which the United Irishmen now fully expected the following summer.

In Dublin Emmet assembled a hard-core cadre of middle-level activists. These men included: James Hope, William Putnam McCabe, Michael Quigley, William Hamilton, Malachy Delaney and Nicholas Grey. Although his name was never directly linked to that of Emmet, at least in the extant sources, it is all but certain that Daniel Cullinan should be added to this list. In April, Thomas Russell, a founding father of the movement as well as its most socially radical member, returned from France. Planning remained centred on the arrival of a French force with the United Irishmen playing an auxiliary role. From March, preparations for the impending rising were under way in a number of counties. These efforts utilized the links that had been re-established from 1800, as trusted and highly capable activists were dispatched to a number of key counties where they contacted known republicans. The conspiracy centred on the capital, where the Castle was to be seized by a *coup de main*. Key support was to be provided by the adjacent counties of Kildare and Wicklow. Yet significantly, contact also was established with sympathizers in all four provinces. Indeed, Emmet believed that if he was successful in Dublin initially, he could ultimately count on nineteen counties.[96]

Agrarianism, 1802–1803

The renewal of hostilities between England and France was mirrored by the return of large-scale agrarian disturbance to Munster, a fact that can hardly be considered coincidental. By November, after a year-long hiatus, outrages again grew frequent in Limerick, south Tipperary, north Cork and northwestern Waterford. Tithes, rents and agricultural wages returned as the primary grievances of the agitators, but local loyalists clearly perceived the hand of outside influences. A deeply concerned John Cooke wrote in a letter to Under Secretary Alexander Marsden:

> If outrages were all I wouldn't trouble you. But their associations seem too general and methodical for the ostensible purposes of them, and if there be a probability of a war with France, experience has convinced us that they claim the attention of [the] government.[97]

Active resistance in Munster centred on the two substantial cities in the region, Cork and Limerick. The case of the disaffection in Limerick is exceedingly complex and demonstrates the difficulties that all concerned parties – the authorities both local and national as well as the leadership of the United Irishmen in the capital – had in ascertaining its true nature. In February 1803 Gen. Payne was assigned to replace a discredited Gen. Morrison as military commander of the city. Morrison had been forced to resign after he responded to, apparently false, rumours of an impending attack on the city on the night of 6 January. He stripped the outlying areas of all military protection in order to reinforce his already formidable garrison. A thorough investigation into the events in Limerick revealed that the pantomime rebellion was in fact the result of local political machinations.[98]

Yet by February 1803, Payne found himself reporting: '[T]here is certainly mischief abroad and a combination between the capital and this entire province – but to what extent I cannot yet venture to hazard an opinion.' The general held interviews with 'confidential spies', who 'positively assert[ed] that they [we]re in the habit of attending nightly meetings'. Moreover, Payne received the names of 'captains of hundreds and lists of arms taken'. He doubted the veracity of much of the intelligence provided to him by informers, with the exception of the accounts of the arms raids he had received. The general reported: 'There are more arms in the county than I at first imagined and the audacity of the people to acquire more is unbounded.'[99]

With mounting consternation, Marsden replied to another of Payne's communiqués in March, stating:

> I am sorry to find your district so much disturbed … The picture you give is very serious, and the robbing of arms which you mention is quite beyond anything we have heard of since the rebellion, take most effectual courses, and give us information, whatever money wanted for information and rewards you may have.[100]

Gen. Payne continued to struggle to determine the motivations that lay behind the acts of outrage that manifested themselves in Limerick during the winter 1802–1803 and which, despite his best efforts, persisted into the spring and summer. He was duly cautious in attributing the distress to overtly political factors and continually acknowledged the traditional nature of most of the offences. Yet Payne also was deeply concerned with certain aspects of the agitation, particularly the highly focused determination demonstrated by the arms raiders. Like many other observers in Ireland that spring, he identified the renewal of war with France as the primary cause of the increased activity he was witnessing in his own district: '[T]he probability of war has already produced symptoms of mischief – such as riding at night-flogging.'[101] Similar accounts came from Tipperary. James Perry, a local landowner near Clonmel, described 'nightly outrages' in a note to Marsden. These assaults also took the form of arms' raids. Like Payne in Limerick, Perry saw a direct correlation between the 'commencement of hostilities' and events in Tipperary.[102]

United Irish efforts to prepare Munster for a supportive rebellion date from at least mid-April 1803. On 14 May Payne reported to Dublin Castle, 'I have heard in the last four weeks a good deal of a certain Mr Jones passing thro the counties of Cork and Kerry.' This man was most certainly the proven united activist Richard Todd Jones, who played a key part in maintaining contact between the conspirators in the capital and Munster. The general added that Jones was now in Limerick, while 'three men have been sent to Tralee Gaol' in Kerry 'for conducting illegal oaths'.[103] Similarly in June, Henry Harding informed William Wickham that County Clare, as well as eastern and central Limerick, were 'supposed to be ... quiet', although the same could not be said for western Limerick and north Cork. In these latter areas, Harding feared that 'the disaffected ha[d] ... active agents'. Additionally he found that 'the people in that part [we]re ready for enterprise on the first opportunity'.[104]

Revealingly, Cullinan was in Munster that spring and was undoubtedly one of the agents utilized by Emmet to prepare the south to rise in conjunction with the expected French invasion. Cullinan contacted Timothy Conway, a Cork watchmaker and a central figure in the city's Republican movement through 1798, who unbeknownst to him had been turned by the government in 1799. Conway duly notified Gen. Myers of Cullinan's presence in the city, and he was narrowly able to elude capture.[105]

The early summer of 1803 was relatively quiet in much of Munster, although rumours of impending rebellion continuously plagued Gen. Payne at Limerick. Two days before the solstice, he replied to an earlier communication by acknowledging his pleasure over the apparent good dispositions of 'the people of Ireland'. But in spite of the calm, he warned his correspondent, 'I would not be too sanguine as to the province of Munster.' Payne anticipated no immediate threat, yet further cautioned: 'Do not calculate too much upon our dispositions if we have an opportunity of showing them.'[106] In the weeks immediately preceding Emmet's rebellion, Munster retained the appearance of placidity although tantalizing hints of preparations are undeniably discernible. On 13 July, Payne once more reported his district tranquil, with the notable exception of 'some rumours relative to associations and the administering of the United oath in Kerry'.[107]

All was thrown into chaos by an accidental explosion on 16 May at one of the several munitions depots established by the conspirators in the capital. With the government thus alerted, the rebels were forced to move quickly before the inevitable purge. Emmet dispatched messengers to alert the provincial organizations. On the evening of 23 July 1803, a hastily conceived attempt, known since as Emmet's rebellion, rapidly was quelled in the streets of Dublin. Nonetheless, limited reactions did occur in Munster. On the day of the rebellion, Gen. Payne at Limerick received intelligence of the attack on the capital. Significantly, this information was obtained prior to the actual rising, which, considering the extreme secrecy maintained by the conspirators through the spring and summer, can in turn only be explained by participatory foreknowledge of parties in the city.[108] More impressively, Payne learned a surprising number of specifics about the conspiracy, including the existence of the Thomas Street depot. Apparently, like Michael Dwyer in Wicklow, the rebels in Limerick, Cork and Kerry were only expected to rise upon news of success in the capital. Indeed, five 'rebel captains were said to have been in the city on the night of the twenty-third and only departed the following day, after receiving news of Emmet's failure in Dublin'.[109] Finally, three rockets were fired off in the environs of Limerick that night while events were unfolding in Dublin, and although their source has never been identified positively, it can hardly have been a coincidental occurrence.[110]

In Cork, the reactions to the events of 23 July were even more muted than in Limerick. Yet, it is clear that up until a few days prior to the rising Emmet had anticipated that city to rise after receiving news that Dublin was taken.[111] Confirmation of a republican conspiracy came in the following weeks and months as the authorities in Cork city successfully rounded up a number of important radicals. One such individual, a twenty-eight year old merchant named John O'Finn was a possible United Irish activist. His brother Edmund had played a key role in establishing Cork's United Irish organizational structure before fleeing to England early in 1797. The brothers escaped to the continent in 1799, where they settled at Bordeaux. Importantly, John O'Finn returned to Ireland from Lisbon at some point shortly prior to Emmet's rebellion. The sheriff of Cork City arrested him on 3 August, and the news of his capture was considered to be of sufficient merit to be passed on to Whitehall by Under Secretary William Wickham, who added: 'Edmund O'Finn appears to have been in correspondence with the principle conspirators here.' John O'Finn was confined in the Provost prison at Cork on charges of high treason.[112] By early December six additional men had been imprisoned at Cork 'on treasonable charges'. Included in this number was the attorney, William Todd Jones, an early and prominent member of the United Irishmen and known to be still highly active. Jones was arrested on the specific orders of the government, which were contained in a letter from Mr Marsden to Lt Gen. Myers, dated 29 July 1803.[113] Jones's prompt incarceration confirms the government's awareness of his part in the conspiracy. In all probability William Todd Jones is the Mr Jones refereed to in Payne's report of May.[114] Eventually, upwards of forty people were arrested in the city and county of Cork.[115] The authorities clearly took the threat posed by these individuals seriously as ten of the men incarcerated during the winter of 1803–1804 were still in the Provost prison in July 1805.[116] At Limerick, John Farrell was executed in February on charges of high treason and two other individuals, John Dwyer and Dennis Murphy, were confined from 8 August 1803 and 8 March 1804, respectively, through at least 1805.[117] Finally, David Dickson concludes of Cork's involvement in the Emmet plot: '[W]hen news of Emmet's rebellion broke the calm in the summer of 1803, a number of leading United Irishmen in the city and west Cork were immediately detained for some months there were grounds for the suspicions.'[118]

The presence of Cullinan and other united activists in Munster in the spring and summer of 1803 lends credence to the supposition that Emmet, at least until shortly prior to the rebellion, had anticipated support from the province. This expectation in its own right alters the perception that the planning for the rebellion of 1803 was confined to Dublin and two or three adjacent counties. The major failing of 1803 in the southwest was one of false expectations; the radicals of Munster expected to rise in conjunction with a French invasion force in August, not in July on their own. Anecdotal evidence of revolutionary preparations in Munster continued to reach Dublin Castle for months after Emmet's rebellion. The Dublin rising triggered a subsequent wave of rumours in Limerick, as Payne explained: 'I have lately received fresh and frequent informations relative to the old story of an attack on Limerick.'[119] Yet by the twenty-seventh, he had become sincerely concerned: 'I really begin to think there is a great probability of a rising in this quarter, [and] I ... believe that meetings in this county have been [in?] the last week frequent.'[120] The primary cause of the general's worries was intelligence obtained from a correspondent whom he trusted implicitly. This man had recently been in Clare, where he discovered that agents of the disaffected were swearing the people to the 'Finisher' oath. Furthermore, the informer claimed to have been drinking on the night of the twenty-sixth with a number individuals who revealed to him that they intended to 'meet their captain', a pub owner named Brennan. The man, supposedly, then accompanied his drinking companions to the banks of the Shannon, east of Castletroy, where they joined an assembly of between 400 and 500 men. Heated exchanges within this body occurred over the issue of command. There was also some question as to the timing of an attack planned on the city of Limerick. In addition, the rebels determined that on the given morning signal fires would be lit at a number of locations in order to mobilize the people for a night assault. On the Limerick side of the river, such fires were to be set near the town of Newcastle, another on Pallis Hill, outside the city, and a third at the Fourth of Craig. A further beacon was to be placed at Trough on the County Clare side. Finally, the assembled rebels agreed that 'whether [the] Leinster people succeeded or not they would rise, for they were thought cowards by the Leinster people for not rising during the last rebellion.[121] In a like fashion on 29 July, Payne was 'informed by a person on whom [he] place[d] great reliance that an attack [wa]s to be made on the city of Limerick in the course of a few days in great force'. The source of this information was 'a Catholic and his [own] informant ... a United Irishmen', who had 'constant intercourse with all the societies'. Chosen to command the rebels were Gen. Fitzgerald from the confluence of the borders of Counties Kerry and Limerick and a Mr Holmes.[122] In fact, as late as 5 August, the informer claimed :'this country is determined to rise'. Yet, it is clear that if the disaffected ever seriously contemplated an attack on the city – and this remains highly questionable – important elements within their ranks correctly discerned the suicidal impracticality of such an attempt. Payne's source inadvertently pointed to this fact when qualifying his assessment of the likelihood of a rising: 'However, in consequence of the failure in the capital there is a strong party against it.'[123] The veracity of the intelligence received by Payne in Limerick that summer is impossible to determine; self serving informers, paranoid loyalists and political manipulation all served to cloud the picture.

Severe doubts as to the loyalty of the population of County Cork also persisted through the late summer and autumn of 1803. In the third week of August, Mr Townshend, a local landowner, transcribed the following account of the disloyal tendencies of the population of west Cork:

> the present state of this wretched country is truly deplorable, the loyal consisting of not more than one in one-hundred ... [and are] ... at the mercy of a barbarous peasantry, who, there is every reason to believe would, in case of a French landing be ready to join them and commit atrocious acts. From Kinsale to Bantry Bay, forty miles or so, with many small harbours where an enemy may land without difficulty, is defenceless. Only protection is a few undisciplined yeomen.[124]

Other gentlemen concurred with this bleak assessment and, more pointedly, frequently ascribed the prevalence of disaffection to an organized radical structure still dedicated to supporting a French landing. From Castlemartyr in east Cork, Mr Barnard warned: '[that] a system of organization is carrying on in parts of this county is certain', and a man confessed to having recently sworn 'to assist the French were they to land'. Additionally, meetings of between twenty and forty rebels were convened throughout the county on a regular basis. At these gatherings the principal business was the administration of oaths to aid the French and the planning of arms raids. While Barnard allowed that he had 'no positive proof of there being any connection between [the] disaffected here and those in Dublin', he nonetheless believed: '[T]here can be no doubt but that when disaffection exists there is some chain of communication with the capital.'[125] A similar account came from the city of Cork on 23 November, when an informer James Fitzmaurice explained to William Wickham that the 'county appear[ed] to be absolutely organized, nineteen of twenty being sworn rebels'.[126] Finally, as late as

Christmas 1803, William Wickham was forced to admit to Whitehall that he was 'very uneasy about the counties of Cork, Limerick and Kerry'.[127]

Daniel Cullinan remained at large in Munster for several months following the suppression of the Dublin rising. In August, local authorities arrested five men at a pub near Adair, County Limerick. One of the individuals had in his position a concealed document of a highly seditious nature. Under examination the man, a local farmer, revealed that he had received the paper from an armed and 'well-dressed' stranger, who informed him that 'it would secure him in the worst of times'. When asked his identity the stranger had cryptically replied, 'Have you ever heard of General Clarke?'[128] The end came in December 1803, when James Hanning, the deputy postmaster of Cashel and a yeomanry lieutenant, learned of Cullinan's presence in the town. The day following Christmas Hanning arrested Cullinan and turned him over to the local military commander Lord Enniskillen. Quite amazingly, in light of the fear he had engendered over the previous five years, Cullinan managed to effect an escape the next night. However, Hanning accompanied by a corporal's guard drawn from the Fermanagh militia was able to rapidly retake him.[129] The news of General Clarke's capture was promptly forwarded to Dublin and from there to London. William Wickham, the Under Secretary, summarized the significance of the event as follows: '[F]rom circumstances that have lately transpired, there is great reason to believe he is one of the adventurers to whom the lower orders look as a principal leader. I consider his being apprehended a very fortunate event.'[130]

Shortly after his arrest, the authorities transferred Cullinan to the capital. His importance in the government's eyes was confirmed by the fact that they lodged him in the tower of Dublin Castle. On the night of 4 January 1804, 'General Clarke' undertook the final daring act of his lengthy career. Having somehow made his way up the chimney of the room in which he was being held, he lowered himself down from the roof by means of a leaden drainpipe to the terrace below. There, he encountered a sentry. In the ensuing struggle, he received a blow to the head, which proved fatal.[131]

Over the years, a number of ranking officials, however begrudgingly, acknowledged the tenacity and ability of Daniel Cullinan. For instance, Gen. Myers, who commanded the garrison at Cork, blandly observed of Cullinan in 1801: '[T]his traitor is said to possess talents.' More tellingly, shortly after his capture in 1804, Chief Secretary Alexander Marsden conceded that although he was 'a low contemptible fellow', he nonetheless seemed 'to have talent, and by comparison, may not be undeserving of the title of General which he assume[d]'.[132] Indeed, the authorities clearly recognized the importance of the role he played in the post-1798 republican movement. A memorial from Cashel written in early 1804 described Cullinan as 'a noted rebel and leader of insurgents in several parts of the Kingdom ... who for five years had escaped the hands of justice notwithstanding a reward of £500 or upwards'.[133]

The fact that Daniel Cullinan has slipped through the ever narrowing historiographical cracks of the 1790s is in itself an impressive feat. In reality his rightful place is alongside the far better known Ulster activists William Putnam McCabe and James Hope. Over the past ten years, the definitive role played by these extraordinarily capable and highly versatile emissaries in extending and organizing the United Irish movement through much of Ulster and Leinster has come to light.[134] Paradoxically, Cullinan's very success in carrying out the mission of the United Irishmen in secrecy, while eluding the authorities for over five years, is the very cause of his relative historiographical obscurity.

Ultimately, the course of events in County Cork between 1798 and 1803 are illustrative of a number of key issues about the nature and extent of post-1798 resistance throughout Ireland. First and foremost, they confirm the essential fact that extremely large sections of the Irish population were overtly hostile to the system of governance. Thus, the ascendancy and the British connection were maintained not by consent, or more primitively by deference, but by superior firepower. More problematic is the question of ideological motivation, for it is highly unlikely that the redresser movements in Munster were driven by a desire to establish the non-sectarian, middle-class dominated Republic conceived of by the United Irishmen. Yet the presence of the radical centre at Cork city, and to a lesser extent Limerick, combined with the widespread discontent reflected by the prevalence of agrarianism in the region, demonstrate that Robert Emmet could legitimately anticipate the support of substantial elements of south Munster's population.

Notes

1 For socio-economic backgrounds, see David Dickson, *Old world colony: Cork and south Munster 1630–1830* (Madison, 2005). David Dickson, 'South Munster region in the 1790s', in John A. Murphy (ed.), *The French are in the bay: The expedition to Bantry Bay 1796* (Dublin, 1997), 85–8; Kevin Whelan, 'Bantry Bay: The wider context', in Murphy, *French are in the bay*, 95–6.

2 Nancy J. Curtin, *The United Irishmen: Popular politics in Ulster and Dublin, 1791–1798* (Oxford, 1994), 118–19.

3 Kevin Whelan, *The tree of liberty: Radicalism, Catholicism and the construction of Irish identity* (Cork, 1996), 34–5; Dickson, 'South Munster region', 86–7.

4 Whelan, 'Bantry Bay', 95–7.

5 James S. Donnelly, 'The Whiteboy movement, 1761–1765', in *Irish historical studies* 21, no. 81 (1978), 20–54.

6 Ibid; Maurice Bric, 'Priests, parsons and politics: The Rightboy protest in County Cork, 1785–1788', in *Past and present*, no. 100 (1983), 100–23.

7 Bric, 'Priests, parsons and politics', 104–7.

8 Dickson, *Old world colony*, 469–70; David Dickson, 'Paine and Ireland', in David Dickson, Dáire Keogh and Kevin Whelan (eds), *The United Irishmen: Republicanism, radicalism and rebellion* (Dublin, 1993), 145–6.

9 Quoted in Dickson, 'Paine and Ireland', 145–6.

10 Whelan, *Tree of liberty*, 83.

11 Dickson, *Old world colony*, 458.

12 Marianne Elliott, *Partners in revolution: The United Irishmen and France* (New Haven, 1982), 108. Also see, Dickson, *Old world colony*, 462; David Dickson, 'Smoke without fire? Munster and the 1798 rebellion', in Thomas Bartlett, David Dickson, Dáire Keogh and Kevin Whelan (eds), *1798: A bicentenary perspective* (Dublin, 2003), 156–7.

13 Dickson, 'Smoke without fire?' 157–60.

14 Ibid., 158; Whelan, 'Bantry Bay', 118–19; Dickson, 'South Munster region', 93.

15 Dickson, 'South Munster region', 93–4; Whelan, 'Bantry Bay'.

16 Quoted in Elliott, *Partners*, 129.

17 Quoted in David Dickson, 'The State of Ireland before 1798', in Cathal Póirtéir (ed.), *The great Irish rebellion of 1798* (Dublin, 1998), 24–5.

18 Allan Blackstock, *An ascendancy army: The Irish yeomanry, 1796–1834* (Dublin, 1998), 139.

19 Dickson, *Old world colony*, 468.

20 Dickson, *Old world colony*, 459–65.

21 Elliott, *Partners*, 206.

22 Whelan, 'Bantry Bay', 111.

23 Ibid., 101, 108–9, 111; Dickson, 'South Munster region', 91.

24 For the disarming, see Dickson, 'Smoke without fire?', 167–70; Dickson, 'South Munster region', 91; Philip M. O'Neill, *The barrow uncrossed* (Dublin, 1998), 65.

25 Dickson, *Old world colony*, 472.

26 NAI RP 620/52/137, Robert Harding to Cooke, Cork, 7 Mar. 1799. For the Harp of Erin, see Elliott, *Partners*, 175; Jim Smyth, *The men of no property: Irish radicals and popular politics in the late eighteenth century* (New York, 1992), 158.

27 Elliott, *Partners*, 250.

28 TNA HO 100/86/242–3, Castlereagh to Wickham, Dublin Castle, 2 Apr. 1799.

29 NAI RP 620/7/74/22, Pollock, 15 Apr. 1799.

30 For the agrarian secret societies, see Donnelly, 'Whiteboy movement', 20–54; James Donnelly, 'The Rightboy movement', in *Studia Hibernica*, nos. 17 and 18 (1977–1978), 120–202; Donnelly, 'Hearts of oak, hearts of steel', in *Studia Hibernica*, no. 21 (1981), 7–75; Smyth, *Men of no property*, 33–45; Bric, 'Priests, parsons and politics', 100–23.

31 Donnelly, 'Whiteboy movement', 20–54; Smyth, *Men of no property*, 33–45; Thomas Bartlett, 'An end to the moral economy: The Irish militia disturbance of 1793', in *Past and present*, no. 99 (May 1983), 42–3.

32 Bartlett, 'End to moral economy', 42–3.

33 The targeting of horses was tied to the owners' use of the animals to carry away tithes, many of which were still paid in kind. NAI RP 620/40/61, Harding, Cork, 16 Sept. 1798.

34 For the anti-tithe farmer agenda exhibited by the Whiteboys and Rightboys, see Donnelly, 'Whiteboy movement', 20, 34–6; Bric, 'Priests, parsons and politics', 112.

35 NAI SOC 1018/2, Mr Longfield, Cork, 24 Jan. 1799.

36 NAI SOC 1018/2, Mr Freeman, 24 Jan. 1799.

37 Marquis Cornwallis to Portland, 14 Feb. 1799, C. Stewart (ed.), *Memoirs and correspondence of Viscount Castlereagh, second marquis of Londonderry*, 4 vols (London, 1848–1849), vol. 2, 174.

38 NAI RP 620/46/23, Lord Hamilton to Castlereagh, Cork, 29 Jan. 1799; ibid. 620/56/59, 'Outrages committed in the Diocese of Cloyne', Bishop of Cloyne, 29 Jan. 1799.

39 Ibid. 620/46/23, Hamilton to Castlereagh, Cork, 29 Jan. 1799.

40 Bric, 'Priests, parsons and politics', 112.

41 For Limerick and Tipperary, see Thomas Bartlett, 'Clemency and compensation: The treatment of defeated rebels and suffering loyalists after the 1798 rebellion', in Jim Smyth (ed.), *Revolution, counter-revolution and union: Ireland in the 1790s* (Cambridge, 2000), 106–11.

42 NAI RP 620/66/196, Thomas Prendergast to Marsden, Clonmel, 14 Dec. 1803.

43 Bartlett, 'End to moral economy', 42–3.

44 Smyth, *Men of no property*, 43.

45 NAI RP 620/46/23, Hamilton to Castlereagh, Cork, 29 Jan. 1799.

46 Ibid. 620/7/73, Lt Gen. Lake, Limerick, 25 Mar. 1799.

47 Donnelly, 'Whiteboy movement', 20–1, 34–6.

48 Donnelly, 'Rightboy movement', 120–202; Bric, 'Priests, parsons and politics', 101–7.

49 Whelan, 'Bantry Bay', 118.

50 Ibid.

51 Quoted in ibid.

52 The phrase 'educated Whiteboy' was coined by John Fitzgibbon, quoted in Whelan, 'Bantry Bay', 118.

53 TNA HO 100/85/95–6, William Kirby to Castlereagh, 12 Jan. 1799.

54 NAI RP 620 46/80, Harding to Cooke, 19 Mar. 1799.

55 NAI RP 620/52/137, Harding to Cooke, Cork, 7 Mar. 1799; ibid. 620/46/68, Harding to Cooke, 9 Mar. 1799; ibid. 620/46/80, Harding to Cooke, 19 Mar. 1799.

56 Ibid. 620/52/137, Harding to Cooke, Cork, 7 Mar. 1799; ibid. 620/46/80, Harding to Cooke, Cork, 19 Mar. 1799; ibid. 620/7/73, Lake, Limerick, 20 Mar. 1799.

57 Ibid. 620/46/80, Robert Harding to Cooke, 19 Mar. 1799.

58 TNA HO 100/86/242–3, Castlereagh to Wickham, Dublin Castle, 2 Apr. 1799; NAI RP 620/7/73, Lake, Limerick, 20 Mar. 1799; ibid., Cork, 29 Mar. 1799.

59 Ibid., Lake, Cork, 29 Mar. 1799.

60 Ibid., Lake, Limerick, 23 Mar. 1799.

61 Ibid., Gen Myers, Cork, 26 Mar. 1799; TNA HO 100/86/246–8, Myers, Cork, 26 Mar. 1799.

62 NAI RP 620/7/73, Lake, Limerick, 25 Mar. 1799.

63 Other accounts describe Hutchinson being shot with his own pistol, which he had loaned to one of the attackers a few days prior to his murder. TNA HO 100/86/351, Macroom [?], County Cork, 21 Apr. 1799; *BNL*, 30 Apr. 1799.

64 Ibid., 21 May 1799.

65 Ibid., 28 May 1799.

66 Ibid., 16 July 1799.

67 TNA HO 100/89/55, Gen. Henri Clarke, Royal Hospital, 3 June 1799.

68 Ibid.

69 NAI RP 620/56/59, 'Outrages committed in the Diocese of Cloyne', Bishop of Cloyne, 29 Jan. 1799.

70 NAI RP 620/63/6, Richard Orpen to Hardwicke, Cork, 24 Mar. 1802.

71 TNA HO 100/87/200, Myers to Lake, Cork, 15 Sept. 1799.

72 NAI SOC 1018/3, Lord Longueville, Cork, 7 Oct. 1799.

73 Ibid., Longueville, 27 Dec. 1799.

74 Ibid.

75 Helen Landreth, *The pursuit of Robert Emmet* (New York, 1948), 145.

76 Ibid.

77 TNA HO 100/115/68, Wickham to King, Dublin Castle, 28 Dec. 1803.

78 For Clarke, see Elliott, *Partners*, 85–8.

79 In fact Harding's letter is dated 22 August, the very day of Humbert's landing. NAI RP 620/39/194, Harding to Cooke, Cork, 22 Aug. 1798.

80 TNA HO 100/87/85, Castlereagh to King, Dublin Castle, 5 Aug. 1799.

81 Ruán O'Donnell, *Aftermath: Post-rebellion insurgency in Wicklow, 1799–1803* (Dublin, 2000), 51, 54, 84.

82 For the 'New Plan of Organization', see examination of NAI RP 620/47/100, Henry, County Antrim, 23 July 1799; ibid. 620/7/74/6, McGucken, 2 Feb. 1799; ibid. 620/7/74/11, Pollock, 15 Feb. 1799; ibid. 620/7/74/15, McGucken to Pollock, 19 Feb. 1799.

83 Ibid. 620/10/118/1, McGucken to Cooke, Belfast, 3 Jan. 1801.

84 Ibid. 620/49/47, McGucken to Pollock, 20 Sept. 1800.

85 Ibid. 620/10/118/1, McGucken to Cooke, Belfast, 3 Jan. 1801.

86 Landreth, *Pursuit*, 145.

87 Elliott, *Partners*, 258, 274.

88 NAI RP 620/59/82, Harding to Archer, Cork, 28 May 1801.

89 Ibid. 620/60/44, Myers to ?, Cork, 19 July 1801.

90 Ibid.

91 Ibid. 620/53/39, 'Plan of Organization', n.d.

92 Ibid.

93 Ibid. 620/49/116, Judkin Fitzgerald, 12 Aug. 1801.

94 Ibid. 620/49/119, Myers to Charles Abbot, Cork, 19 Aug. 1801.

95 Ibid. 620/49/130, Fitzgerald to Cooke, Lisleagh, 16 Sept. 1801.

96 The definitive account of Emmet's rebellion is Ruán O'Donnell, *Robert Emmet and the rising of 1803* (Dublin, 2003)

97 NAI RP 620/61/110, Cooke to Marsden, 8 Nov. 1802.

98 TNA HO 100/112/5–6, Hardwicke to Chief Secretary Thomas Pelham, Phoenix Park, 9 Jan. 1803; ibid. 100/112/42–8, Hardwicke to Pelham, Dublin Castle, 25 Jan. 1803. For the rebellion scare in Limerick in Jan. 1803, see ibid. 100/112/5–6, Hardwicke to Pelham, Phoenix Park, 9 Jan. 1803; ibid. 100/112/42, Hardwicke to Pelham, Dublin Castle, 25 Jan. 1803; ibid. 100/112/84–5, extract of a letter from Gen. Payne to Col. Beckwith, Limerick, 21 Feb. 1803; ibid. 100/112/90–3, Payne to Beckwith, 5 Mar. 1803.

99 Ibid. 100/112/84–5, extract of a letter from Payne to Beckwith, Limerick, 21 Feb. 1803.

100 NAI RP 620/66/133, Marsden to Payne, Dublin Castle, 4 Mar. 1803.

101 Ibid. 620/66/139, Payne to Marsden, Limerick, 14 May 1803.

102 Ibid. 620/66/167, James Perry to Marsden, 6 June 1803; ibid. 620/66/168, Perry to Marsden, 8 June 1803.

103 Ibid. 620/66/139, Payne to Marsden, Limerick, 14 May 1803. For Jones' role in

the Emmet conspiracy, see O'Donnell, *Emmet and the rising*, 128–9.
104 NAI RP 620/65/42, Harding to Wickham, 18 June 1803.
105 Landreth, *Pursuit*, 224.
106 NAI RP 620/65/42, Harding to Wickham, Limerick, 18 June 1803; ibid. 620/66/142, Payne to ?, 19 June 1803.
107 Ibid. 620/66/143, Payne to ?, 13 July 1803.
108 Ibid. 620/66/146, Payne, Limerick, 27 July 1803.
109 Landreth, *Pursuit*, 220; also see NAI RP 620/64/214, J. D., 27 July 1803.
110 Ibid. 620/66/144, Payne, Limerick, 24 July 1803.
111 Landreth, *Pursuit*, 223. For Cork's supportive role, see O'Donnell, *Emmet and the rising*, 43.
112 TNA HO 100/112/139, Wickham to King, Dublin Castle, 6 Aug. 1803; ibid. 100/118/244, list of prisoners on charges of high treason and suspicion of treasonable practices, Cork, 3 Dec. 1803.
113 Ibid. 100/118/244, list of prisoners on charges of high treason and suspicion of treasonable practices, Cork, 3 Dec. 1803; ibid. 100/118/220, Wickham to King, Dublin Castle, 9 Dec. 1803. For Jones' early membership in the United Irishmen, see Elliott, *Partners*, 26.
114 NAI RP 620/66/139, Payne to Marsden, Limerick, 14 May 1803.
115 Landreth, *Pursuit*, 223.
116 NAI RP 620/14/184/3, prisoners confined in the Provost Prison, Cork, 13 July 1805.
117 Landreth, *Pursuit*, 370.
118 Dickson, *Old world colony*, 472.
119 NAI RP 620/66/144, Payne, Limerick, 24 July 1803.
120 Ibid. 620/66/146, Payne, Limerick, 27 July 1803.
121 Ibid. 620/64/214, J. D., 27 July 1803.
122 Ibid. 620/66/147, Payne, Limerick, 30 July 1803.
123 Ibid. 620/66/149, Payne, Limerick, 5 Aug. 1803.
124 Ibid. 620/67/130, Mr Townsend to Marsden, Skibbereen, 21 Aug. 1803.
125 NAI SOC 1025/10, Mr Barnard, Castlemartyr, 12 Oct. 1803.
126 TNA HO 100/115/5, James Fitzmaurice to Wickham, Cork, 23 Nov. 1803.
127 Ibid. 100/115/57–8, Wickham to King, Dublin Castle, 26 Dec. 1803.
128 NAI RP 620/66/153, Payne, Limerick, 21 Aug. 1803.
129 Ibid. 620/50/53, Memorial of James Hanning Deputy Postmaster of the city of Cashel and a second lieutenant of the yeomanry, 1803.
130 TNA HO 100/115/67, Wickham to King, Dublin Castle, 28 Dec. 1803.
131 Ibid. 100/119/21, Marsden to Pole Carew, Dublin Castle, 5 Jan. 1804.
132 NAI RP 620/60/44, Myers to ?, Cork, 19 July 1801; TNA HO 100/119/21, Marsden to Carew, Dublin Castle, 5 Jan. 1804.
133 NAI RP 620/50/53, Memorial of Hanning, 1803.
134 O'Donnell, *Emmet and the rising*, and Ruán O'Donnell, Robert Emmet and the rebellion of 1798 (Dublin, 2003).

6

Galway and Mayo

On 22 August 1798, the United Irishmen's long-term efforts to obtain French assistance finally came to fruition with the appearance of three frigates in Killala Bay on the north coast of County Mayo. Unfortunately for them, their allies had come too late, for the rebellion of 1798 had been suppressed several weeks earlier.[1] Moreover, the French landing force numbered barely 1,000 men.[2] Nonetheless, this belated and undersized army was joined by thousands of Irish volunteers and scored several local victories before being overwhelmed at Ballynamuck in County Longford on 8 September.[3] Events ran full circle, and the last significant action of the western rising also took place at Killala on 23 September, where in under an hour another 400–600 rebel dead were added to the roughly 2,000 slaughtered at Ballynamuck. In a final act of brutality, the military swept through the Barony of Erris, burning cottages and murdering some fifty or sixty 'unresisting peasants in the process'.[4] The Republic of Connacht had survived barely a month. In the succeeding 200 years, historians have failed to explain satisfactorily what drove as many as 10,000 supposedly complacent Irish peasants (in reality artisans, farmers, labourers and shopkeepers) to partake in such an apparently ill-conceived endeavour.

The Church of Ireland Bishop of Killala, Joseph Stock, himself only a recent arrival to the area with a limited knowledge of the Irish language, described the people who flocked to join General Humbert's tiny army as motivated by a desire to 'to take arms for France and the Blessed Virgin'.[5] In a similar vein, Captain Jobit, an officer in the French expeditionary force, derisively depicted the natives he encountered: 'they throw themselves in front of us, head in the mud, and long prayers for our success. All men and women wear, suspended around their necks, large, dirty, ugly scapulars and rosary beads'.[6] The influence of these outsiders' accounts on the historiographical interpretations of the western rebellion has been enduring. For example, Marianne Elliott describes the people who joined the French as 'clasping rosaries and scapulars' in an obvious paraphrasing of Jobit before going on to quote Stock on the influence of 'France and the Blessed Virgin'. In a like fashion, S. J. Connolly, after also quoting Stock on the 'Blessed Virgin', concludes that the Mayo rising can most accurately be viewed as 'the last rising of traditional Ireland' with its foundations laid firmly in sectarian and 'dynastic loyalties'. Thus, in Connolly's eyes, the western rebellion is more reflective of an atavistic loyalty to the Catholic Church, the historic French alliance and even the Stuarts than of the ideals of the Enlightenment and the French Revolution.[7]

This chapter argues that such views oversimplify a highly complex situation. In reality, the west had experienced a period of prior politicization by the Defenders and United Irishmen, which in turn was shaped by preexisting, regionally specific socio-economic and cultural factors. More precisely, the existence of an underground Catholic gentry with long-term connections to the continent and the interrelated presence of a pervasive smuggling culture, coupled with traditional agrarian discontent, had produced a deeply rooted, albeit unfocused, anti-state *mentalité* into which the radical organizations tapped. This reality is evident both in who turned out in 1798 and how long they remained active after the rebellion.

Furthermore, the remarkably broad-based popular resistance to the state that manifested itself in a number of divergent veins in the west of Ireland during the closing decade of the eighteenth century can only begin to be properly understood when placed in the wider context of the Atlantic revolutions. Indeed for a ten-year period between 1795 and 1805, the hope, promise or actuality of French assistance, coupled with the existence of an Irish revolutionary expatriate community in France, drove events in the west of Ireland.

Radical backgrounds

The leading Catholic families of the region had extensive cultural, economic and religious ties to France. Trade, both legal and illicit, had been carried on with French ports for centuries, while cadet branches of Irish-Catholic maritime families were a fixture at places like Bordeaux and Nantes.[8] Given these strong Franco-Irish connections, it strains credulity to argue that the ideals of the Enlightenment and French Revolution failed to influence elements of the younger generation of the cosmopolitan elite. The republican tendencies of families like the MacDonnells, Gibbons, O'Malleys and Jordans are clearly suggestive of such an ideological link.

Defenders

The traditional interpretation of the western rising hinges on the argument that there was little, if any, radical penetration of the province of Connaught during the 1790s. However, there is sufficient evidence to suggest that this view bears qualification. For instance, as early as 1793 Denis Browne, MP and high sheriff of Mayo, pointed to United Irish efforts to politicize the county:

> the new political doctrines which have pervaded the lower classes – that ... spirit has been produced by the circulation of Paine's *Rights of Man*, of seditious newspapers, and by shopkeepers who having been in Dublin to buy goods have formed connections with some of the United Irishmen.[9]

Additionally in 1796, an unnamed activist traversed County Galway 'with the sole purpose of providing rural dwellers with oral readings of the radical press'.[10] Meanwhile in November 1796, Arthur O'Connor was believed to have travelled to Galway 'to complete the division of the country into United Irish executive departments'.[11]

Yet despite the fact that the United Irishmen were present, albeit in a nascent form, from an early date it is apparent that the key to the development of broad-based popular antipathy to the state in the far west of Ireland was the expansion of the Defenders into the region, which began in the autumn of 1795. Although Defenderism existed in north Connaught by 1793, the movement's expansion into the extreme west of the province directly coincided with the arrival of thousands of Catholic refugees from the sectarian cockpit of mid-Ulster from the autumn of 1795.[12] The majority of these northern exiles settled in Counties Galway and Mayo as a result of the 'Armagh Expulsions' of 1795–1796.[13] In turn, the expulsions themselves were the end product of long-term social, economic and political competition between Protestant and Catholic weavers in north Armagh. Open conflict of varying intensity between Catholic Defenders and Protestant Peep O'Day Boys in that county dated from 1784. These stresses came to a head at the Battle of the Diamond near Loughgall on 17 September 1795. In the immediate aftermath of the clash, triumphant lower-class Anglicans established the Orange Order and initiated a brutal campaign of ethnic cleansing.[14] The visceral sectarian animosity under-pinning this drive is transparently evident: 'Go to Hell or Connacht. If you do not, we are all haters of the papists, and we will destroy you', exhorted one of the countless notices affixed to Catholic dwellings by the Orangemen.[15] Families that failed to comply had their homes burned and their possessions, including irreplaceable looms, stolen or destroyed. Some heads of households were simply murdered.[16] To Catholics on the ground, underlying political and economic factors can hardly have registered. In popular memory it was overt sectarian hatred that drove the people from their homes. The inactivity of the magistrates in response to this aggression, often shading into tacit approval of the Orangemen's activities, created the impression amongst the Catholic population of mid-Ulster, and much of the rest of the country, that the Orange atrocities had the de-facto sanction of the government.[17] That this belief was patently false is irrelevant. It was the perception that mattered, and along with their meagre belongings, the Ulstermen carried to the west a deep-rooted animosity towards the Protestant ascendancy and the state that supported it.

Ultimately, between the autumn of 1795 and the end of 1796, some 7,000 Catholics became unwilling participants in a mass exodus to the west, with up to 4,000 of them settling in County Mayo alone.[18] The impact of these people on the political landscape of the region was enormous as an important recent study confirms: '[T]hese northern exiles played a critical role in spreading both the revolutionary ideology and organizational structure of the Defenders and the Society of United Irishmen to the west of Ireland.'[19]

Indeed, the radical organizations' recruitment efforts amongst the indigenous population were dramatically assisted by the deplorable appearance of the new arrivals. Compounding the visual effect were the harrowing accounts of Orange atrocities told by the northern refugees. The Lord Lieutenant, Camden, pointed to the danger posed by this latter phenomenon in a communication to his Chief Secretary Thomas Pelham: 'They related their sufferings and I fear excited a spirit of revenge among their Catholic brethren.'[20]

Local loyalists clearly identified the danger posed to the region's stability by the northern refugees.[21] Particularly disconcerting was the large colony of emigrant weavers established in the tight triangle formed by the towns of Ballina, Foxford and Crossmolina in north Mayo. The majority of these people had fled the epicentre of the Orange outrages in Armagh and South Down, and it is hardly surprising then that they were known to be 'addicted to speculate in politics'. More ominously, the weavers ideologically seduced indigenous 'shopkeepers, mechanics and servants' in taverns and alehouses.[22] Indeed, the political orientation of the Ulstermen was confirmed in August of 1798 when large numbers of them rushed to 'join the rebels in Mayo'.[23] During the rising, weavers from the Ballina triangle serving under the command of their fellow northerner Bartholomew Teeling, proved to be the most disciplined and effective indigenous unit in the Franco-Irish army.[24]

Following Ballynamuck, a number of these unfortunate people were once again forced to flee their homes. Eventually, some two hundred families sought refuge in Connemara, where a number found employment with the smuggling captains of the region. An example of their continued audacity came in 1802 when 'a party of these fellows ... attacked and disarmed fifty soldiers from Westport'. As late as July 1803, the Ulstermen were 'armed and employed by William Coneys, Ian Coneys, the Rev Russell and the other smugglers in discharging cargoes and escorting the smuggled goods in open daylight'.[25] Although the accommodation reached between the Ballina weavers and the Connemara smugglers cannot definitively be attributed to pre-existing political connections, it strongly suggests mutual sympathy.

That the most significant radical inroads in the west, at least at the grass-roots level, were made by the Defenders is indicated by a number of observations. The rapid expansion of Defenderism in Galway and Mayo directly coincided with the arrival of northern refugees in the autumn of 1795. Additionally, the majority of the exiles were from Armagh, the birthplace of the Defenderism, and sworn members of the movement were the obvious, if by no means exclusive, targets of the Orangemen responsible for the expulsions. The United Irishmen only reached out to the Defenders in late 1795 as a direct result of the opportunities created by the Armagh outrages.[26] In fact, it was not until mid-1796 that an alliance between the two movements was effectively in place.[27] In the end, it is highly probable that a large, if indeterminate, percentage of the people who turned out in August 1798 were politicized weavers, engaged at the time, or previously, in production for the market. Pointedly, these Defenders were not apolitical primitives blindly following their priests and chieftains to destruction.

The radical gentry

Near the apex of the social pyramid in County Mayo stood an influential Catholic gentry family, the MacDonnells. Joseph MacDonnell was active in the 'patriot' politics of the 1770s and 1780s; he raised a Volunteer corps and, more importantly, played a key role in Grattan's 'patriot' movement, which culminated in the 'constitutional revolution' of 1782.[28] His son, James Joseph, was educated in Austria, where a number of relatives held influential positions in the imperial military and governmental bureaucracy. The younger MacDonnell studied law in London, where he established a close relationship with a kindred spirit, Wolfe Tone. On his return to Ireland in 1791, MacDonnell joined Tone on the Catholic Committee.[29] In 1792 –1793, he represented Mayo at the Catholic Convention, and most significantly, became an early and influential member of the Society of United Irishmen. He was heavily involved in the preparations for the rising of 1798, meeting frequently in the months prior with Lord Edward Fitzgerald, the United Irishmen's military commander, in Dublin. MacDonnell narrowly missed being swept up in the raid on Oliver Bond's house in March of that year. This event crippled the rebellion by robbing the republicans of most of their leaders.

Nonetheless, MacDonnell utilized his extensive local influence to bring some thousand men to join the French when they landed in August. Humbert, quite logically, placed MacDonnell in command of the native contingent of the Franco-Irish army, and several French officers reported that he served during the doomed campaign with great skill and bravery. Following the catastrophe at Ballynamuck, MacDonnell managed to escape the field and made his way to western Galway, where he contacted sympathetic smugglers who arranged his passage to the continent. In France, MacDonnell rapidly became a central figure in the Irish republican expatriate community centred in Paris. Indeed, Robert Emmet developed a close relationship with MacDonnell in 1802 while he was planning the rising that later bore his name.

By 1805, MacDonnell had grown bitterly disillusioned with the despotic tendencies of Napoleon Bonaparte and, like so many other Irish republicans, moved on to the North American Republic, where he died in 1849.[30] This highly educated, cosmopolitan barrister had spent 14 years of his life working to bring about a radical transformation of the Irish political environment. The North Atlantic revolutionary nexus through which he moved included France, America and, importantly, at least for a time, the west of Ireland.

The radicalism of James Joseph MacDonnell was not an isolated phenomenon in Connaught. Charles O'Conor, the scion of a leading Catholic family from Mount Allen in County Roscommon, had channelled his mounting frustration with the government's fiscal policies in a decidedly radical direction by 1791. In the late summer of that year he turned his back with disdain on the Catholic Committee and made contact with extremist elements in the Volunteer movement that favoured Catholic emancipation. O'Conor's correspondence with Thomas Russell played a key role in persuading recalcitrant members of the newly founded Society of United Irishmen that Catholics were worthy of full participation in civic life. A short time later he became a founding member of the United Society in Connaught, and before the year was out he had travelled 'throughout Galway and Mayo' spreading the radical gospel. As with many other Connaught families, the O'Conors' membership in the United Irishmen was an intergenerational phenomenon. Tone personally administered the society's oath to Charles's son Thomas in December 1791, and another son, Denis, was sworn a short time after. Although the extent of the family's role in the events of 1798 is unclear, it is certain that Thomas O'Conor became a central figure in the post-rebellion republican diaspora. He made his way to America in 1801, where in 1814 he became a co-editor of the first Irish-American newspaper, the Shamrock.[31]

Other prominent individuals were active participants in the reform politics of the closing decades of the eighteenth century. Valentine Jordan from Forkfield was a member of an Old English gentry family of considerable influence in Mayo. His father, Col. Edward Jordan, had been active in the Volunteer movement and attended the Dungannon Convention as a delegate from County Mayo.[32] The younger Jordan joined the French at Castlebar, serving as a colonel in the republican army of Connaught.[33]

Thus, an important evolution is revealed. Members of the generation that reached political maturity in the 1770s and 1780s were active in the reforming politics of the Volunteer movement. A transition phase is evidenced by participation in the Catholic Committee, which sought to remove the remaining restrictions imposed on the nation's religious majority by the Penal Laws. With the frustration of these efforts, and inspired by events in France, members of the younger generation, exemplified by James Joseph MacDonnell, Valentine Jordan and Thomas O'Conor, moved towards separatist republicanism.

Nor was membership in the United Irishmen confined entirely to the young. The patriarch of the formidable Gibbons family, John Gibbons, Sr, whom Lord Sligo described as an 'old shrewd man', played a pivotal role in establishing the western branch of the movement.[34] He was both secretary and treasurer for the Mayo society and served as treasurer of the Connacht Provincial Committee. In the early spring of 1798, he was appointed by MacDonnell to head the organization's pike manufacturing efforts, which preceded the outbreak of open rebellion in May.[35] Gibbons had served for twenty years as Lord Sligo's land agent, and that position had made him both 'very wealthy' and 'influential'. Yet despite the fact that he had a great deal to lose by opposing the government, Gibbons, accompanied by his sons Edmund and John, Jr, as well as his brother Thomas and nephew Austin, rushed to join Humbert. The elder Gibbons (nearly seventy years of age at the time) proved an invaluable asset to the republican cause, utilizing his considerable local influence to bring in hundreds of recruits to the Franco-Irish army. After the collapse of the western rising, Gibbons remained in hiding for over a year until November 1799 when he surrendered under the condition that he be allowed to transport himself from the country.[36] The Marquis of Sligo, who later had cause to regret the decision, used his influence with the government to save the life of his former agent. Gibbons duly removed himself to Nantes and eventually moved on to Amsterdam, maintaining written communications with John, Jr, who was still at large in Ireland, until shortly before his death in 1807.[37]

A radical vein ran deeply in the Gibbons family. Edmund was sentenced to death for his role in the rising, although this sentence was commuted at the eleventh hour to transportation for life. He eventually made his way to France, where he served for years as an officer in the Irish Legion.[38] Thomas Gibbons was also ranking rebel officer in 1798. Imprisoned after the rising, he voluntarily transported himself to France at some point after October 1799.[39] Austin Gibbons lived at Newport, where he had 'great influence with people in that area'. He participated in the Battle of Ballynamuck and, like other fortunate rebels, escaped to the western coast in its aftermath. A ship's captain involved in the smuggling trade, Austin utilized his maritime connections to escape to France. While in France, he held 'frequent conferences' with James Joseph MacDonnell and remained in contact with Myles Prendergast, the United Irish priest, well into the 1800s.[40]

The O'Malleys were another wealthy and influential western family, many of whose members risked all in supporting the radical cause. At the head of this extensive familial grouping stood Alexander O'Malley, a loyalist Catholic magistrate whose seat was at Edenpark, County Mayo. But several members of the family, particularly of the younger generation, took part on the rebel side in the events of 1798. First among these were Austin O'Malley and his brother Joseph, sons of an important Catholic gentleman, Owen O'Malley of Burrishoole. Both men joined the French at Ballina and served with distinction in the actions that followed. Joseph was slain at Ballynamuck, while Austin managed to fight his way through the government lines and made his way to Achill Island. He was eventually taken to France, most likely by the Connemara smuggler George O'Malley. Austin was commissioned a captain in the Irish Legion and awaited the opportunity to return to Ireland in an anticipated second invasion. When hope of such a turn of events finally evaporated in 1805, he chose to remain in the French military and served throughout the Napoleonic Wars, eventually rising to the rank of colonel.[41]

A smuggling culture

An examination of the pervasive smuggling culture that held sway in the west of Ireland is also essential in developing an understanding of the region's deep-rooted alienation from the state. The work of S. J. Connolly demonstrates that in parts of Ireland 'the resources of the state repeatedly proved inadequate to secure the enforcement of unpopular laws' well into the middle of the eighteenth century.[42] Furthermore, this lawlessness was particularly acute in west Galway, which as late as 1759 was said to be 'inhabited by the ancient Irish, who never yet ha[d] been made amenable to the laws'.[43] Moreover, the population of the region did not view smuggling as criminal, for such activity lay within accepted norms of local behaviour. As Connolly notes, the trade in contraband reflected the 'denial of the legitimacy of particular laws'.[44]

> Many of the leading smugglers were drawn from prominent Galway families including the O'Malleys and Gibbons. Moreover, the interwoven stratum of Catholic gentry, mercantile and middlemen families enjoyed relatively high social status and were, in fact, perceived as the "natural" rulers by much of the native population of the region.[45]

Indeed, it is apparent that commerce in untaxed goods continued to permeate all levels of Connemara society well into the new century. Economic incentives as well as traditional ties of deference and patronage further bound the 'lower orders' of the region to the head-tenant/merchant families. Richard Martin, the largest landowner in Connemara, explained the persistence of this phenomenon to the Lord Lieutenant in July 1803:

> The mode in which those smugglers carry on the trade contributes to organize the whole country; those who have ships, about twenty-five ... [allow the] poor [to] invest trifling amounts in brandy and tobacco, which is delivered on landing. By this means, I may say the general population of the two Baronies of Ballynahinch and Moycullen [are] smugglers.[46]

Similarly, in October of 1803, Denis Browne observed of Connemara:

> [A]ll the lower people are engaged, more or less, in the smuggling trade. Consequently, they are professionally outlaws due to [the presence of the] sea and the interior being no more object to the laws of Ireland than Ireland is [to the laws of] France.[47]

Sympathy for the United Irishmen on the part of elements of the merchant, middleman and smuggler class is suggested in a number of instances. For example, a Protestant head tenant of Richard Martin's, Walter Coneys, permitted his home to serve 'during the late rebellion and since' as a 'resort of all the chiefs of the Mayo rebels'. In a like manner, the local Church of Ireland clergyman, Russell, who resided at Cleggan, also on the Martin estate, 'entertained the chiefs of the Mayo rebels in his house both during and since the rebellion'.[48] When Valentine Jordan returned from transportation, he settled on land held by Russell. He was also the brother-in-law of one of the Coneys, a 'wealthy tenant' of Martin's, 'which insured him protection'. On this land, Jordan ran a store and public house, which provided him with the 'excuse' he needed to hold 'general intercourse with all the lower orders'.[49] Russell and a number of the Coneys were deeply immersed in the smuggling trade.[50]

The smuggling ships offered a vital means of escape to hunted rebels. James Joseph MacDonnell escaped to France, depending on the version told, in the sloop of a Galway man named Agnew, or the smuggling bark of one of the Coneys. He remained in communication with the west coast through the medium of smuggling vessels during the years that followed. As Richard Martin explained, 'James MacDonnell corresponds with persons in this kingdom, and letters are conveyed from France by some of the smuggling barks'.[51] Reports of smugglers transporting firearms to the rebels persisted well into 1805.[52]

Agrarianism / the houghers

A massive wave of agrarian agitation manifested itself in western Connaught during the winter of 1798–1799. This phenomenon took the traditional form of 'houghing', the hamstringing of livestock, particularly cattle, resulting in the beast's destruction. Organized agrarianism is first seen in Connaught in the early years of the eighteenth century when Connemara was the epicentre of the only pre-1761 example of activity that would latter fall under the rubric of Whiteboyism. These early Houghers of 1711–1712 have been viewed as reactive in their attempts to block the conversion of land from tillage to less labour-intensive commercialized grazing.[53] It is, however, much more difficult to tease out the motivational forces that underlay the agrarian agitation of 1798–1799 because of the existence of pockets of rebels operating in the same geographical area, combined with evidence that many of the houghers believed they were acting under the auspices of the United Irishmen.

In early December 1798, Richard Martin of Ballynahinch, who held several thousand acres in west Galway, complained to Dublin Castle about the 'disturbed state' of Connemara. The Lord Lieutenant responded by granting Martin permission to place the yeomanry corps he commanded on permanent duty. A similar request came from Denis Bingham of Holymount in southeast Mayo.[54] However, the situation continued to deteriorate, and by February 1799, 'not a night passed without the houghing of cattle to a very large amount' in both Galway and Mayo. The nocturnal raiders left threatening notices demanding that the flesh of the maimed cattle be distributed to the poor and intimidated witnesses into silence. On the evening of 8 February houghers engaged in a massive assault on the livestock of a farmer named Walsh, slaughtering some 250 of his bullocks. Later that month Malachy Tahey lost sheep and cattle worth £540.[55] The prime sergeant and MP for Mayo, St George Daly, warned Castlereagh that 'if [the] depredations' were permitted to 'go unchecked', it would 'end in the total destruction of those rearing counties'.[56] Cornwallis concurred with this bleak assessment, explaining, in a report to the Home Secretary, the Duke of Portland: 'in the west the old system of houghing cattle has been of late revived and carried to an extent which threatens the most serious consequences not only to this kingdom, but to the empire'.[57]

The vast scale of the destruction became clear at the Lent assizes of County Galway in April 1799, when £12,800 in compensation was granted to the victims of the hougher attacks. This sum was 'to be levied off different parts of the county under the Acts to Prevent Malicious Houghing and Maiming'. At the same time, the grand jury also clearly recognized that Galway would be completely unable to raise such an amount.[58]

The primary objective of the houghers was the reduction of rent and the elimination of 'intermediate tenants' or middlemen.[59] Further clouding the picture is the fact that it was in the obvious interest of the region's gentry to encourage the government to send troops to suppress the outrages, and overstating the political orientation of the houghers was an obvious means to this end. In any case, the authorities at all levels believed that the houghers were operating under the auspices of the United Irishmen. St George Daly asserted: 'the people have been told that it [houghing] will occasion the lowering of rents, but the scheme has ... originated from our internal enemies [desire] to prevent victualing of [the] fleet'.[60] The Marquis of Buckingham offered a similar interpretation: 'The mischief done to private property by the new system (as ordered by the directory here) of plunder and destroying cattle is out of all calculation.' He added, 'The system is openly talked of as being more certain, and more destructive, than that of open force till their friends arrive [the French]'.[61]

Significantly, such interpretations of a political orientation on the part of the houghers were not confined to local loyalists, for even the calm and rational Cornwallis was convinced the houghing in Galway and Mayo masked a republican conspiracy – 'I have mentioned the pretences for the outrages, but I have every reason to believe that they are connected to the system of the United Irishmen' – with the goal of denying provisions to the Royal Navy.[62]

Ultimately, while it is unlikely that the attacks on livestock were directly targeted at the imperial war effort, it is apparent that, as Under Secretary Edward Cooke stated, 'The insurrection [wa]s certainly combined with an expectation of the French fleet.'[63] This interpretation is strengthened by the comment of the Mayo MP Dennis Browne that juries in the region would not convict individuals on charges of houghing or 'any kind of treason'. Browne also complained, '[the people] cannot be persuaded that aiding the French is any crime', and added, '[while they acknowledge that] robbers ought to suffer ... the moment you speak to them of rebels they begin to plead for them'.[64]

Eventually the extent of the turmoil that prevailed in the countryside and the belief that the system was 'great and spreading rapidly' led the magistracy of Galway to request the proclamation of the entire county. Similarly in Mayo Dennis Browne insisted that courts martial were 'absolutely necessary'.[65] The Lord Lieutenant responded by dispatching troops 'to repress, as far as possible, this mischief'. Nevertheless, he admitted that he had little faith in the military's ability to 'prevent the commission of crimes perpetrated, at night, over the face of so extended a district'. Galway and Mayo were placed under the Insurrection Act on 20 February, and Cornwallis ordered martial law to be exerted with 'vigour' as courts martial duly assembled.[66] In a matter of three or four weeks, these measures appeared to have the desired effect, and by mid-March after a number of executions, Castlereagh reported that the destruction of livestock in Mayo and Galway had 'entirely ceased'.[67] Unfortunately for local graziers, this assessment was somewhat premature. Towards the end of April Lord Altamont informed Dublin Castle: 'the houghing of cattle has begun again in Galway'. On the night of 19 April, the houghers slaughtered three-hundred sheep and forty bullocks on the property of a Mr Losdall; several days later another attack occurred.[68]

Some sense of the scale of the agrarian discontent that gripped the west can be gleaned from the efforts required to break its hold on the region. The government assembled courts martial at Galway town, as well as Castlebar and Ballinrobe in Mayo. These trials revealed a good deal about the activities and motivations of the houghers. At Galway six men were charged 'with being united men and with forcibly and unlawfully tendering illegal oaths'. Four others were charged with 'having assembled at an unlawful hour, tendering and taking unlawful oaths, and ... houghing cattle on the lands of Ballygar'. John and James Hardiman stood accused of 'treason and rebellion against 'our' sovereign ... carrying arms against him, imagining his death ... administering unlawful oaths and forcibly taking away arms'. Thady O'Shaughnessy, Edward Conway and Dennis Cannon were accused simply of being United Irishmen.

Four of these men were acquitted. One was sentenced to transportation, three others to service abroad for life, and Michael Kearns, Patrick Naughten, James Winn and John Hardiman were condemned to death. Special weight was given to the 'treason' of the Hardimans. Before service abroad James was sentenced 'to receive 1000 lashes on his bare back with a cat-o-nine tails, while after execution John's head was to be severed from his body and exposed in some conspicuous place'. Another series of courts martial occurred at Galway in April. Martin Kelly was 'charged with being a United man appearing in military array', arms' robbery and the attempted murder of a yeomanry officer. Finally on 18 April, seven men defended themselves against charges of membership in the United Irish Society, administering 'unlawful oaths and houghing cattle' as well as conspiracy to murder.[69]

Eventually, some seventy-three cases were heard at Galway between 25

February and 18 April. The trials resulted in eighteen capital convictions. Another seven individuals were sentenced to transportation for life, and fifteen men were condemned to general service. Similarly at Ballinrobe, eleven men were charged with houghing and administering unlawful oaths, resulting in two capital convictions. Six others were sentenced to general service for life, while three were acquitted. More striking are the number of death sentences meted out at the courts martial convened at Castlebar under Maj. Maxwell. It is apparent that local authorities took advantage of the crisis precipitated by agrarian unrest to try a number of former rebels under martial law, thereby avoiding the possibility that they would be acquitted by sympathetic juries in civil trials. Most of the accused at Castlebar were charged with having actively cooperated with the French in the summer of 1798. The trials continued from April to September, resulting in twenty death sentences. Remarkably, only five of the accused were convicted of houghing; the remainder were victims of a purge made possible by the proclamation of the west.[70]

Perhaps the most important question raised by the hougher movement of 1798–1799 is that of the relationship between the obviously traditional nature of the insurgents' activities and the anti-state motivations attributed to them by contemporary observers. More specifically, why did the houghers refer to themselves as United Irishmen, and why did courts martial try and convict so many of them on charges of being oath-bound members of the society, if this agitation was merely the latest regional manifestation of the long-term phenomenon of Whiteboyism? It is argued here that the presence of Defenderism in Galway and Mayo offers the most satisfactory explanation.

An alliance between the United Irishmen and the Defenders had been effectively forged in mid-1796.[71] Soon afterwards the extraordinarily competent United Irish activists James Hope and William Putnum McCabe followed the 'refugee trail' from mid-Ulster into Connaught. These Belfast emissaries had a good deal of success in 'converting' beleaguered members of the Defender movement in the north Connaught counties of Leitrim and Roscommon. And by the end of 1796, as Liam Kelly has written, 'many of the people throughout the county [Leitrim] were "up and up"-sworn Defenders and United Irishmen. From this time onwards, they were usually referred to as United Irishmen.'[72]

Here is the likely key to the problem of the houghers referring to themselves as United Irishmen and swearing United Irish oaths in 1799. Although, admittedly, there is no extant evidence of United Irish activists from Ulster penetrating as far west as Galway and Mayo, they did reach tantalizingly close in Roscommon. Furthermore, given the fact that the Defenders had established a national structure and communications networks by 1795, it strains credulity to argue that the movement's policy of merger with the United Irishmen failed to cross the border from Roscommon into Galway and from thence to Mayo.[73]

Thus, the apparently contradictory mixture of economic and political
motivations exhibited by the houghers in 1798–1799 actually dovetails
nicely with the broad-range of activities and motivations incorporated in
Defenderism. Alongside their atavistic sectarian and millenarian veins, the
Defenders also adopted the revolutionary rhetoric of the French and American Revolutions. This complex hybridization continued to accommodate
the traditional economic grievances of the redresser movements, the major
distinction being that, as Jim Smyth has astutely observed in reference to
Defenderism in the 1790s, 'the political dimensions of agrarian protest
implicit in Whiteboyism were now explicit'.[74]

In the end, the houghers of 1798–1799 are perhaps best defined as
Defenders engaging in Whiteboy-like agrarian agitation while loosely identifying themselves as United Irishmen. None of this is meant to suggest that
the Houghers/Defenders had absorbed the ideological nuances of the United
Irishmen's secular republicanism. But what can be established with more
certainty is a desire to support the radical goal of overturning the system of
governance through the medium of a French invasion. At least for a time, an
overtly political objective was grafted onto the traditional concerns of the
redresser movements in Galway and Mayo.

Despite the crushing losses of the late summer of 1798, active resistance,
albeit on a vastly diminished scale often shading into desultory brigandage, continued in Counties Galway and Mayo into the following winter.
Although it is impossible to conclusively draw a connection between the
houghers and the surviving pockets of rebels, the fact that both groups operated in the same areas lends credence to the argument that there was a
United Irish role in the outrages.

One example of the continuing efforts to 'mop up' the remains of the
rebel army came in the early morning of 10 January 1799 when Captain
Roxburgh of the dragoons stationed at Ballinrobe received an urgent mes-
sage from Fairhill reporting that a sizable body of some 100 'armed rebels
were plundering the houses in that neighbourhood'.[75] These men had sought
refuge in the mountains of Erris after the defeat at Ballynamuck, but were
driven to less-forbidding terrain 'for a want of substance'.[76] Roxburgh
moved to Fairhill with a party of troops, where he learned he had missed
the insurgents by less than an hour. As evening approached he came upon
forty rebels on mountain slopes near Lough Corrib. After a brief skirmish
the rebels escaped, taking advantage of the encroaching darkness and the
cavalry's inability to negotiate the rocky terrain. The net result of this twilight encounter was the death of a solitary man, although he proved to
be 'a noted leader' named Welsh, a native of Ballinrobe.[77] In late March
government forces cornered and killed another 'notorious rebel leader'
named Faherty. The dispatch from Gen. Trench, which carried the news
of Faherty's demise to Dublin, further reported the capture of 'seven rebel
chiefs ... in the mountains'.[78] As part of the ongoing cleansing campaign,
the general dispatched units to drive a body of rebels from their sanctuary

in the mountains between Lough Conn and Barnageeha near Foxford. The soldiers successfully forced this group from the high country, compelling them to disperse in the process. One of the rebel commanders, 'commonly stilled Captain Timlin ... notorious for ... robberies and acts of cruelty', but also 'a remarkably able, active man', was spotted by loyalists coming out of the mountains with a companion in early April. A patrol from Turlough captured the pair after a brief skirmish near Balla, during which Timlin 'shot dead [a] lad named Clark'. A deserter from the elite King's Lifeguards, Timlin was wearing a French uniform when captured. He was brought to Castlebar at about ten on a Monday morning and, as Gen. Trench calmly observed, '[t]ried and executed before twelve', adding, 'he made no discovery and died extremely hardened'.[79] Near the end of April, Capt. Denis Bingham, an ardent loyalist of the Erris yeomanry, surprised a 'small ... rebel picket', killing two and capturing Hugh McGuire. McGuire, a well-to-do farmer and brewer, had marched to Killala accompanied by his three sons to join the French in August 1798. His sons were all eventually transported, while McGuire was tried at Castlebar, found guilty of 'being actively concerned in the late rebellion ... being a rebel leader', and sentenced to die.[80] Despite these successes, Bingham observed that a number of 'rebel chiefs' remained in the mountains of Erris.[81]

United Irishmen in the aftermath of 1798

It is apparent that the United Irishmen managed to maintain a rudimentary presence in the west for a number of years following the rebellion of 1798. This lends some credence to the reports that agrarian disaffection had ties to the republican cause. Edward Cooke received intelligence in January 1799 from an anonymous source at Loughrea informing him of the 'desperate condition' that existed in County Galway. He believed there was 'a connection kept up with France' via a Mr Burke, who was a cousin of Gen. Kilmaine (of the French army). Accordingly, he advised that the Burkes, prominent merchants of Galway city, should be 'carefully examined.' The informant added that a number of houses in Loughrea, which he described 'as a dangerous and seditious town', should be searched. Included in the list were the homes of Joseph Brennan, a shopkeeper, James McHugo, Lawrence Quinn and Walter Hardman, as well as the Friary at Loughrea, where Father Long, a 'banished priest' and known United Irish organizer, resided. The informer concluded his account by asserting that 'a back room' of the house of a yeomanry sergeant named Lawler was a 'resort' of the United Irishmen and that Mr Andrew Hardman was 'an active traitor'.[82]

More important, the most effective remaining government informant, the Belfast attorney James McGucken, reported in the spring of 1799 that Francis O'Flaherty, a Galway attorney, had been appointed the United Irish leader for that county. O'Flaherty, who resided in Dublin at the time, was instructed to maintain contact between the republicans of Galway and the

new executive in the capital.[83] Communications were to be transmitted
orally via trusted couriers; 'a young man named Madden' from Loughrea
filled this role for County Galway.[84] Additionally, McGucken recommended
having several westerners arrested in the event of an invasion, including a
man named Malone from Mayo, who was 'in the confidence of the Dublin
executive', and a Galwegian named Moore, a relative of Councillor John
Moore who had served as the President of the 'Republic of Connacht'
during the French occupation.[85]

In the late summer of 1799, a Mr Mahon of Galway received information that 'a considerable part of the command of this province [Connaught]'
had been given to 'two gentlemen, with whom he ha[d] frequent communication'. These men were believed to be in contact with the 'president of
the directory' in Dublin 'from whom they g[o]t their commissions'. Mahon
added: 'They are organizing this province, and making pikes with more
industry, than at any period hitherto'.[86] Cornwallis believed this information sufficiently important to be forwarded to Whitehall:

> [T]he disposition to disturbance although most strongly manifested
> throughout the County Waterford and parts of Tipperary, is not altogether
> confined to that quarter of the Kingdom; but ... a corresponding move-
> ment has shown itself in Galway and a similarity of plan is traceable in the
> statements which are transmitted by Mr Greene from Waterford and Mr
> Mahon from Galway.[87]

Finally, Francis O'Flaherty's name reappears with sufficient frequency
in government documents to suggest that concerns over his activities on
the part of local loyalists were legitimate. Shortly after Emmet's rebellion,
Richard Martin informed Dublin Castle:

> Some months ago I wrote Marsden of my fears that Francis O'Flaherty, an
> attorney and notorious rebel, who swore almost every rebel in Galway and
> confessed and obtained protection, was again employed ... [I] have good
> information that there are private meetings in Galway, loyalists resent his
> still practicing, inquire striking him off the roll of Attorneys.[88]

Myles Prendergast and Johnny the outlaw

By June 1799, local loyalists and the military had significantly degraded
the rebels' military capability in County Mayo, although a small hard-core
cadre of leaders escaped into Galway, where they were to prove remarkably
resilient. In January, parties of soldiers were stationed at Loughrea and Gort
as a result of the 'rebel parties ... known to march at night through many
parts of the country'. These bands operating in eastern Galway supported
themselves by 'petty robberies', and their depredations were dismissed as
'rare and trifling'.[89] Of far greater concern to the authorities was 'a party of
rebels' that had found shelter in the isolated baronies of Connemara. Gen.

Trench correctly observed that the 'wild mountainous nature of the country they now inhabit[ed] would render any attempt to apprehend the individuals of the party very difficult'.[90]

The identity of the leaders at large in Connemara was firmly established in the autumn of 1799 when Cornwallis issued a proclamation requiring that every person in the county who had 'been engaged in the late rebellion' apply for a pardon under the Act of Amnesty. Those individuals not entitled to pardon were to surrender themselves within a month and provide 'security to depart forthwith in a vessel to be provided'. Finally because of the 'enormity of their crimes', eight men were exempted from the pardon. Among others identified were Dr Christopher Crump, of Orrery, John Gibbons, Sr, of Westport and his son John Gibbons, Jr, Father Myles Prendergast, and Peter Gibbons of Newport. A reward of £500 was offered for the capture of MacDonnell and £200 for each of the others. Additionally, harbourers were to be punished under martial law.[91] The threat posed by the rebels was clearly recognized by Lord Sligo, the most powerful magnate in the region, who complained: 'these parts can never be secure till something is done to drive the rebel chiefs from Connemara'.[92]

Over time, Father Myles Prendergast and John Gibbons, Jr, proved to be the most recalcitrant of the Connemara holdouts. The heart of the region where Gibbons and Prendergast found shelter was known to locals as the 'Island', consisting of 'the whole country bounded on the north by Lough Corrib, Mask and Carra ... [and] on the south and west by Galway Bay and the ocean'.[93] Although the paucity of extant sources precludes drawing more than a rough outline of the activities of these men, it is possible to tease out answers to several questions raised by their long-term survival. Of central importance is the issue of motivation. In the case of Myles Prendergast, an overtly political orientation is established by his status as a United Irish activist prior to the rebellion of 1798. As Denis Browne explained to the Viceroy, Hardwicke, '[Prendergast] was very deep in the mischiefs of the country previous to the invasion, [and] was a confidant and partner of power with the MacDonnells, Gibbons and O'Malleys.'[94] Similarly, Lord Sligo described Prendergast as 'a most daring villain [of] desperate courage', who played a central role in rallying the people to the French at the time of the invasion.[95] Furthermore, Richard Hayes noted in his 1937 history that Prendergast 'had been associated with the United movement for several years and ... hurried into Castlebar to welcome Humbert'.[96] Perhaps of greatest significance, Prendergast himself acknowledged that his 'persecution' by the loyalist Browne family pre-dated the rebellion by more than a year.[97] This in turn strongly suggests that the Brownes were reacting to his role as a United Irish activist. Prendergast turned out in 1798 and served a key role in drawing recruits to the Franco-Irish army due to his influence with the people. Loyalists captured Prendergast in the aftermath of Ballinamuck, yet the priest managed to escape from Castlebar jail, killing a guard in the process. During his protracted stay in Connemara, Prendergast was maintained by the Provincial of the Augustinians, and members of the order interceded on more than one occasion with the Church hierarchy on his behalf.[98]

'Johnny the Outlaw' was the son of the leading Westport United Irishman John Gibbons, Sr. The younger Gibbons joined the French in August and fought in a number of engagements, surviving the massacre after Ballynamuck by concealing himself for several hours in a bog hole.[99] After the battle Gibbons escaped to Connemara, where he joined Myles Prendergast at the head of a small band of rebels.[100] His conduct after 1798 reflects a complexity of motivation: although a descent into extreme violence, banditry and probably alcoholism is suggested, Gibbons' actions also encompass aspects that can be construed as political.

Between 1798 and 1800, Gibbons' name remained consistently near the top of the government's list of wanted rebels. In July 1800 he drew further attention when he killed a man named Patrick Gibbons during a drinking session. This murder appears to have been the result of a fusion of political and personal motivations. An informant later explained: 'every person he saw' reported that the murder occurred when John Gibbons proclaimed 'he would shoot some of the O'Flahertys of Ballynakill as they were Orangemen and tyrants', and the victim attempted to restrain him.[101] As a result of these threats to the lives of this influential family, James O'Flaherty had Gibbons tracked down by a bounty hunter. He was taken at a home in Ballynakill and handed over to the Ballynahinch yeomanry, who lodged him in Castlebar jail.[102] Although Gibbons' arrest was the result of his own rashness in threatening the life of a prominent member of the local gentry, it is also evident that the authorities had stepped up their efforts to capture the outlaw in the spring of 1800. On 20–21 June, a general court martial was convened at Castlebar for the purpose of trying two of his associates. Daniel and John McGloughlin were charged with 'harbouring and associating with John Gibbons, Jr, a proclaimed rebel ... and for aiding in his escape on or about the second of June'. The court sentenced John McGloughlin to twelve months in prison, while Daniel, who was 'guilty to a greater extent ... as the constant associate of John Gibbons', was condemned to 'be transported beyond the seas' for life.[103]

Despite the authority's preoccupation with his arrest, Gibbons managed to effect a dramatic escape from Castlebar jail in the autumn of 1800. With classic understatement, Lord Altamont described Gibbons's flight as 'very unfortunate'. It had involved a substantial number of prisoners who scattered throughout the countryside in its aftermath. Gibbons himself was soon reported to be 'robbing in the mountains', and as a result, local loyalists no longer dared to 'venture out unarmed'.[104]

In the winter of 1801–1802, Gibbons and Prendergast 'plunder[ed] a vessel at anchor of everything' on board.[105] Several months later a party consisting of 'eight yeomen and loyalists' commanded by Patrick McCabe confiscated an illegal cargo of 'thirty bales of tobacco and two kegs of spirituous liquors', which had been concealed in the house of a smuggling captain, William O'Malley. A short time later Gibbons and Prendergast at the head of 'numerous' armed followers, including Edward, George and Austin O'Malley, forcibly repossessed the confiscated goods. Indeed, the party of '100 plus [men] armed with guns' and other weapons included a number of individuals drawn from the 'higher class'.[106] By 1801, therefore, Gibbons and Prendergast had integrated themselves fully into the region's smuggling community. This relationship offered them a high degree of security, for a culture based on illicit trade bred a strong antipathy to informers by necessity, which greatly enhanced Gibbons and Prendergast's ability to evade capture.[107] In fact, Prendergast remained deeply immersed in the Connemara smuggling community through 1808 and quite probably a great deal longer.[108]

On 13 June 1802, Lord Sligo issued a report on the state of Connemara. In this document he explained to Under Secretary Alexander Marsden that 'rewards and troops' had eliminated most of the rebels. In fact, 'only a few of the most desperate' remained, of which 'the two most daring were Father Myles Prendergast and John Gibbons'. He cautioned that 'they still ke[pt] up a very dangerous influence' with the people.[109] Here lies the key to Prendergast and Gibbons' ability to remain at large for so long. Although the isolated nature of Connemara, combined with the prevalence of a regional commerce in illicit goods, proved invaluable assets to the fugitive rebels, the single most important factor in their continued survival was the protection offered by the local community.

The fact that Prendergast and Gibbons remained 'inaccessible to the King's troops' while keeping 'all the loyalists there under contribution [and] even the magistrates' houses open to them', implies the existence of a high degree of popular sympathy.[110] Lord Sligo confirmed this reality when he observed: '[T]hey have friends enough to give notice … [when] … measures from hence are in contemplation against them.' Significantly, the people did not merely remain passively silent as to the rebels' whereabouts, which could be attributed to physical intimidation; instead they served as active sources of intelligence. Sligo also acknowledged that, as a priest, Prendergast had 'some influence arising from his sacred function'.[111]

Prendergast was not only sheltered in the homes of members of the 'lower orders', as might be expected if popular support were merely a reflection of an atavistic tendency on the part of a Catholic peasantry to protect their priests. Richard Martin revealed the presence of an important phenomenon when he stated: 'Prendergast says mass twice a month at the house of Walter Coneys, who I am sorry to say is a tenant of mine.' What made this observation so surprising was the revelation: 'Coneys is a Protestant, which makes his encouraging this rebel, who by his own admission murdered two [men] since his flight from Mayo, the more remarkable'.[112] Similarly, Lord Sligo wrote: 'It is a shame that outlaws, murderers and traitors should be allowed to remain openly everywhere in the king's dominions unmolested.'

He believed, erroneously, that Prendergast had been sent to Rome 'by a sub-scription from the Bishops and Priests'. Yet, he wrote, 'John Gibbons, Jr., Valentine Jordan, and two or three others whose names I could not spell or write, being Irish, still live openly in Connemara'.[113] The persistent willing-ness of the people of Connemara to protect the fugitive rebels was confirmed in 1805 when an informer reported that Prendergast, 'a man much looked up to by the disaffected, [wa]s constantly concealed by Colonel Martin's tenantry'. He added that Prendergast and Gibbons 'seldom remain[ed] more than a day and a night at any house', suggesting that they were welcome in a large number of homes.[114]

Emmet's rebellion

Despite the existence of tantalizing rumours to the contrary, there is no real evidence of contact between Prendergast and the conspirators responsible for Emmet's rebellion.[115] Only nineteen days before Emmet's rebellion, Lord Ashtown, a Galway magnate, wrote from his seat at Woodlawn: '[T]his part of the County Galway is perfectly quiet ... [and] the disturbances in Connemara ... have been much exaggerated.' As confirmation that the 'lower classes of people' were 'peaceably disposed', Ashtown pointed out: 'they also get drunk and break heads now and then, as usual, at fairs and hurling matches'. In turn, these activities reassured the peer because they were 'extraordinary proof of a peaceable disposition, and such as none but an Irishman would give'. Thus in Ashtown's mind, the absence of such behaviour was a sign of disaffection. As he explained, '[It is] unquestionably true, that for some months previous to the late rebellion when they were immediately to disturb the public peace, drunkenness was almost unknown, and private quarrel, extremely rare'.[116]

Yet, the news of Emmet's rebellion quickly revealed the shallowness of the regional gentry's confidence in the loyalty of the common people. Before the month was out, in consequence to events in Dublin, a meeting of the 'Gentlemen of the Barony' of Erris was convened. It was agreed that there were insufficient troops in the region, and a request was made to permit the distribution of arms to loyalists and the yeomanry. Significantly, this appli-cation was made not as a simple preventative measure but as a direct result of the belief that 'if a rising of the people was to take place here, which it [wa]s the general opinion that their minds [we]re perfectly prepared, the consequence would be [disaster?]'.[117] The importance of this assessment should not be underestimated, for it reveals that the 'ruling class' was firmly convinced of the willingness of the general population to actively participate in the violent overthrow of the existing government.

Nor was this state of alarm confined to Mayo. On the day of the rebel-lion, before he can have obtained knowledge of the event, Richard Martin wrote to the Lord Lieutenant, with the following observations:

When last I saw you I was of the opinion that no rebellious disposition existed in Connemara. I really thought [the] natives [were] loyal, and I now believe they have been misled by the long residence of the rebel chiefs who were expelled by General Trench from Mayo.[118]

On 1 August 1803, Lord Sligo reported: 'there did not appear to me to be any expectation here at all' of the rising in Dublin. Yet this fact offered no comfort to the Marquis, for he also observed of the Dublin 'riot': '[T]he public mind seems alive to our danger. [T]he unequivocal result of my observations is that in the event of a serious French invasion of Ireland the lower order of Catholics would join the French. [T]hose possessing property of that persuasion will for a considerable time stand neuter, privately wishing it well, and ultimately joining to overturn the establishment.' Furthermore, 'the priests in whom' Sligo confided 'agree[d] in that opinion'. He went on to state that 'an emissary' arrived from Galway the day after the rebellion whom he 'narrowly' missed capturing. In fact on the twenty-fourth, 'the rebel chiefs from Connemara crossed ... into the mountains of Mayo, which they had not ventured on for the last three years'. Sligo concluded, 'They will shoot three or four loyalists ... and then go to their home again.'[119]

Prendergast and Gibbons, 1803–1808

Even after the final collapse of the United Irishmen signalled by the failure of Robert Emmet's rebellion in July 1803, the Connemara fugitives continued to create anxiety in the hearts of local loyalists. In mid-October 1803 Lord Sligo described Prendergast and Gibbons as 'the only leaders of these parts', and stating: 'their present bodyguard is formed of deserters, and it is a great shame they should be allowed to roam at large in Connemara'.[120]

Two weeks later Denis Browne reported: '[P]eople have fled here after 23 July [and] two [have] met Prendergast and since associated [with him].' He requested that a force of 200 volunteers drawn from the Mayo Yeomanry be stationed 'in and [on] the coast of Connemara'. By implication, the yeomen of Galway were unable or, more pointedly, unwilling to deal with the problem themselves.[121]

Prendergast 'was run about' by loyalists near Thomastown in Connemara in mid-December 1803 but, as always, successfully eluded his pursuers.[122] February of 1804 found Richard Martin requesting that the government establish military posts in the 'mountains of Connemara with a view to the expulsion of the Banditti in that quarter'.[123] The necessity of seeking outside assistance again emphasized the inability of the local magistrates and yeomanry to come to grips with the rebels.

As the spectre of a French return to the west of Ireland receded, accounts of the disaffected state of Galway declined in tandem. All this while, however, Prendergast and Gibbons remained safely ensconced in the wilds of Connemara. Indeed the occasional alarm bell still chimed. On the final day of April 1805 secret information received in Dublin from Galway city revealed that loyalists there remained highly suspicious about a number of individuals. A roll was enclosed of 'persons suspected of aiding treasonable plans' and 'who should be closely watched'.[124] A similar list was compiled for Connemara. Three men, Austin Gibbons, Luke Lee and William Crawford, were thought to 'correspond' with Prendergast, while the Rev. Mr Russell and Messrs Agnew, Lynch, Bourke, O'Donnald and O'Mealy were all suspect. A number of these men were known smugglers.[125] From Mayo, Denis Browne still bemoaned the state of Connemara, where the Magistrates dared not act against Prendergast and Gibbons for fear of their lives.[126] Thus as late as mid-1805, western Galway remained outside the effective control of the government.

In April of 1806, Brigade Major Marshall requested that the Lord Lieutenant pardon Prendergast under the condition that he transport himself from the country. An important factor in Marshall's recommendation was his belief that, if pardoned, Prendergast would 'give [him] such information as w[ould] enable [him] to take that most infamous character Gibbons'. Behind Marshall's concern lay the increasing audacity of John Gibbons, who in early 1806 attempted to assassinate Denis Browne. Moreover, Gibbons boldly stated he would 'not be happy until he t[ook] another shot' and threatened to 'have a shot' at Maj. Marshall if he 'ever came his way'.[127]

By the spring of 1806, Prendergast had enough of life as a fugitive and opened negotiations with the government. In a remarkable series of communications, he offered to remove himself from the country in exchange for a general pardon. At the prompting of Mr Boyd, a Galway magistrate, he composed a memorial to Lord Cathcart and a letter to Gen. Hill; both documents asserted that Prendergast's name had been falsely tarnished. A witness swore in Boyd's presence that he had been robbed by a man named McNichols, who had pretended to be Prendergast during the commission of the crime. Moreover, Prendergast insisted that McNichols 'had robbed many more also in [his] name'. There appears to have been some validity to this claim, as is demonstrated by the willingness of Boyd and Maj. Marshall to intercede on Prendergast's behalf. On 20 April Marshall forwarded a communication he had received from Prendergast to Alexander Marsden at Dublin Castle. The letter sought to 'answer … queries' that had been posed by Marshall at an earlier date. First, Prendergast 'agree[d] to go to America and not return'. He went on to explain how his name had been used falsely by McNichols in a number of robberies. Finally, while he did not deny that he had committed 'offences', he felt that the troubled conditions of his present existence, combined with the persecution he had suffered for years at the hands of the Browne family, were punishment enough:

> In [my] forty-ninth year of life, [with] torments of mind and body of past years [from being] unjustly persecuted by the Westport Browne family. [F]ifteen months before the invasion [I was] obliged to live in the mountains [and] used to lurk about home when said family would happen to be in Dublin or elsewhere, so that if eight years and a few months punish-

ment would be thought sufficient for my offences, with a loss of upwards of £1,000 ... me thinks sufficiently punished, but thy will be done not mine.[128]

Ultimately, Prendergast withdrew his offer of transportation, or it was rejected by the government. He stayed in Connemara for the rest of his life, another thirty years or more.[129] Certainly by 1808, and probably much earlier, Prendergast had abandoned all revolutionary pretensions. This fact was confirmed that year when the former republican-turned informer, Bernard Duggan, travelled to Connemara where he was able to arrange a meeting with 'Prendergast the priest'. Duggan informed his handlers that Prendergast 'd[id] not stay in a house more [than] a night or two', implying that he was still being pursued by the authorities. Moreover, Prendergast acknowledged himself 'to be a smuggler – but d[id] not pretend to know anything of politics'.[130]

At some point after the spring of 1806, Johnny the Outlaw ventured from his sanctuary in Connemara to attend a wedding at Roonah near his former home in Mayo. 'Worn out with fatigue' and probably quite drunk, he fell asleep. Individuals seeking the bounty offered for his capture damped his powder and notified the authorities of his presence. The house in which he slept was surrounded by a party of troops; he was captured and taken to Westport. With grim irony, on the following day it was Denis Browne who affixed the noose around Johnny the Outlaw's neck. Browne was John Gibbons Junior's godfather.[131]

The traditional historiographical view that focuses on the 'clasping of scapulars and crucifixes' as proof of an atavistic, almost primitive sectarian orientation on the part of the people who rose in 1798 misses the point.[132] Admittedly, it is unlikely that the common people of Mayo rebelled in 1798, or that that those of Galway sheltered the rebels of Connemara in the years following the rebellion, as a result of overt popular support for the creation the secular republic envisioned by the leadership of the United Irishmen. Yet at the same time it is apparent that an ideologically driven cadre of gentry, middlemen, merchants and Catholic priests did in fact exist. Moreover, politicized Defenders had also penetrated the region. This in turn begs the admittedly unanswerable question of what might have resulted had the French sent a viable army in 1798.

Notes

I would like to thank Breandán Mac Suibhne for his valuable comments on an earlier draft of this chapter.

1 Nancy J. Curtin, *The United Irishmen: Popular politics in Ulster and Dublin, 1791–1798* (Oxford, 1994); Jim Smyth, *The men of no property: Irish radicals and popular politics in the late eighteenth century* (New York, 1992); Kevin Whelan, *The tree of liberty: Radicalism, Catholicism and the construction of Irish identity* (Cork, 1996).

2 For the French invasion see, Richard Hayes, *The last invasion of Ireland:*

When Connacht rose (Dublin, 1937); Thomas Pakenham, *The year of liberty: The history of the great Irish rebellion of 1798* (New York, 1969), 278–335; Marianne Elliott, *Partners in revolution: The United Irishmen and France* (New Haven, 1982), 214–40; Harman Murtagh, 'General Humbert's campaign in the west', in Cathal Póirtéir (ed.), *The great Irish rebellion of 1798* (Dublin, 1998), 115–24; Harman Murtagh, 'General Humbert's futile campaign', in Thomas Bartlett, David Dickson, Dáire Keogh and Kevin Whelan (eds), *1798: A bicentenary perspective* (Dublin, 2003), 174–87.

3   Estimates as to how many Irish actually joined the French, unsurprisingly, vary extensively. Marianne Elliott claims the number 'never exceeded 3,000', while Harman Murtagh's figures approach 4,200. At the high end Kevin Whelan states that 'over 10,000 Irish volunteers joined this tiny raiding party'. Elliott, *Partners*, 231; Murtagh, 'Humbert's futile campaign', 180; Kevin Whelan, 'Introduction to section II', in Bartlett *et al.*, 1798, 101.

4   Pakenham, *Year of liberty*, 334–5; Murtagh, 'Humbert's campaign in the west', 115–24.

5   For examples of Stock's continuing influence on the historiography of the western rising and the use of this specific quotation, see Pakenham, *Year of liberty*, 306; Elliott, *Partners*, 224; S. J. Connolly, *Religion, law and power: The making of Protestant Ireland, 1660–1760* (Oxford, 1992), 248–9; Murtagh, 'Humbert's futile campaign', 180.

6   Quoted in Liam Kelly, *A flame now quenched: Leitrim in the 1790s* (Dublin, 1998), 77–8.

7   Connolly, *Religion, law and power*, 248–9. Alternatively, Dáire Keogh has argued that 'the substantial evidence of priests swearing and marshaling their flocks behind the French and the distances some traveled to join with Humbert's army indicates principled motivation'. Moreover, he cites 'Myles Byrne's account of the close ties between the former rebels and clerical exiles in Paris' as 'further testimony of their sympathies for the United Irish cause'. Dáire Keogh, *The French disease: The Catholic Church and radicalism in Ireland, 1790–1800* (Dublin, 1993), 182–6.

8   For a recent work on the Catholic gentry of County Galway in the eighteenth century, their continental ties as well as the centrality of mercantile activity in their ability to remain solvent, see Karen Harvey, *The Bellews of Mount Bellew* (Dublin, 1998), particularly 144–81.

9   Quoted in Smyth, *Men of no property*, 103; also see Whelan, *Tree of liberty*, 64.

10 Elliott, *Partners*, 108.

11 Curtin, *The United Irishmen*, 178–9.

12 NAI SOC 3493, Richard Martin to Hardwicke, Ballynahinch Castle, 23 July 1803; Hayes, *Invasion*, 32; Murtagh, 'Humbert's campaign in the west', 117.

13 For the Armagh expulsions, see David Miller, 'The Armagh troubles', in Samuel Clark and James Donnelly (eds), *Irish peasants: Violence and political unrest, 1780–1914* (Madison, 1983), 155–91; David Miller, 'The origins of the orange order in County Armagh', in A. J. Hughes and William Nolan (eds), *Armagh history and society* (Dublin, 2001), 583–608; Kelly, *Flame*, 47–55; Smyth, *Men of no property*, 110–12; Sean Farrell, *Rituals and riots: Sectarian violence and political culture in Ulster, 1784–1886* (Lexington, KY, 2000), particularly Chapter 2.

14 For the compelling argument that the original Orangemen were members of

the established Church and not Presbyterians, see Miller, 'Origins of the orange order'.

15 J. Short to G. Geraghty, 6 Jan. 1796 quoted in Kelly, *Flame*, 48–9.

16 Miller, 'Origins of the orange order', 590–1; Kelly, *Flame*, 48.

17 Curtin, *The United Irishmen*, 156.

18 For varying estimates of the number of Ulster refugees, ranging between 4,000 and 10,000, see Curtin, *The United Irishmen*, 156–7; Smyth, *Men of no property*, 110–12; Kelly, *Flame*, 50; Farrell, *Rituals and riots*, 26–7.

19 Farrell, *Rituals and riots*, 10–11 and 26–7. Similarly in his examination of Leitrim in the 1790s, Liam Kelly observes of the Ulster exiles that 'they brought with them a detailed knowledge of the workings of such secret societies as the Defenders and United Irishmen, and a determination to combine once more in these secret societies in their new location'. Kelly, *Flame*, 50.

20 Lord Lt Camden to Home Secretary Pelham, 6 Aug 1796, quoted in Kelly, *Flame*, 50.

21 Curtin, *The United Irishmen*, 156.

22 Murtagh, 'Humbert's futile campaign', 180; Murtagh, 'Humbert's campaign in the west', 117.

23 NAI SOC 3493, Martin to Hardwicke, Ballynahinch Castle, 23 July 1803.

24 Ibid.; Hayes, *Invasion*, 32; Murtagh, 'Humbert's campaign in the west', 117.

25 NAI SOC 3493, Martin to Hardwicke, Ballynahinch Castle, 23 July 1803.

26 Curtin, *The United Irishmen*, 157.

27 Ibid., 165.

28 In the last quarter of the eighteenth century, long-term grievances over constitutional domination by Whitehall and the subsidiary status of Ireland's economy led to a reform movement within the Irish Parliament. Backed by the Volunteers, local military units nominally raised to defend Ireland from the French during the conflicts centered on the American Revolution, these 'patriots' took advantage of the crisis created by events in America to obtain legislative independence for the Irish Parliament and the lifting of trade restrictions. These dual objectives were achieved in 1779 and 1782 respectively. Yet, the executive branch of the Irish government headed by the Lord Lieutenant remained responsible to the Imperial cabinet. Moreover, the Lord Lieutenant retained the ability to manipulate the corrupt Irish Parliament through the liberal distribution of patronage. Most importantly, the Reform Act of 1782 failed to address the aspirations of the middle classes, which remained largely excluded from the political process.

29 The Catholic Committee sought to remove the remaining restrictions of the Penal Laws, which had been imposed on the Catholics of Ireland in the aftermath of the Williamite War of 1689–1691.

30 For MacDonnell, see Smyth, *Men of no property*, 60, 75–6; Pakenham, *Year of liberty*, 298, 335; Hayes, *Invasion*, 275–80.

31 Luke Gibbons, 'Republicanism and radical memory: The O'Connors, O'Carolan and the United Irishmen', in Jim Smyth (ed.), *Revolution, counter-revolution and union* (Cambridge, 1998), 211–37.

32 Hayes, *Invasion*, 186.

33 Ibid., 62, 186–8.

34 For John Gibbons Sr, see NAI RP 620/18A/7, Lord Sligo, 18 Sept ?; NAI SOC 1021/21, Sligo to Marsden, Westport House, 23 June 1802; NAI RP 620/7/76/7, secret information, Martin's estate, 14 April 1805.

35 Hayes, *Invasion*, 61, 182, 276, 302–3.
36 NLI KP MS 1200, Gen. Trench to Cooke, Castlebar, 3 Mar. 1800; NAI RP 620/7/76/7, government proclamation, County Galway, 22 Sept. 1799.
37 Ibid. 620/18A/7, Sligo, 18 Sept. ?; NAI SOC 1021/21, Sligo to Marsden, Westport House, 23 June 1802; NAI RP 620/7/76/7, government proclamation, County Galway, 22 Sept., 1799; ibid. 620/14/189/1, secret information, Martin's estate, 14 April 1805.
38 Hayes, *Invasion*, 182.
39 For Thomas Gibbons, see NAI RP 620/12/141/33, Denis Browne, Clare, 26 Oct. ?; ibid. 620/18A/7, Sligo, Westport House, 5 July 1802; NAI SOC 1021/20, NAI State Prisoners Petition 600, Sligo to Marsden, 13 June 1802; 18 Oct. 1799; also see, Helen Landreth, *The pursuit of Robert Emmet* (New York, 1948), 226.
40 NAI RP 620/189/1, secret information, Martin's estate, Connemara, 14 April 1805; NAI RP 620/14/189/3, secret information, Town of Galway, 30 April 1805.
41 For Austin O'Malley, see Hayes, *Invasion*, 32, 62, 146, 263–5.
42 Connolly, *Religion, law and power*, 211–12.
43 Quoted in ibid., 212.
44 Ibid., 213–14.
45 Whelan, *Tree of liberty*, 12–22.
46 NAI SOC 3493, Martin to Hardwicke, Ballynahinch Castle, 23 July 1803.
47 Ibid. SOC 1023/5, Browne, Westport, 30 Oct 1803.
48 NAI RP 620/64/30, to Littlehales, 1803.
49 NAI SOC 3493, Martin to Hardwicke, Ballynahinch Castle, 23 July 1803.
50 NAI RP 620/64/30, Littlehales, 1803; for Coney's and Russell's role as smugglers, also see NAI SOC 3493, Martin to Hardwicke, Ballynahinch Castle, 23 July 1803.
51 For letters from MacDonnell, see TNA HO 100/114/85, Wickham to King, Dublin Castle, 18 Oct. 1803; NAI SOC 1023/4, Martin, 30 Aug. 1803; for John Gibbons Sr's communications to both his son John Jr and nephew Austin, see NAI RP 620/14/189/1, secret information on Connemara, Martin's estate, 14 April 1805; for MacDonnell's escape, see ibid. 620/48/31, 21 Dec. 1799; for other rebels, see NAI SOC 1023/2, Martin, 14 July 1803.
52 NAI SOC 1023/2, Col. Robinson to William Cummins, 4 Aug. 1803; NAI RP 620/66/197, information relative to the organization of the people of Connemara by Prendergast, the priest, a leader of the County Mayo rebels likely 1803; ibid. 620/14/189/1, secret information on Connemara, Martin's estate, 14 April 1805; ibid. 620/64/117, Browne, to Wickham, Galway, 28 Jan. 1803.
53 For the houghers of the early eighteenth century, see Connolly, *Religion, law and power*, 130, 198–262.
54 NLI KP MS 1206, 44, Taylor to Martin, Dublin Castle, 13 Dec. 1798; ibid. MS 1202, 21, to Dennis Bingham, 7 Dec. 1798.
55 NAI RP 620/57/102, memorial of Malachy Tahy of Dalgin in County Mayo, 18 June 1800.
56 TNA HO 100/85/237, extract of a letter from St George Daly, esq. to Castlereagh, Galway, 9 Feb. 1799; for Daly, also see Hayes, *Invasion*, 272–3.
57 Cornwallis to Portland, 14 Feb. 1799, C. Stewart (ed.), *Memoirs and correspondence of Viscount Castlereagh, second marquis of Londonderry*, 4 vols (London, 1848–1849), vol. 2, 174.

58 NAI RP 620/46, memorial of the Grand Jury of County Galway, 20 April 1799; for the assessment of damages caused by the rebellion in Down, see Pakenham, *Year of liberty*, 342–3.

59 For the objectives of the houghers, see extract of a letter from TNA HO 100/85/237, St George Daly to Castlereagh, Galway, 9 Feb. 1799; ibid. 100/85/259, Cornwallis, Dublin Castle, 23 Feb. 1799.

60 Ibid. 100/85/237, extract of a letter from St George Daly to Castlereagh, Galway, 9 Feb. 1799.

61 The Marquis of Buckingham to Lord Grenville, 11 Mar. 1799 in *The manuscripts of J. B. Fortescue, esq.* preserved at Dropmore, 4 vols (London, 1892–1894), vol. 4, 496–8.

62 TNA HO 100/85/259, Cornwallis, Dublin Castle, 23 Feb. 1799.

63 Ibid. 100/85/287, Cooke to Wickham, Dublin Castle, 28 Feb. 1799; for the anticipation of French assistance, also see Buckingham to Grenville, 11 Mar. 1799 in *Manuscripts Fortescue*, vol. 4, 496–8.

64 TNA HO 100/86/272–4, extract of a report from Browne, Castlebar, Mar. 1799.

65 Ibid. 100/85/237, St George Daly to Castlereagh, Galway, 9 Feb. 1799; ibid. 100/86/272–4, Browne, Castlebar, Mar. 1799.

66 Ibid. 100/85/261, Gen. George Hewitt to Gen. John Moore, Dublin Castle, 20 Feb. 1799; ibid. 100/85/259, Cornwallis, Dublin Castle, 23 Feb. 1799.

67 Ibid. 100/86/137–8, Castlereagh to Portland, Dublin Castle, 11 Mar. 1799; ibid. 100/86/351, Lord Altamont, County Mayo, 24 April 1799.

68 Ibid. 100/86/351, Altamont, County Mayo, 24 April 1799.

69 NLI KP MS 1199, 52–121.

70 NLI KP MSS 1199–1200.

71 Curtin, *The United Irishmen*, 165.

72 Kelly, *Flame*, 56–8. The phrase 'refugee trail' is Kelly's.

73 For the national structure and communication networks of the Defenders, see Smyth, *Men of no property*, 140.

74 Ibid., 45.

75 TNA HO 100/85/93, Capt. Roxburgh to Trench, Ballinrobe, 11 Jan. 1799.

76 Ibid. 100/85/91, Trench to Littlehales, Castlebar, 12 Jan. 1799.

77 Ibid. 100/85/93, Roxburgh to Trench, Ballinrobe, 11 Jan. 1799.

78 Ibid. TNA HO 100/86/246–8, Trench, Castlebar, 30 Mar. 1799.

79 NAI RP 620/46/112, Trench, Castlebar, 3 April 1799; TNA HO 100/86/272–4, Trench, Castlebar, 3 April 1799; for Timlin, also see NLI KP MS 1199, 17, Littlehales to Trench, Dublin Castle, 7 April 1799.

80 Ibid. MS 1199, 194–6, Castlereagh to Trench, 28 May 1799; for McGuire, also see Hayes, *Invasion*, 22, 181, 188–9, 302.

81 TNA HO 100/86/354, Trench, Galway, 24 April 1799.

82 NAI RP 620/46/18, anonymous, Loughrea, 25 Jan. 1799.

83 Ibid. 620/7/74/6, McGucken, 2 Feb. 1799; ibid. 620/7/74/8, McGucken, 7 Feb. 1799.

84 Ibid. 620/7/74/15, McGucken to Pollock, 19 Feb. 1799.

85 Ibid. 620/7/74/11, McGucken, 15 Feb. 1799.

86 TNA HO 100/87/162, Mr Mahon, Galway, 7 Sept. 1799.

87 Ibid. 100/87/138, Cornwallis to Portland, Dublin Castle, 9 Sept. 1799.

88 NAI SOC 1023, Martin, 30 Aug. 1803.

89 NAI RP 620/46/18, anonymous to Cooke, Loughrea, 25 Jan. 1799.

90 TNA HO 100/89/49, Trench, Castlebar, 3 June 1799.

91 NAI RP 620/7/76/7, Government Proclamation, Galway, 22 Sept. 1799; also see NAI RP 620/56/12, Robert Aylmer to Castlereagh, near Lisburn, 5 Oct. 1799.

92 Sligo to Marsden, Westport House, 1 Aug 1803, in Michael MacDonagh (ed.) *The Viceroy's post-bag: The correspondence hitherto unpublished of the Earl of Hardwicke, the first Lord Lieutenant after the union* (London, 1904), 315–17.

93 NAI RP 620/46/149, Robinson to Cummins, Galway, 29 April 1799.

94 Cited in Hayes, *Invasion*, 193.

95 NAI RP 620/18A/7, Sligo, Westport House, 11 June 1803.

96 Hayes, *Invasion*, 192.

97 NAI SOC 3732/2, Myles Prendergast to Brigade Maj. Marshall, April 1806.

98 Keogh, *French disease*, 186.

99 Hayes, *Invasion*, 61.

100 Hayes, *Invasion*, 303–4.

101 NAI SOC 3415/5, Edward Blake, J. P., County Galway, 25 July 1800.

102 Ibid. 3415/2, Gen. Meyrick to Trench, Galway, 26 July 1800; ibid. 3415/4, Meyrick to Trench, Galway, 26 July 1800; ibid. 3415/5, Blake, County Galway, 25 July 1800.

103 NLI KP MS 1201, 19–21, Castlereagh to Trench, Dublin Castle, 28 June 1800.

104 NAI RP 620/9/104/3, Altamont, Westport House, 25 Oct. 1800.

105 NAI SOC 1021/20, Sligo to Marsden, Westport House, 13 June 1802.

106 Ibid., information of Patrick McCabe, 12 June 1802; ibid. 1021/21, Sligo to Marsden, Westport House, 23 June 1802.

107 David Dickson, Hugh Dorian, and Breandán Mac Suibhne (eds), *The outer edge of Ulster: A memoir of social life in nineteenth-century Donegal*, 'Introduction'.

108 For Prendergast's status as a smuggler in 1808, see NAI SOC box 159, 21 Dec. 1808.

109 Ibid. 1021/20, Sligo to Marsden, State of the district, Westport House, 13 June 1802.

110 NAI RP 620/18A/7, Sligo, Westport House, 11 June 1803.

111 Ibid. 620/18A/7, Sligo, Westport House, 11 June 1803; ibid., Sligo, 18 Sept. ? [after Dec 1800].

112 NAI SOC 3493, Martin to Hardwicke, Ballynahinch Castle, 23 July 1803.

113 Sligo to Marsden, Westport House, 1 Aug. 1803 in MacDonagh, *Viceroy's post-bag*, 315–17.

114 NAI RP 620/14/189/1, secret information, Martin's estate, Connemara, 14 April 1805.

115 NAI RP 620/66/197, information relative to the organization of the people of Connemara by Prendergast the Priest, a leader of the County Mayo Rebels, n.d.; ibid. 620/11/160/21, Browne, Westport, 24 Aug. 1803.

116 Lord Ashtown to Hardwicke, Woodlawn, 4 July 1803, in MacDonagh, *Viceroy's post-bag*, 267–8.

117 NAI SOC 1025/37, [Gore?] to Marsden, Ballina, 29 July 1803.

118 Ibid. 3493, Martin to Hardwicke, Ballynahinch Castle, 23 July 1803.

119 NAI RP 620/18A/7, Sligo to Marsden, Westport House, 1 Aug. 1803.

120 Ibid. 620/67/76, Westport House, 14 Oct. 1803.

121 NAI SOC 1023/5, Browne, Westport, 30 Oct. 1803.

122 NAI RP 620/50/46, Gen. Hill to Wickham, Galway, 1 Jan. 1804.
123 NLI KP, MS 1018, 475, Beckwith to Littlehales, Royal Hospital, 18 Feb. 1804.
124 NAI RP 620/14/189/3, secret information, Town of Galway, 30 April 1805.
125 Ibid.
126 Ibid. 620/14/189/5, Browne, 1 May 1805.
127 NAI SOC 3732/1, Marshall to Marsden, Tuam, 20 April 1806.
128 Ibid. 3732/2, M. Prendergast to Marshall, enclosed in ibid. 3732/1, Marshall to Marsden, Tuam, 20 April 1806. Prendergast died in 1842 at the age of 82.
129 Keogh, *French disease*, 184.
130 NAI SOC box 159, 21 Dec. 1808.
131 Landreth, *Pursuit*, 226; Hayes, *Invasion*, 183.
132 Elliott, *Partners*, 224.

Part III
South Leinster

7

South Leinster

On 21 June, the decisive engagement of the Wexford campaign was fought at Vinegar Hill, where the rebel army was routed, although surviving elements stayed in the field until mid-July.[1] After this point, the most significant remaining rebel forces in Leinster were those in the mountains of County Wicklow headed by Joseph Holt and a less well-documented entity, which became known as the 'Babes in the Wood'. From within these groups emerged smaller bands that continued to offer resistance for the ensuing six years. Several key issues are raised by the persistence of these bands. Of central importance is the question of motivation. It is argued here that the ability of these rebels to remain at large for so extended a period is a reflection of the broad-based support they received in wide swaths of south Leinster. In turn, popular disaffection was the result of two inter-related processes. First, the long-term efforts of the United Irishmen to disseminate their secular, Enlightenment-influenced, republican ideology took a deeper hold on the region than is sometimes appreciated. Second, the role of repression as a catalyst for continued resistance is of central importance in the development of an understanding of the post-1798 period. In fact, it will be argued here that it was the persistence of counter-revolutionary violence, or 'white terror', a phenomenon with both political and sectarian manifestations, which ultimately crippled Dublin Castle's efforts at reconciliation with the defeated republicans. Furthermore, the government's inability to curb loyalist atrocities created the impression within much of the Catholic population of south Leinster that these depredations had the *de-facto* support of the central authorities. This perception served to void the legitimacy of the state in the eyes of thousands of its non-Protestant citizens.

Further complicating the picture is the presence of gangs that took advantage of the general chaos following the rising to engage in acts of common criminality. In turn, even apparently clear-cut cases of brigandage are not necessarily indicative of an apolitical agenda. There is strong evidence that extreme loyalist elements of the yeomanry, with the tacit approval and even direction of ultra-conservative officers and magistrates, utilized armed robbery as part of a wider campaign of political and sectarian intimidation lasting until 1801. Finally, the activities of a rebel band headed by Joseph Cody and James Corcoran, at least on the surface, appear to mirror many of the theoretical aspects of the phenomenon of social banditry as laid out in Eric Hobsbawm's influential, albeit dated, studies, *Primitive rebels* and *Bandits*.[2] An examination of this party also demonstrates some of the difficulties that emerge in attempting to determine the ultimate nature and motivations of bands, most of which were dismissed as thieves or bandits by the authorities then and historians now.[3]

Counter-revolutionary violence: the white terror

The origins of the white terror in County Wexford can be traced to the expansion of the Orange Order into south Leinster in early 1798. This growth was part of a wider counter-insurgency campaign on the part of conservative elements within the Irish government. Centred on the unofficial cabinet of Cooke, Fitzgibbon, Beresford and Foster, these ultras endeavoured to create a counterweight to the United Irishmen who, starting in north Wexford in early 1797, had been spreading throughout south Leinster with increasing rapidity. The driving force behind this policy was the Under Secretary Edward Cooke, who organized pro-government factions from within the loyalist gentry and magistracy of the affected counties. By the spring of 1798, there were a number of Orange lodges in Carlow, Wexford and Wicklow.[4] In describing this process L. M. Cullen notes, 'We are faced with a hidden agenda in the Irish politics of the day.'[5]

The new lodges were sponsored by a group of hard-line magistrates from the confluence of the borders of Wexford, Carlow and Wicklow. Many of these men commanded highly sectarianized yeomanry corps that comprised like-minded Orangemen. The most notorious individuals in this collection were the Wexford middlemen Hunter Gowan, Hawtry White and Archibald Hamilton Jacob. Other members included the high sheriff of Carlow, Robert Cornwall, the brothers John and Robert Rochfort, also of that county, as well as John James from Ballycrystal in Wexford. Gowan was particularly prominent in the movement, and in addition to his own lodge at Mount Nebo near Gorey, he helped to establish a number of others in south Wicklow and north Wexford.[6]

The first substantial episodes of counter-revolutionary violence occurred in Wexford during mid-May shortly before the outbreak of open rebellion. For example, Hawtry White's Ballaghkeen Cavalry 'began to burn [on] Saturday, 26 May and before'.[7] As a result of the rebel occupation of much of Wexford, many of the counties yeomanry corps prudently withdrew to the relative safety of adjacent counties. With the defeat of the republican army at Vinegar Hill on 21 June, loyalist forces initiated a vengeance-fuelled campaign of terror that was to continue for the next three years. Miles Byrne, a long-time north Wexford United Irishman, described the opening phases of this campaign in his memoirs explaining:

> [W]hen the government forces left in reserve at Gorey learned that our army was dispersed and nearly exterminated ... they took courage and

sallied out ... They began to murder all they met, crossed and scoured the country in every direction, entered houses, killing.[8]

Shortly after his arrival in late June, the new Lord Lieutenant, the Marquis Cornwallis, made an assessment of the military and political environment of Ireland. In his initial report to the Home Secretary, the Duke of Portland, Cornwallis denounced the ferocity of government forces, which in the case of the Irish units at least, he feared was not confined to the private soldiers. The Viceroy went on to explain his plans to end the rebellion by offering protections to rebels who would surrender their arms and swear an oath of allegiance. Finally and most pointedly, Cornwallis concluded that he would use the 'utmost exertions to suppress the folly ... of substituting the word Catholicism instead of Jacobinism as the foundation of the present rebellion'.[9] Three days later, he expanded on his initial impressions in a letter to Gen. Charles Ross in which he stated, 'The violence of our friends, and their folly in endeavouring to make it a religious war, added to the ferocity of our troops who delight in murder, most powerfully counteract all plans of conciliation.'[10] The Viceroy was not alone in recognizing the danger of indiscriminate repression. While stationed in Wexford in early July, the highly competent and humane Gen. Moore found his efforts to conciliate the minds of the people frustrated by the actions of the less tolerant Gen. Eustace, who was 'sending out detachments from Ross to burn and destroy'. Moore believed that Eustace's conduct was 'extremely criminal' and insisted that 'it must be stopped'.[11] Additionally, the general, who had the dubious pleasure of commanding units of the Irish militia earlier in the Wexford campaign, summed up his impressions of this key element of the Irish security apparatus as follows: '[T]he officers of every description are so bad that it is quite discouraging. Except that they are clothed with more uniformity, they are as ignorant and as much a rabble as those who have hitherto opposed us.'[12] This negative view of the militia was shared by Cornwallis. He described the Irish militia as 'totally without discipline, contemptible before the enemy ... but ferocious and cruel in the extreme when any poor wretches c[a]me within their power', and concluded: 'In short, murder appears to be their chief pastime.'[13]

Nor were the militia the only loyalist forces that bore watching as, ominously, the 'yeomen were beginning to vex the people by casting up against them what had passed and threatening revenge; to burn'.[14] Additionally, there was the quandary posed by the gentlemen of Wexford, most of whom had fled the countryside during the rebellion. While Moore saw the utility of the gentry returning to their homes, stating: 'their presence would do much if they were under the control of prudent military officers', he also cautioned that if left to themselves, 'they [we]re apt to revenge past injuries and counteract the spirit and effect of the proclamation'.[15]

Significantly, it was not only the Irish military or local extremists who hindered the Lord Lieutenant's efforts to end the rebellion and restore tranquillity. At the national level, the ultra-conservative members of the

Protestant ascendancy, who dominated both houses of the Irish parliament and who were also strongly represented in the cabinet, did all in their power to impede this process. When, in early July, Cornwallis issued a proclamation of general pardon 'that proposed to exclude from the security of life only those who ha[d] been guilty of cool and deliberate murder and the leaders to banishment', ranking loyalists were outraged.[16] In a letter to the Duke of Portland, the long-term danger posed by the militant attitude of these elements of the ascendancy was prophetically delineated by the Viceroy:

> The principal persons of this country and members of both houses of parliament are in general adverse to all acts of clemency ... and [are] perhaps too heated to see the effects which their violence must produce ... [it can] only terminate in the extirpation of the greater number of the inhabitants, and in the utter destruction of the country: the words Papist and Priest are forever in their mouths and by their policy, they would drive four-fifths of the community into irreconcilable rebellion.[17]

In the early morning hours of 6 July, the remnants of the once formidable republican army of Wexford withdrew from the county on a final desperate march across the midlands. With this departure, organized resistance collapsed and disbanded rebels as well as their families were left defenceless in the face of loyalist extremists who now raped, robbed and burned at will.

On the fourteenth Cornwallis confessed to Gen. Ross that he was ashamed at the condition of Ireland, not as a result of the rebellion, but because of the 'numberless murders' that were being 'committed hourly by [the] people, without any process or examination whatever'. He attributed the worst offences to the yeomanry, whom he described as ferocious. After making allowances for their having 'saved the country', the Lord Lieutenant observed that they 'now t[ook] the lead in rapine and murder'. The militia was little better, and the passions of the leading people of the country remained heated, as was established in conversations where he found all of them in favour of a continuing 'system of blood'.[18]

Thus, prior to the cessation of open rebellion in mid-July, Cornwallis and Moore had identified the sources of the violence that was to so torment the rural population of south Leinster in the months and years that followed the rebellion of 1798. Moreover, they clearly recognized the danger posed by the continuance of a policy of unrestrained repression and also correctly identified the three-tiered foundation on which the white terror was based. On the local level, lower-class Protestants, who constituted the rank-and-file of the yeomanry, were already exacting revenge on those they suspected of participating in the rebellion. On a regional basis extremist members of the gentry, who invariably were also commanders of the more violent yeomanry corps, often directed these efforts. As the moderate Anglican cleric James Gordon asserted, the depredations of lower-class loyalists were 'suspected to have been most unwisely encouraged by the connivance of some yeoman officers'.[19] Nationally, powerful and influential ultra-conservatives gave their tacit approval, and possibly their active support, to this still evolving campaign of intimidation. Significantly, a number of these ranking Orangemen were members of the same Dublin grand lodge.[20] This fact demonstrates that these men were organized, which in turn implies that their efforts had a higher degree of coordination than has been previously appreciated. Moreover, the role of Cooke in establishing the Orange Order in south Leinster, coupled with his ties to Carlow and his relationship with Cornwall and the Rochforts, suggests that the Order was under the control of ultra-conservative elements in the Irish government.

Throughout the winter of 1798–1799, as Gordon observed, '[The country was] miserably afflicted ... by gangs of nocturnal marauders.' Additionally, he found those responsible to be 'the lower classes of loyalists', motivated by a desire for revenge.[21] Similarly, Luke Cullen, in his account of the rebellion's aftermath drawn from his interviews with surviving eyewitnesses in the 1840s and 1850s, stated:

> [I]n the last months of 1798 and early 1799, the Orange yeomen did as they pleased. The lands [and the] properties [of Catholics] and Catholic chapels were free warren, and their persons free game, old grudges were settled ... Court-martials were held mostly by young subalterns from the yeomanry and militia. The whole (hanging) was substituted for the half, the pitch cap for enlistment, flagellation gave way to transportation for life and with these terrible penalties ... came the dark nights of January 1799, with the heart rending loss of houses and property, sons, brothers and fathers ... old and dreadful animosities in the revengeful wantonness of a lawless society.[22]

The activities of a gang of loyalist extremist yeomanry that operated in north Wexford, the so-called 'Black Mob', are illustrative of both the form taken by loyalist atrocities and the mentality that lay behind them. The notorious leader of this group was the fanatical Protestant middleman, Hunter Gowan, with his seat at Mount Nebo near the Wicklow border. Gowan founded one of the first Orange lodges in south Leinster and played a prominent role in the Orange Order's expansion into Wexford in the first half of 1798. The forty or so supplementary yeomen who comprised the Black Mob began terrorizing the area around Gorey in the third week of June and were already responsible for a number of murders before the end of the rebellion in mid-July. Through the autumn well into the winter, these 'low Orangemen' murdered and burned.[23]

Writing from Gorey in January 1799, Annesley Brownrigg, a long-time Wicklow magistrate, gave a graphic account of the Black Mob's depredations. He opened by stating, 'This part between Gorey and Wexford is in such a state that I shall thank you to have a representative laid before the Lord Lieutenant.' He further stated that at the fair of Ballycanew on 30 November 1798, 'great abuse was given ... to several country people, without any provocation'. Those responsible were Hunter Gowan's yeomanry, who later 'burned above nine houses that night'. Brownrigg believed that because these transgressions had failed to draw any response from the authorities, they might well make the rebels rise again. Additionally, he felt that they served as an 'encouragement for the most wanton barbarity', which occurred on the night of Wednesday 16 January. In a rampage that lasted from approximately 7 p.m. to 12:30 a.m., two Catholic chapels, a priest's house and nine other dwellings were plundered and put to the torch. A servant girl was killed at the home of the priest. One unfortunate resident, 'a shoemaker, [was] shot and ... thrown into the flames'. The 'conflagration extended six miles from the first house [attacked]'.[24]

The immediate cause of this nightmarish turn of events was the shooting death of Sgt Johnson, a non-commissioned officer in Hawtry White's Ballaghkeen yeomanry. This killing took place three days earlier on the morning of Sunday 13 January, when a fugitive rebel fleeing a cavalry patrol sought shelter in the home of Capt. Sparks, who unfortunately was attending church at the time. Sgt Johnson and another trooper entered the house, and the man fired upon them. The captain commanding the patrol ordered the house to be burned, and the fugitive was killed. Two servants were also shot in the process. A dangerous confluence of yeomanry corps occurred at the funeral of Sgt Johnson on 16 January. In addition to the Ballaghkeen troop, the Wingfield and Gorey Yeomanry as well as the Black Mob and others were in attendance. A local magistrate obtained information that John Redmond and William Porter, both of the Ballykeen Yeomen, knew the identity of every man who had participated in the mayhem. Yet none of the numerous witnesses to the affair would dare to give evidence. More significantly, Brownrigg himself requested that 'my name ... be kept secret'. He based his reluctance on the fact that another 'gentleman of this neighbourhood has been and is yet in continual fear of his life for forwarding a prosecution against a yeoman for [a] night murder'. This hesitancy on the part of Brownrigg is extremely revealing of the climate of fear that existed in north Wexford, and to varying degrees, throughout south Leinster half a year after the rebellion was crushed. If a wealthy member of the local establishment, who additionally had been a magistrate for upwards of twenty years dared not prosecute, or even to have his name associated with the case, Catholics from the lower orders stood no chance whatsoever.[25]

Brownrigg attended the wake of the girl slain during the January rampage, where he saw her body and noted that 'a great number of people were there quite peaceable'. Yet he also recognized the danger posed by these unrelenting assaults on the non-loyalist majority, stating: '[The] said flagrant acts endanger the peace of the country and the lives of us several loyal inhabitants now living at our places of abode'. 'It is a shame', he continued, 'that not just [the] military has [the] power to execute.' Brownrigg concluded by stating that he was sending to Wexford for military assistance 'to save the country' as, ominously, 'more burning [wa]s expected'.[26] In

1801, Gowan was accused of thirty-four murders, although the failure of a key witness to appear resulted in a dismissal.[27]

Despite the determined efforts of the executive branch of the Irish government headed by the extremely capable Cornwallis and Castlereagh, as well as endeavours of the talented and humane army officers such as Generals Hunter and Moore, loyalist depredations continued unabated. Significantly, the white terror was not directed solely against the persons and property of defeated rebels. Instead, Catholic society as a whole was targeted. The sectarian focus of the terror was illustrated with remarkable clarity by the destruction of Catholic chapels, some thirty of which were ultimately burned in nocturnal raids during the three-year period that followed the rebellion.[28] As Luke Cullen noted, 'On the fifteenth of January 1799, commenced the burning of Catholic chapels ... and for the first eight and a half months not less than eighteen chapels ... were destroyed by fire- most ... twelve [of these] in Wexford.'[29]

The Babes in the Wood

In the aftermath of the battle of Vinegar Hill, a number of the defeated rebels fled west to the Wood of Killoughrum. The forest already sheltered several deserters from various militia regiments. A short time later, these refugees were joined by survivors of Father John Murphy's rebel column, which had failed in its efforts to carry the rising to the midlands after Vinegar Hill. In the turbulent and dangerous climate that followed the cessation of open warfare, elements of the disparate parties hiding in the forest coalesced into a loose body that became known as the 'Babes in the Woods'.[30]

The Babes offered the only protection available to the Roman Catholic population of the region against the emerging white terror. Exemplifying the defensive role played by the group was the capture and execution of five yeomen, who had been raiding Catholic houses in the neighbourhood of Killoughrum.[31] Unsurprisingly in such an environment, the Babes enjoyed the support of much of the local population. They maintained themselves by levying small contributions, which met with little opposition. Families living near the forest supplied provisions in kind, while those further away contributed small amounts of hard currency.[32]

In late September the Babes sallied from the woods, attacking, and utterly destroying the home of an influential local magistrate, Caesar Colclough, at Mocurry in the Barony of Scarawalsh.[33] This was not an isolated incident. A party from Killoughrum marched from the forest on the night of 25 September. The band of rebels passed through the border village of Ballymurphy into south Carlow, where they 'committed several robberies', then crossed the Barrow and entered the town of Graigenamangh on the Kilkenny side of the river. There, with 'a most incredible audacity', they dragged a shopkeeper named Singles from his bed and 'massacred' him in the street in front of his home. In reality, this murder is best viewed as a retaliatory political action. Singles was targeted because he was a yeoman who had played a central part in the pursuit and capture of a deserter, whom the authorities had executed at Kilkenny 'a few days before'.[34]

The Babes continued to operate in western Wexford throughout the autumn of 1798, and contemporary accounts described the group as 'very formidable'. In a letter composed on 22 September, a correspondent from Naas in south Kildare wrote that he had received news 'from County Wexford that the rebels [we]re in considerable force there, especially in the woods of Killoughrum and that part of the country called Bantry'.[35] Similarly, the Rev. Daniel McNeille informed Lord Monck that the area around Killann was in the 'possession' of 'rebels and deserters'. Indeed, loyalist farmers who had flowed from the countryside at the time of the rebellion had begun to trickle back to their homesteads during the late summer in hope of salvaging their crops. Yet although these planters were safe by day, the night remained bitterly contested by the rebels. For example, a Protestant farmer named Parslow worked his land during the daylight hours and then retired at dusk to what he believed to be the safety of a nearby town. There, he spent his evenings at the home of a loyalist widow named Dobbyn, whose husband and three sons had been burned by rebel extremists at Scullabogue. Parslow's sense of security proved false. The Dobbyn house was broken into one night; both Parslow and his son were shot and wounded. The two Dobbyn widows residing in the home were beaten severely, as was Parslow's wife, who was additionally denigrated as 'an Orange whore'. That same evening, five men entered the house of John Whitney, a loyalist also burned at Scullabogue, where they robbed and 'cruelly beat' his widow. McNeille cautioned Monck, a powerful north Wicklow magnate who also held land in Wexford, about the impact of these assaults on his tenants: '[I]n consequence of the outrages the Protestants on your lordship's estate have been compelled to desert their harvests and take refuge here [Adamstown].' The reverend concluded that unless detachments of troops were stationed at Adamstown and Killann there would be 'no safety for a Protestant this winter' in Wexford 'west of the Slaney'.[36]

The persistence of this activity is further illustrated in a letter written by John James, a magistrate from the Wexford border village of Ballycrystal, to his influential brother, Alderman James in Dublin. James requested that his brother caution Lord Castlereagh that unless he 'put some yeomanry on permanent duty, no loyal person of the smallest property' would be able to 'remain in this parish'. James directly attributed the precarious position of local loyalists to the activities of 'the rebels' passing and re-passing from Barony of St. Mullins in County Carlow to the woods of Killoughrum and Ferns [and] lurking there in'.[37] Similarly, the *Belfast News-Letter* reported the same month: 'From Enniscorthy, we learn that the few inhabitants remaining in that town are exposed to perpetual alarms from the rebels in Killoughrum wood.'[38] The veracity of these loyalist warnings was born out on Christmas Eve 1798, when the Lord Lieutenant Cornwallis confessed to the Home Secretary, the Duke of Portland, that in a number of counties, including Wexford, Wicklow, Kildare and most parts of Carlow, Kings, Queens and Kilkenny, 'no Protestant or person suspected to be well-affected to the government can venture to sleep in a house that is not protected by the neighbourhood of the soldiery'.[39]

In reality throughout the autumn and winter of 1798, an undeclared civil war continued to be waged between surviving bands of rebels and loyalist irregulars in the mountains and forests of western Wexford. Although no field armies were involved, the intensity of this guerrilla war should not be underestimated. Some idea, albeit from a loyalist perspective, of the nature and extent of this warfare can be gleaned from an article that appeared in the *Courier* on 8 October:

> [T]he most shocking enormities are daily committed by the rebels against the yeomen and the Protestant Orange families in Wicklow and neighbouring counties. These enormities are committed not by an army of rebels, but by detached parties assembling in the dead of night perhaps, and dispersing when the business of murder is dispatched; to prevent them, has been thought impossible – to punish them in a legal way, impracticable. Nor is Holt and his followers alone, who has dealt in those murderous deeds. The savage spirit has infected the mass of the peasantry; who notwithstanding his excellency's leniency, seem to consider themselves as a forlorn hope in an enemy's country, and think only of wrecking vengeance on that enemy – the only means they possess of doing so, are the firebrand and the pike.[40]

This article reveals several key aspects of the continuing resistance in south Leinster. First, the perpetrators are described as rebels (not robbers) or as the more generic, banditti. Furthermore, the targets of rebel violence are identified as Orange families and yeoman. Thus, even in the face of highly sectarianized attacks by conservative extremists, the rebels continued to make some distinction between active loyalists and Protestants in general. Additionally, and of greatest import, the paper recognized that the mass of the peasantry now viewed itself as existing in an enemy's country. The form taken by this nocturnal war is further illustrated in a letter from Castlereagh to the Under Secretary, William Wickham: '[L]atterly, the rebellion has degenerated, particularly in the counties of Wicklow, Wexford, Kildare, Westmeath and Dublin into a petty warfare, not less afflicting to the loyal inhabitants, though less formidable to the state.'[41] Thus, even after making allowances for exaggerations on the part of overly alarmed loyalists, it is undeniable that the rebels remained a formidable presence on the local level.

A hard-core of well-trained deserters, keenly aware of the fate awaiting them if captured, made the Babes a force to be reckoned with. Contemporary accounts of the Babes' numbers vary from a high of 1,500 men, down to a more realistic figure of somewhat under 300. The band appears to have been able to raise approximately 150 men for a single operation as late as the second half of September, and about ninety men surrendered to Capt. Robinson in mid-November.[42]

The continued resistance of the Babes in the Wood can be attributed to a variety of causes. First, so-called 'protections', slips of paper signed by military officers to guarantee the safety of rebels who agreed to surrender their arms and return home, were frequently ignored by loyalists on the local level. More dangerously, these protections were sometimes used against former rebels as evidence of their participation in the rising, with inevitable results.[43] For many, the option of surrender did not exist as death sentences were mandatory for any individual who had burned a house or who had committed murder (suspicion of having killed a loyalist, even in combat, appears to have met the criterion for this latter charge). As Luke Cullen noted, 'Those who took up in the Killoughrum Woods ... only sought protection.'[44]

Yet beyond the impulse for self-preservation, which led many of the former rebels and deserters to band together in the summer of 1798, a more overtly political motivation can be discerned. Significantly, the Babes maintained contact with the largest surviving rebel force in Ireland, that of Joseph Holt, which continued to hold out in the mountains of neighbouring County Wicklow. The government received intelligence during the last week of September, which established that the Babes 'h[e]ld communication with Holt and the Wicklow rebels'.[45] Similarly, Edward Hay asserted in his history that the Babes 'were occasionally visited by [Andrew] Hackett and Holt'.[46] Information provided to the government by William Hacket, a County Wexford farmer and also 'a principal leader and captain of the rebels', also provides some insight into the motivational forces that drove the holdouts in the wood. He claimed in a memorial addressed to the Lord Lieutenant that the news of the French invasion in August 1798 had led the 'party of rebels and deserters then in considerable force in the woods of Killoughrum' to plan to 'renew the attack on several places of strength in the hands of the King's troops'.[47] Confirmation of Hacket's assertion that the Babes still hoped to act came on 6 October when Patrick Fitzsimmons, whom Ruán O'Donnell identifies as a member of the 'core-group' in the woods, informed the loyalist magistrate, Robert Cornwall, that they would 'keep themselves as quiet as possible until joined by General Holt and then make a general attack' on Dublin.[48]

Government forces made a concerted effort to destroy the Babes during the autumn of 1798. Soldiers surrounded the Wood of Killoughrum in September and a small, savage, action took place at the foot of the Blackstairs Mountains on Saturday 5 October. This engagement occurred when Gen. Taylor led a mixed body of regulars, militia and yeomen on a sweep through the area. The military party came upon a large body of rebels about a mile from Woodbrook in the parish of Killann. Gen. Taylor captured seven of the rebels and claimed to have killed sixty more, most of whom were carrying protections. The surviving insurgents attempted to flee over the mountains into Carlow but were met by elements of Capt. Cornwall's yeoman cavalry and the Killedmond infantry, who claimed to have killed a further 150 of the rebels.[49] Although the officer's assessments of rebel casualties in this engagement were certainly exaggerated, it is nonetheless obvious that the Babes had suffered a catastrophic defeat. Further reductions in rebel strength came as the military continued to kill, capture and accept the surrender of members of the Killoughrum band. On 16 November, thirty rebels surrendered to Capt. Robinson of the south Cork militia, and another sixty capitulated a short time later. The authorities executed a number of these unfortunate men at Newtownbarry. They condemned others to serve in the Prussian army, while some of the rebels were compelled to join the fleet.[50]

Yet despite the efforts of the military, resistance of a sort continued as winter approached. In mid-November, Castlereagh described the counties of Wexford and Wicklow as remaining in a state of rebellion, and the rebels 'still acting upon treasonable and systematic principles'.[51] In December, Cornwallis found it necessary to continue martial law in Wexford and Wicklow, although he now felt the remainder of the country could return safely to civil justice. He explained that in the two counties 'the peace ... c[ould] by no means be left to the mere protection of the civil power' and that 'military stations, guards and patrols [we]re in numerous districts necessary for the protection of the inhabitants from outrage'.[52]

In fact as late as April 1799 in response to a request by the Grand Jury of County Wexford, Cornwallis contemplated the establishment of a military post in Wood of Killoughrum as well as the cutting of 'passes through it in different directions'. The Viceroy even dispatched an engineer to the Wood to examine the feasibility of such a project.[53] Yet stability of a sort was gradually returning to western Wexford. The Catholic Bishop of Ferns, James Caulfield, informed Archbishop Troy in March, 'I have not heard of any robberies committed these two months past, by the fugitive rebels, I therefore am inclined to think they have quit this county'.[54] By June, the Lord Lieutenant felt he could safely avoid incurring the expense of having the Killoughrum yeomanry continued on permanent duty. Similarly, the regional commander, Lt Gen. Dundas, believed there were sufficient troops in the county and 'the neighbourhood of the Woods of Killoughrum to prevent their [again] becoming an asylum for deserters'.[55]

Cody and Corcoran as United Irishmen

Among the rebels in the Wood of Killoughrum who surrendered in the autumn of 1798 was a farmer from Ballindaggan named James Corcoran. The parish lay on the western extremity of Wexford adjacent to south Carlow, with which it shared the Blackstairs Mountains. Corcoran was described as five-feet seven inches in height with 'reddish hair' and a 'long nose'. He was also 'slender, straight and well-limbed'. Significantly, he spoke with 'a very good address', suggesting a degree of education and the likelihood that he

came from the upper strata of the Catholic farming community. Furthermore, like so many of the 1798 rebels, Corcoran was a relatively young
man, still under the age of thirty in 1801.[56]

Indeed, James Corcoran fits the pattern of young men recruited by mis-
sionaries from the radical wing of the United Irishmen in 1797. This faction
was responsible for spreading the movement's new military cell structure
into the previously unorganized parishes of western Wexford during the
autumn of 1797. The radical wing distinguished itself by its active recruitment amongst the lower orders. Alternatively, the so-called 'moderates',
who had earlier brought the United system to the eastern districts of Wexford, were primarily concerned with political organization and questioned
the wisdom of broadening the movement's social base. Later on when both
groups came to see the necessity of rebellion, the radicals were willing to
risk an indigenous rising, while the moderates still believed it was necessary
to wait for French assistance (at least partially as a safeguard against the
levelling tendencies of their own lower ranks).[57]

The evidence of Corcoran's membership in the United Irishmen is compelling, and it is apparent that he came to play an important role as an
activist prior to the rebellion. Moreover, the authorities had him arrested
and interned in Wexford jail before the rising.[58] As the government's disarming campaign in the county commenced in late April, it is likely that
Corcoran was taken up during the week that preceded the outbreak of open
rebellion on 26 May.[59] Daniel Gahan notes that it was at this point that
'cartloads of prisoners, many of them active United Irishmen, were drawn
from the northern and south-western parishes of Wexford'.[60] Whatever the
circumstances of his arrest, Corcoran's emergence as a Captain of the Babes
in the Wood suggests that he did in fact hold a position of leadership in the
society's military structure. Finally, Mr Colclough, who was in a position
to be known, asserted, 'I know he was the man who was most active in
fomenting the rebellion in the beginning.'[61]

Corcoran was freed when the rebel army occupied Wexford town, and he
went on to fight at the Battle of New Ross.[62] He also saw combat at Vinegar
Hill and remained in the field until the rebel forces dispersed at the end of
June.[63] During the rebellion, Corcoran appears to have conducted himself
with 'humanity' and later claimed that he could produce 'several Protestants
of that county ... whose persons or property he was the means of saving'.[64]
Considering the latter willingness of a number of influential magistrates and
military officers to intercede on his behalf this claim seems quite plausible.

With the collapse of organized resistance in Wexford, Corcoran sought
sanctuary in the Wood of Killoughrum, where he emerged as one of the
leaders of the Babes in the Woods.[65] At some point during the autumn
of 1798 Brigade Maj. Fitzgerald of the Wexford yeomanry attempted to
arrange Corcoran's surrender. An intriguing account of a series of meetings
between Fitzgerald and Corcoran survives in the material gathered by Luke
Cullen. According to Cullen's source, Corcoran would have a note passed to

one of Fitzgerald's men informing the major that he would 'come to him' at a specified time. Then, 'the Major would sit up [waiting] for him with a case of loaded pistols on his table. Corcoran would come, of course armed, [and] they would debate conditions, and not agreeing the latter would return to his [cover?] and the Major to his bed.' These negotiations ultimately failed, although Fitzgerald's willingness to meet with Corcoran is demonstrative of his importance in the eyes of the authorities.[66]

Following the breakdown of negotiations with Maj. Fitzgerald, the precarious position of the rebels compelled Corcoran to again seek terms. The military had exerted increasing pressure on the Babes from the middle of September, and news of the French defeat at Ballynamuck earlier that month, coupled with the surrender of Holt in Wicklow on 10 November, can only have compounded the hopelessness of the situation. In any event, Corcoran sought terms from Capt. Robinson of the South Cork militia, who commanded the government forces at Grange. On 16 November, Corcoran, described in a newspaper account of the event as a 'rebel chief', surrendered himself. As per the agreement, the following day, after having received assurances for their safety, Corcoran returned to the wood and brought out thirty of his men.[67] Yet his captivity proved to be short lived. Upon learning that, in violation of the terms of surrender, the government planned to transport several of his men and that he was himself to be tried by court martial, Corcoran escaped. He fled to the Barony of St Mullins in south Carlow, where he was to remain a thorn in the side of local authorities and a source of concern to the government for the next five and a half years.[68]

The identity of the band's other leader is more problematic. Gahan identifies James Coady as the co-commander of the Corcoran gang, the two having fought together at New Ross in the rebellion.[69] In his comprehensive work on the rebellion in County Wicklow, Ruán O'Donnell also identifies 'Captain James Cody of Enniscorthy' as the commander of the 'core-group' in the Wood of Killoughrum.[70] Yet all accounts from 1800 on refer to Joseph, not James, Cody. This suggests that we may be dealing with two individuals, although it is more likely that the confusion results from the inaccuracy of contemporary intelligence. In any case, in July 1800, Lt Col. Littlehales received a letter from Robert Cornwall which contained an offer to surrender, 'signed Joseph Cody and James Corcoran'.[71] Similarly in February 1801, Mr Kavanagh, whose seat at Borris House lay in the heart of the region where the band operated, 'obtained the … names of the persons who compose[d] [the] banditti'. The name Joseph Cody appears second on the enclosed list of twelve men.[72] He was also identified as 'a malignant deserter from Cavan regiment of militia [who] fled the woods of Monart and quickly joined Corcoran, whose attached friend and associate he had continued ever since'.[73] Finally, when the band was outlawed on 1 October 1801, the proclamation offered rewards of 200 guineas for Corcoran and Joseph Cody and described the latter as 'a deserter from Cavan Militia' who 'live[d] at Newtownbarry'.[74]

In 1801, Joseph Cody was under thirty years of age, five feet six inches in height, with red hair and freckles.[75] Yet the most significant aspect of his background was his religion. One of Luke Cullen's sources, Mr Foley, claimed: 'I knew Coady's brother he was a slater and Protestant. I know not if Coady was one, I believe their mother was of that breed, I knew him at Newtownbarry, his native place'.[76] More pointedly, Mr Colclough, a local magistrate, stated authoritatively: 'Cody is a Protestant and a deserter from the Cavan militia.'[77] This denominational background is so significant because it eliminates sectarianism as a motivational force in the band's continued resistance. Moreover, it is demonstrative of the broad range of Protestant responses to the events of 1798, even in Leinster.

1798–1799

The activities of the Cody and Corcoran band are difficult to trace for the period between late 1798 and mid-1800. Nonetheless, a rough outline can be drawn. It is apparent that elements of the Babes in the Wood were operating in south Carlow as early as September 1798 and in all likelihood, considering their later activities in St Mullins, this presence included Corcoran and Cody. Thomas Prendergast wrote an account to the Under Secretary, Alexander Marsden, of a three-day stay at Borris House, the home of Walter Kavanagh. He found the Borris area 'on the verge of insurrection'. Furthermore, Kavanagh had received information of an impending assault, and, as a result, the household remained on guard throughout the night of 24 September. Although no attack materialized, a party of fourteen men armed with muskets did pass through the Scullough Gap from Wexford into Carlow that evening.[78] Indeed, the band continued to use the pass in order to move at will between the two counties for much of the ensuing five and a half years.

Although the summer of 1799 was relatively placid, rumours of rebel activity in the Wood of Killoughrum persisted. As a result of these accounts, Mr Colclough searched the forest twice in mid-June and concluded 'with certainty … that there could be no numbers of people there without [his] having seen or heard of them'. In fact, he could not recall a time when the area was 'so apparently tranquil as at present'. Alternatively, he believed that the false reports of rebel activity were 'calculated … to keep up the alarm, to serve private purposes'. The primary motivation behind these alarms was, in Colclough's view, the 'wish [of the local yeomanry] to remain on permanent duty'. This desire, he attributed to a variety of interrelated causes. First, many yeomen could not return to their farms, either because of the destruction of their dwellings during the rebellion or on account of having made 'themselves obnoxious by their conduct to the people with whom they [we]re to reside'. Furthermore, many had grown accustomed to 'the habit of idleness which went with military life'. Finally if they were 'inclined to be … so industrious', the season offered 'no contrary principal to employ them'.[79] The yeomen referred to by Mr Colclough were undoubtedly the members of John James's Killoughrum rangers. This unit was implicated in a number of robberies on both sides of the border, and in all probability, it was men of this corps who had been executed in the wood by the Babes in 1798. James himself was an Orangeman, and the rangers' collective mentality and composition probably mirrored that of their commander (it was the members of this corps who would be the agents of Corcoran's death in 1804). On 27 June, a communication from Littlehales to Alderman James (who was again interceding on his younger brother John's behalf) explained that Cornwallis had denied Capt. James's request to continue his unit on permanent duty. This request was repeated in October.[80] Colclough was politically liberal, while James was a hard-line conservative, and the former's thinly veiled contempt for the Killoughrum corps may partially reflect local political animosities.

Sectarianism and civil war

The lengthening autumnal nights of 1799 witnessed the return of violence giving lie to any perception that peace had permanently returned to Wexford. The parishes west of Enniscorthy were particularly disturbed, and numerous robberies were reported from the region in late September and early October. More significantly, loyalist irregulars burned the thatched chapel at Kiltealy. This action led the local military commander, Gen. Groose, to station seven members of the South Cork militia at Ballindaggan in an effort to protect the slated chapel there.[81] Such attacks understandably drew the attention of Archbishop Troy, who stated on 12 October:

> Excesses are daily committing in County Wexford and in the upper parts of County Wicklow. Within the last and present months, two chapels have been burned and one greatly injured. Attempts were made to destroy others, but frustrated by the exertions of loyal dispassionate Protestants.

Troy held conversations with Lord Castlereagh and Lt Col. Littlehales about taking appropriate measures. A proclamation had been issued for the burning of a chapel at Kilmurry in the County Wicklow, and Castlereagh explained to Dr Troy that the 'principle of reprobation and detestation of such outrages' was therefore 'established' by the government. Moreover, the Chief Secretary recognized the need to address 'similar excesses in the county of Wexford'. Yet to the mounting consternation of Troy, the issuance of a proclamation in County Wexford was delayed.[82]

Murders, house burnings and robberies continued through the winter and into the spring of 1800. Capt. Cornock, a liberal magistrate and the commander of the Scarawalsh yeoman infantry, bemoaned the distressed state of the 'lower order of people' as a result of the 'frequent robberies and murders'. He further maintained that 'hardly a night passes but something new occurs' and regretted the inability of his corps to come to grips with the parties responsible for the raids.[83] In early March 1800, a party of about a dozen armed men robbed and murdered a farmer near Enniscorthy. Gen. Groose had no trouble identifying those behind the 'many robberies and outrages going on among the lower class of people'. While he allowed for the activities of 'a gang of villains … who frequently infest[ed] the country', he concluded that 'ten robberies of eleven [we]re committed by the lower order of yeomen'. The general was sufficiently disturbed by events to propose the disarmament of all yeomen not then on permanent duty.[84] Confirmation of Groose's assessment of the situation came a month later when his immediate superior, Dundas, agreed that owing to the 'murders and robberies', which had 'greatly increased', the weapons of yeomanry corps not on permanent duty should be collected, for 'there [wa]s every reason to suspect the lower class of yeoman [we]re deeply engaged in these depredations'.[85] An example of the form that these assaults took, as well as of the individuals responsible for them, can be found in the case of William Thorpe, a private in the Killoughrum rangers. Accompanied by another man, Thorpe, broke into the house of the family named Bryan at Clonmore in County Carlow on the night of Thursday 17 October 1799. The pair appeared at the bedside of Mary Bryan, described as a 'spinster' aged seventeen from Coolduff in Wexford. Thorpe, whom Bryan had known for years, 'was armed with two pistols and [carried a] lantern with lighted candle under his arm'. The other individual, who had a musket, was believed by Bryan to be John Bayley, a private in the Newtownbarry yeomanry. Bayley assaulted Bryan and 'threatened rape', but the intervention of the other members of the party, who had previously remained outside, 'prevented it'. Ultimately, the raiders took eleven shillings and six pence, and departed. Yet, their night's work was far from over. Between two and three in the morning, Thorpe 'with several others armed', forced his way into the home of George Clinch, a farmer also of Crone More. Clinch shouted out to the robbers that there were armed men in his house. In response, the marauders fired several shots into the home before they broke down the door. The gang took £13 in cash and a watch before moving on. Peter Nowlan, a farmer at Aclare, was also attacked that night. The raiders hanged Nowlan 'until senseless' in an unsuccessful effort to get him to disclose the location of his money. They then turned their attentions on Nowlan's son, from whom they demanded twenty guineas. The son replied that he did not know where his father 'hid his money'; he was half-hanged twice as a result.[86]

Mr Cornock did not 'consider these depredations to be in the least concerned with the former rebellion' and instead felt that the fact that the 'freebooters' attacked only Catholics could be explained by the latter's want of arms. As evidence he cited the 'absence of assaults on any of the Protestant houses of the county where arms were supposed to be'. Yet Cornock was also sincerely concerned that if the attacks were left unchecked, they would 'destroy the tenantry of the county'. He went so far as to suggest that 'wealthy and well-disposed Roman Catholics' be allowed to arm themselves in self-defence.[87]

It is vitally important to remember that although loyalist depredations frequently took the form of armed robbery, this fact in no way necessitates that the perpetrators were motivated solely by opportunistic greed. The goals of political-sectarian intimidation and personal gain are by no means mutually exclusive. When the identities of the individuals involved in such attacks can be established, they are invariably found to have been members of hard-line yeomanry corps. Units commanded by political moderates or liberals are noticeably absent. Furthermore, surviving rebels had no trouble identifying extremist corps, and arms raids were primarily targeted at the rank-and-file of such units.

Loyalist depredations did not entirely go unanswered, and in the parishes of west Wexford and south Carlow, the nocturnal civil war continued through the autumn and winter of 1799–1800. On the night of 6 November, the house of John Whelan (a private in the arch-conservative Robert Cornwall's 1st Carlow Yeomanry Cavalry) was entered by Henry Benett 'and others unknown'. The assailants took 'away a musket and bayonet ... [and] fourteen rounds of ballcartridge'. Elizabeth Whelan's account of the attack on her home provides some insight into the motivations that lay behind it. She testified that after Benett, who was 'armed with a rusty sword', located John Whelan's gun and ammunition he exclaimed that 'he supposed it was for killing croppies, but swearing violently it should kill some bloodybacks (in obvious reference to the colour of loyalist uniforms) first'. John Joyce was charged with 'being a rebel and associating with rebels in arms' as a result of having participated in a similar assault on the home of Samuel Kearney, also a member of the 1st Carlow corps. Kearney testified that at about six on the night of Friday 6 December, he was working at his loom when three armed men entered his home. He positively identified Joyce and James Cody, 'having known them intimately for several years'. Cody pointed a pistol at Kearney's head, while the others carried off his musket, bayonet and yeomanry accoutrements. The trio who had entered the house then joined three others waiting outside and departed.[88] These arms raids worked on a number of levels. Most basically, they provided much-needed weapons. Yet more importantly, they can be viewed as acts of political theatre, in which the primary badge of citizenship was stripped from the loyalist and bestowed on the rebel. The fact that this scene was played out in the victim's home before his family served to intimidate and enrage not only the individual targeted but also the entire loyalist community.

The sectarian focus of the loyalist attacks that continued to plague west Wexford is most clearly demonstrated by the acts of incendiary violence directed against Catholic places of worship. Following the destruction of the chapel at Kiltealy in the autumn of 1799, another Catholic chapel was burned near Ross on 19 December.[89] Indeed, these attacks continued well into the new century. In July 1800, 'a new slated chapel' at Ballymackesy, between Enniscorthy and New Ross, suffered immolation, and the chapel at Caim was put to the torch.[90] Nor were the attacks confined to inanimate objects, as Archbishop Troy related: 'In many parts of the ill-fated County [Wexford] no priest dare officiate. In others, they cannot even appear. In all, they are daily threatened.'[91] The attack on the chapel at Ballymackesy was particularly bold, for the new chapel there had been constructed on the estate of Mr Carew, a whiggish member of the gentry. Carew 'had liberally contributed' to the expense of the building, and its destruction is demonstrative not only of a continuing process of sectarian intimidation but also of a contempt for the liberal establishment of the county, no matter how high its social status.[92] It is doubtful that the ultra-conservative gentry took an active part in the assaults themselves; yet it is equally improbable that lower-class Protestant extremists would have dared to launch such attacks without, at the very least, the tacit approval of their social superiors.

Lower-class loyalism embodied in the yeomanry was the primary vehicle of ultra-conservative violence. This is not to say that all corps, or even every member of the more notorious units, participated in sectarian attacks. Instead, certain yeomanry corps, or cliques within individual companies, came to serve as the paramilitary wing of Protestant extremism. The desire for revenge was a key element of the white terror, and it must be remembered that many loyalists had suffered very real losses during the rising. As Gen. Moore observed, 'Some of the yeomen of this neighbourhood [Taghmon] had been driven from their habitations and plundered by the rebels; their relations and friends had been murdered by them in the most inhuman manner.'[93] Vengeance alone, however, fails to explain the persistence of loyalist violence, which continued for at least three years after the defeat of the rebellion. In fact, the terror is best viewed as a coordinated campaign of political and sectarian intimidation. Moreover, there is indirect evidence of a guiding hand in the form of extremist magistrates and yeomanry officers. It is hardly coincidental that the worst atrocities were committed by units commanded by known Orangemen and often took place in close proximity to such magistrates' homes.[94] Indeed, Bishop Troy pointed to 'a party particularly hostile to Catholics in that County [Wexford] as being behind the attacks against his priests and chapels.[95] As Daniel Gahan notes:

> All these incidents occurred at night and took place at a fairly constant rate throughout the period, a month or two usually intervening between them, indicating that it was the work of a small but closely-knit and secretive group, acting in a calculating rather than impetuous manner.[96]

Alternatively, Mr Cornock's attempt to stem the attacks demonstrates the danger of viewing these events as part of a monolithic assault by all elements of Protestant Wexford society upon the Catholic population of the county. Yet, the reality that the terror was directed not only against former rebels but at Catholics generically was not lost on the people. Dr Troy described the danger posed by allowing this perception to continue unabated: 'The disaffected avail themselves of the occasion to impose on the ignorant, by artfully insinuating the government is indifferent about them and their chapels, and leaves them defenceless.'[97] This phenomenon is further illustrated in an anonymous report on the state of the Roman Catholics of the country, dated Dublin, March 1800. The author observed: 'The generality of the common people ... retain[s] the most rancorous antipathy against the Orangemen, and every act of outrage adds fuel to their passion and their desire for revenge.' That the government was viewed as culpable is also borne out:

> being made to that those outrages are committed on them under the authority and sanction of the government, their antipathy against it and against the Orange party is exactly the same for they conceive on this account [the] government to be the real source of all their real or [ideal?] suffering.

Furthermore, the anonymous composer observed:

> from the mode that had been pursued by the yeomen of not discriminating the innocent from the guilty and not respecting protections granted to individuals, [t]he people are taught to believe their lives and properties are still at the discretion of their enemies.[98]

The extent and impact of this sense of alienation should not be underestimated. In September of 1800 more than two full years after the defeat of the rebellion, Cornwallis gave a lengthy and dismal assessment of the state of Ireland. He felt that the existing tranquillity hinged solely on the continued absence of invasion. If the French landed with a sizable force, he had 'cause to believe that the ill disposition of a great majority of the Irish would be manifested by every act of hostility and outrage'. Furthermore, Cornwallis stated:

> I am persuaded that the mass of the Irish people may be reclaimed, but it must take time to effect this salutary change in their temper, and a very different system must be pursued from that which has hitherto been practiced in the greater part of this wretched country. We must therefore, I am afraid, at least, so long as the present war shall last, feel ourselves under the melancholy necessity of considering the majority of the Irish people as enemies.[99]

Notes

1   For the still limited historiography of the post-rebellion period, see Liam Chambers, *Rebellion in Kildare, 1790–1803* (Dublin, 1998); Daniel Gahan, 'The "black mob" and the "babes in the wood": Wexford in the wake of the rebellion, 1798–1806', in *Journal of the Wexford historical society* 6, no. 13 (1990–1991); Thomas Bartlett, '"Masters of the mountains:" the insurgent careers of Joseph Holt and Michael Dwyer. County Wicklow, 1798–1803', in Hannigan and Nolan (eds), *Wicklow history and society: Interdisciplinary*

essays on the history of an Irish county (Dublin, 1994); Ruán O'Donnell, *Aftermath: Post-rebellion insurgency in Wicklow, 1799–1803* (Dublin, 2000); Ruán O'Donnell, *The Rebellion in Wicklow 1798* (Dublin, 1998).

2 For the Social Banditry Model applied to post-1798 resistance in Carlow and Wexford, see Gahan, 'The black mob', 92–110. For the refutation of the model in the cases of Michael Dwyer and Joseph Holt in Wicklow, see Bartlett, 'Masters of the mountains', 390–5.

3 The historiography of the Cody and Corcoran band is extremely limited. Being confined to a few pages of Daniel Gahan's groundbreaking article on the aftermath of the Wexford Rebellion, 'The black mob', 92–110; also see O'Donnell, *Rebellion in Wicklow*, 329–30, 346. For Dwyer and Holt, see O'Donnell, *Rebellion in Wicklow* and Bartlett, 'Masters of the mountains'.

4 L. M. Cullen, 'Politics and rebellion in Wicklow in the 1790s', in Ken Hannigan and William Nolan (eds), *Wicklow history and society: Interdisciplinary essays on the history of an Irish county* (Dublin, 1994), 411–502; Kevin Whelan, 'Reinterpreting the 1798 rebellion in County Wexford', in Dáire Keogh and William Furlong (eds), *The mighty wave: The 1798 rebellion in Wexford* (Blackrock, 1996), 18–20.

5 Cullen, 'Politics and rebellion', 432.

6 Ibid., 411–502; Whelan, 'Reinterpreting the 1798 rebellion', 18–20.

7 NAI SOC 3271, Annesley Brownrigg to Col. [?], Gorey, 17 Jan.

8 Miles Byrne, *Memoirs of Miles Byrne*, 2 vols (Paris, 1863), 251.

9 TNA HO 100/77/200–1, Cornwallis to Portland, Dublin Castle, 28 June 1798.

10 Cornwallis to Gen Ross, Dublin Castle, 1 July 1798, in Charles Ross (ed.), *Correspondence of Charles, first Marquis Cornwallis*, 3 vols (London, 1859), vol. 2, 255.

11 Maj. Gen. Sir J. F. Maurice (ed.), *Diary of Sir John Moore*, 2 vols (London, 1904), vol. 1, 303.

12 Ibid., 302–3.

13 TNA HO 100/77/214, Cornwallis to Portland, Dublin Castle, 8 July 1798.

14 Maurice, *Diary Moore*, vol. 1, 303.

15 Ibid., 302.

16 TNA HO 100/77/214, Cornwallis to Portland, Dublin Castle, 8 July 1798.

17 Ibid.

18 Cornwall to Ross, Dublin Castle, 14 July 1798, in Ross, *Correspondence Cornwallis*, vol. 2, 368.

19 Rev. James Bently Gordon, *History of the rebellion in Ireland in the year 1798* (Dublin, 1801), 242–3.

20 Cullen, 'Politics and rebellion', 469–72.

21 Gordon, *History of the rebellion*, 241.

22 NLI Cullen Papers MS 8339, 298, 309–10.

23 For Hunter Gowan, see O'Donnell, *Rebellion in Wicklow*, 99, 118–21, 125; Gahan, 'The black mob', 95–6; Cullen, 'Politics and rebellion', 464–72.

24 NAI SOC 3271, Brownrigg to Col [?], Gorey, 17 Jan. 1799.

25 Ibid.; also see Trinity College Library (hereafter TCL), Cullen Papers, MS 1472, 8, 167, 207.

26 NAI SOC 3271, Brownrigg to Col [?], Gorey, 17 Jan. 1799.

27 Gahan, 'The black mob', 96.

28 Ibid., 94.

29 NLI Cullen Papers, MS 8339, 309–10.
30 Gordon, *History of the rebellion*, 236–7; Edward Hay, *History of the insurrection of the County of Wexford, A.D. 1798* (Dublin, 1803), 297.
31 Gahan, 'The black mob', 97.
32 Hay, *History of the insurrection*, 297.
33 *BNL*, 2 Oct. 1798.
34 *BNL*, 2 Oct. 1798.
35 NAI RP 620/40/85, Naas, 22 Sept. 1798.
36 NAI RP 620/40/84, Rev. Daniel McNeille to Lord Monck, Adamstown, 21 Sept. 1798.
37 Ibid. 620/56/112, John James to Alderman James, Ballycrystal, 12 Oct. 1799. For the Jameses, see Cullen, 'Politics and rebellion', 421, 472; O'Donnell, *Rebellion in Wicklow*, 17.
38 *BNL*, 16 Oct. 1798.
39 TNA HO 100/79/280, Cornwallis to Portland, Dublin Castle, 24 Dec. 1798; also see, Gordon, *History of the rebellion*, 237.
40 NLI Holt Letters MSS 4720–1, 347–8, Memoirs and undated autographed letters by Joseph Holt.
41 Castlereagh to Wickham, Dublin Castle, 16 Nov. 1798, Stewart, *Memoirs Castlereagh*, vol. 1, 445–6.
42 For estimates of the strength of the Babes in the Wood, see NAI RP 620/40/85, Naas, 22 Sept. 1798 and Gordon, *History of the rebellion*, 236. Gordon believed that the combined number of rebels in Killoughram and Wicklow probably did not exceed three hundred.
43 Hay, *History of the insurrection*, 271–3; Maurice, *Diary Moore*, 311.
44 NLI Cullen Papers, MS 8339, 426.
45 NAI RP 620/40/85, Naas, 22 Sept. 1798.
46 Hay, *History of the insurrection*, 298.
47 NAI RP 620/46/156, 'The Memorial of William Hacket', 28 Feb. 1799; ibid., Charles Tottenham to Cornwallis, Ross, 21 Mar. 1799.
48 Quoted in O'Donnell, *Rebellion in Wicklow*, 329–30.
49 BNL, 23 Oct. 1798; NAI RP 640/41/28, Fraser to Hacket, 11 Nov. 1798. Also see, O'Donnell, *Rebellion in Wicklow*, 329–30.
50 Hay, *History of the insurrection*, 298; Gordon, *History of the rebellion*, 237; NLI Cullen Papers, MS 9760, 193–5.
51 Castlereagh to Wickham, Dublin Castle, 16 Nov. 1798, C. Stewart (ed.), *Memoirs and correspondence of Viscount Castlereagh, second marquis of Londonderry*, 4 vols (London, 1848–1849), vol. 2, 445–6.
52 TNA HO 100/79/243–5, Cornwallis to Portland, 10 Dec. 1798.
53 NLI KP MS 1206, 334, Littlehales to Edward Perciville, esq., Dublin Castle, 7 Apr. 1799.
54 NAI RP 620/46/96, James Caulfield to Dr Troy, Wexford, 27 Mar. 1799.
55 NLI KP MS 1207, 195, Littlehales to Alderman James, Dublin Castle, 27 June 1799. For the returning calm throughout Ireland, also see TNA HO 100/87/31, Castlereagh to Portland, Dublin Castle, 29 June 1799; ibid. 100/87/65, Cornwallis to Portland, Dublin Castle, 20 July 1799.
56 NAI SOC 1020/3, Proclamation outlawing James Corcoran and 17 others, County Carlow, 1 Oct. 1801. For the relative youth of many of the 1798 rebels, see Daniel Gahan, *The people's rising: Wexford, 1798* (Dublin, 1995), 9.
57 Whelan, 'Reinterpreting the 1798 rebellion', 15–17; L. M. Cullen, 'The United

Irishmen in Wexford', in Keogh and Furlong, *Mighty wave*, 5–6, 60–3; Cullen, 'Politics and rebellion', 427–8, 435–51.

58 NAI RP 620/60/4, Names, descriptions and some accounts of the banditti who have infested the parish of St Mullins in County Carlow since Oct. 1798, enclosed in Walter Kavanagh to Marsden, Borris, 30 Sept. 1801. This lengthy document is invaluable in following the activities of Cody and Corcoran through the autumn of 1801.

59 For the disarming campaign in Wexford, see Cullen, 'United Irishmen in Wexford', 62.

60 Daniel Gahan, 'The military planning of the 1798 rebellion in Wexford', in Keogh and Furlong, *Mighty wave*, 100.

61 NAI RP 620/57/55, Mr Colclough, Wexford, 3 Oct. 1800. For Colclough's background, see Thomas Pakenham, *The year of liberty: The history of the great Irish rebellion of 1798* (New York, 1969), 139, and Cullen, 'Politics and rebellion', 414.

62 Names descriptions and some accounts, enclosed in NAI RP 620/60/4, Kavanagh, to Marsden, Borris, 30 Sept. 1801. For Cloney and Kelly, see Cullen, 'United Irishmen in Wexford', 55–6.

63 Names descriptions and some accounts, enclosed in NAI RP 620/60/4, Kavanagh, to Marsden, Borris, 30 Sept. 1801. For Corcoran's role in the rebellion, also see O'Donnell, *Rebellion in Wicklow*, 329–30; Gahan, 'The black mob', 99.

64 Names descriptions and some accounts, enclosed in NAI RP 620/60/4, Kavanagh, to Marsden, Borris, 30 Sept. 1801.

65 NLI Cullen Papers, MS 8339, 628.

66 Ibid., 646–7; Hay, *History of the insurrection*, 298. For Fitzgerald's background, see O'Donnell, *Rebellion in Wicklow*, 238, 306 and Byrne, *Memoirs Byrne*, 157.

67 Hay, History of the insurrection, 298; NLI Cullen Papers, MS 8339, 646–7.

68 Names descriptions and some accounts, enclosed in NAI RP 620/60/4, Kavanagh, to Marsden, Borris, 30 Sept. 1801. Kavanagh dated Corcoran's arrival in St Mullins to October 1798, in which case he was operating in the barony while still a member of the Babes in the Wood. Furthermore, Kavanagh believed that Corcoran's move to south Carlow occurred shortly after his escape from Newtownbarry. In reality, Corcoran did not surrender until mid-November, and therefore his jailbreak cannot have taken place before that time. In June 1799, Colclough reported in obvious reference to Corcoran: 'Those fellows, who escaped some time since from Newtownbarry [and] who occasionally, at night, steal home to their families. [They] may perhaps – if a pursuit followed them – take shelter in the woods,' NAI RP 620/56/67, Colclough to Marsden, Wexford, 18 June 1799. Therefore, Corcoran's escape transpired at some time between the late autumn of 1798 and the spring of 1799.

69 Gahan, 'The black mob', 99.

70 O'Donnell, *Rebellion in Wicklow*, 329.

71 NLI KP MS 1209, 298, Littlehales to Robert Cornwall, esq., Dublin Castle, 28 July 1800.

72 TNA HO 100/103/77, Kavanagh to Gen. Brydges Henniker, Borris, 21 Feb. 1801.

73 Names descriptions and some accounts, enclosed in NAI RP 620/60/4, Kavanagh, to Marsden, Borris, 30 Sept. 1801.

74 NAI SOC 1020/3, proclamation outlawing Corcoran and 17 others, County Carlow, 1 Oct. 1801.

75 Names descriptions and some accounts, enclosed in NAI RP 620/60/4, Kavanagh, to Marsden, Borris, 30 Sept. 1801.

76 NLI Cullen Papers MS 9760, 224.

77 NAI RP 620/57/59, Colclough, near Enniscorthy, 15 Sept. 1800.

78 Ibid. 620/40/100, Prendergast to Marsden, 25 Sept. 1798.

79 Ibid. 620/56/67, Colclough to Marsden, Wexford, 18 June 1799.

80 Ibid. 620/56/112, John James to Alderman James, Ballycrystal, 12 Oct. 1799; NLI KP MS 1207, 195, Littlehales to Alderman James, Dublin Castle, 27 June 1799.

81 NAI RP 620/56/112, John James to Alderman James, Ballycrystal, 12 Oct. 1799.

82 Troy to Mr R. Marshall, Dublin, 12 Oct. 1799, Stewart, *Memoirs Castlereagh*, vol. 2, 420.

83 NAI SOC 1018/31, Capt. Cornock to Gen Groose, Ferns Barracks, 19 Dec. 1799.

84 NLI KP MS 1209, 15, Littlehales to Alderman James, Dublin Castle, 6 Mar. 1800.

85 TNA HO 100/93/265, monthly report of Lt Gen. Dundas, Kilcullen, 3 Apr. 1800.

86 Charges against William Thorpe, private in the yeomen corps of Killoughram rangers, commanded by Capt. John James, enclosed in NAI RP 620/48/27, Henniker to Littlehales, Carlow, 13 Dec. 1799.

87 NAI SOC 1018/31, Cornock to Groose, Ferns Barricks, 19 Dec. 1799.

88 NAI RP 620/48/27, charges against John Joyce, 13 Dec. 1799; ibid, charges against Henry Bennett.

89 NAI RP 629/48/41, Tottenham to Castlereagh, 24 Dec. 1799.

90 Ibid. 620/58/100, Troy to Castlereagh, Annfield near Luttrellstown, 5 Aug. 1800; TCL Cullen Papers, MS 1472, 3–7, Troy to Castlereagh, 2 Oct. 1800.

91 NAI RP 620/58/100, Troy to Castlereagh, Annfield near Luttrellstown, 5 Aug. 1800.

92 Ibid.

93 Maurice, *Diary Moore*, vol. 1, 303.

94 NLI Cullen Papers, MS 8339, 309–10.

95 Troy to Marshall, Dublin, 12 Oct. 1799, Stewart, *Memoirs Castlereagh*, vol. 2, 420.

96 Gahan, 'The black mob', 94.

97 Troy to Marshall, Dublin, 12 Oct. 1799, Stewart, *Memoirs Castlereagh*, vol. 2, 420.

98 NAI SOC 1019/6, anonymous, Dublin, Mar. 1800.

99 Cornwallis to Portland, Athlone, 2 Sept. 1800, Stewart, *Memoirs Castlereagh*, vol. 3, 374–6.

8

Joseph Cody and James Corcoran

Cody and Corcoran, 1800–1801

The inability of the government to curb loyalist depredations created the impression amongst Catholics that the white terror had the sanction of the central authorities. This perception, in turn, crippled the Cornwallis administration's efforts at reconciliation. In fact, it can be argued that the sectarian focus of the continuing terror, combined with the excesses that preceded the rising and the horror of the rebellion itself, served to void the legitimacy of the state in the eyes of the majority of the rural population of the affected counties. The extensive popular support which Cody and Corcoran received in Wexford, Carlow and Kilkenny can only be understood in this light.

By the late winter of 1800, Carlow was again sufficiently disturbed to draw the attention of Dublin Castle. A number of loyalists had been murdered in the county and several houses burned. The atrocities included the murders of John Nolan, a yeomanry sergeant, and his wife, whom intruders shot in their own bed; three other men, Darby Clowny (a Carlow farmer), John Watson and Thomas Roache were also shot and killed in or near their homes.[1] On 9 March Lt Col. Littlehales informed Sir R. Butler on Cornwallis' behalf 'that every means will be used ... to apprehend the persons, who have lately committed the atrocious murders near Carlow'. The military secretary further related, 'A general officer will be immediately sent to Carlow', and the Viceroy confirmed that he had dispatched a general to the district who had 'hopes of restoring tranquillity and of apprehending some of the principal offenders'.[2]

The officer selected to handle the unravelling security environment in Carlow was Brig. Gen. Brydges Henniker. Henniker had extensive experience in dealing with disaffection, having played a major role in the government's dragooning of Ulster prior to the rebellion. More importantly, the general had been sent to pacify eastern Carlow in November 1797, where he had been granted dual military and judicial authority.[3] Perhaps more importantly, he was described by the United Irishman, William Farrell, as 'a kind and good gentleman' who granted protections to 'everyone that applied (excepting murderers and house burners)'.[4]

Henniker's efforts led Cody and Corcoran to reopen negotiations with the government via the medium of Robert Cornwall, the high sheriff of Carlow. An intriguing letter from Cornwall crossed the desk of the Lord

Lieutenant on 28 July, containing an 'enclosure signed Joseph Cody and James Corcoran'. In their note the pair requested terms of surrender from the Viceroy. The military secretary responded to Cornwall as follows: 'I am commanded by his excellency to acquaint you that he approves of these men being allowed to surrender on the condition of their transporting themselves for life'.[5] The significance of the government's willingness to permit Cody and Corcoran to go into exile should not be underestimated, for it strongly suggests that the authorities viewed them as a political threat. Indeed, the offer mirrors the agreements made with the politically motivated Wicklow insurgents, Joseph Holt and Michael Dwyer. Furthermore, Robert Cornwall was an extreme loyalist who had played a major part in establishing the Orange Order in south Leinster. His intercession on Cody and Corcoran's behalf is difficult to explain on any grounds other than his belief that they posed a threat to the region's security. Cornwall would presumably have preferred to make an example of the pair, but the inability of the authorities to apprehend the men, coupled with their influence on the local population, caused the high sheriff to make the more prudent decision to support their application for a negotiated surrender.

Yet although the 'offers of submission through Mr. Cornwall' were 'accepted by government on condition of transport', Corcoran and Cody ultimately 'declined' the government's terms. They argued 'that neither of them had ever been guilty of murder, robbery, or burning' and told Mr Kavanagh, who had 'several interviews with Corcoran on the subject', their 'hope for a free pardon for their rebellion'. At these meetings, Corcoran explained that he and Cody 'were willing to continue liable to any prosecution for any of these crimes'. Besides rebellion, he confessed to the individual offences of 'cutting off a woman's ear' for having informed on the band and to 'destroying the liquor and utensils of a huckster's tent on the eve of a fair' for a similar offence. Finally, Cody's desertion from the Cavan militia would have to be forgiven.

Later that summer Kavanagh in fact did request a full pardon for Cody and Corcoran.[6] This apparently startling action on the part of a key member of the regional gentry in reality is quite easily explained. Kavanagh was the head of an influential converso family that held sway in the heart of an overwhelmingly Catholic community. Corcoran himself had strong ties to this community, and he was quite likely related to several of the Corcoran's, who were head tenants on the Kavanagh estate. In this light Kavanagh, whatever his personal sympathies, had much to gain by obtaining an accommodation for the pair.

Gen. Henniker appears to have agreed that their were advantages to the government in cutting a deal with Cody and Corcoran as he agreed not to harass the band while such a pardon was under consideration. He insisted, however, that during the process 'they kept quiet and retired'. Despite the General's apparent generosity Cody and Corcoran instead 'became very daring'. They were involved in a 'public affray' at some point in the autumn of 1800, which resulted in Corcoran's capture and confinement in Carlow jail. Remarkably, a short time later, he once again escaped. Furthermore, this jail break was a fairly sizable affair, and three men involved, Patrick Byrne, Edmund Byrne and John Kelly, also joined the band.[7]

Henniker was then forced to renew his efforts to pacify the county. In December, his endeavours finally met with some success. He reported to Dublin that he had taken ten 'notorious offenders' in the vicinity of Carlow town. These prisoners were promptly tried by court martial, and by the end of the month, Henniker's superior, Dundas, claimed that in the district under his command there were no longer any overt symptoms of disloyalty. However, this otherwise positive assessment bore one important caveat; it accepted 'an outlaw banditti who, notwithstanding the [best?] efforts made to suppress them, still continue to place men's property in danger'.[8]

By early 1801, local authorities in Carlow considered the county again 'so disturbed' that the magistracy met to form 'resolutions', which they forwarded to Dublin Castle accompanied by a letter from Henniker.[9] The primary causes of concern were an increase in the Corcoran band's numbers and their mounting audacity. Indeed, the well-armed rebels had begun to move around freely in broad daylight.[10] Walter Kavanagh reported 'a most daring robbery' to Henniker in February. In this incident, which occurred near Bagenalstown, sixteen well-armed men robbed a large sum of money and a gold watch from a man named Thomas Plumber. The victim 'positively' identified James Corcoran and Joseph Cody as 'being among them'. If true, this is the only documented case in which members of the band were implicated in a crime that can be construed as purely criminal. A list containing the names and descriptions of the 'banditti' who continued to 'infest' the 'neighbourhood' accompanied Kavanagh's report of the robbery.[11] This information contained in the document, combined with the descriptions printed in the Proclamation issued in October, allows us to draw a reasonably accurate picture of the Cody and Corcoran band at its height.

Next in importance to Cody and Corcoran was Timothy Brien, aged thirty, from Ballycrystal and Daniel Brennan from Cloroge, both in Wexford. Popular belief held that these men had whipped a loyalist prisoner to death on Vinegar Hill during the rebellion. In order to avoid prosecution on this charge, the 'inseparable' pair fled to south Carlow with Cody and Corcoran in October 1798 (suggesting that they too had been members of the Babes in the Wood). Brennan and Brien acted as bodyguards for Cody and Corcoran, 'from whom they [were] seldom absent', and also served as 'their ministers ... in every vengeance or outrage committed'. John Fitzpatrick, also known as the 'Hessian', from Newtownbarry in Wexford came next. He, like Cody, was a deserter from the Cavan militia. Fitzpatrick was further described as the 'best behaved of the gang', who 'willingly' hired himself out as a labourer to local farmers. Additionally, the 'shabbiness of his dress' was taken as evidence that he had 'not improved his means by dishonesty'. Moses Doyle, thirty-five, and William Reilly, both from the bog of Itty, County Wexford, joined the band after escaping from Wexford jail in 1799. James Hamilton, aged twenty-seven, was wanted for robbery and wore a false hand covered by a glove, having lost the real one during the rebellion. John Meade, aged thirty, and Joseph Farrell, both from Ballycarney in Wexford, were believed to have played a role in the death of Francis Turner, a loyalist, whose residence at Ballingale was stormed by a sizable contingent of rebels at the onset of the rising.[12] Farrell was also thought to have formally have been a member of Michael Dwyer's band in Wicklow. Rounding out the band's Wexford contingent was a man named Mitchell from Ferns, Laurence Morgan, a carpenter from Templeludigan, and Peter Brennan, aged about thirty, of Killann. Finally, there was one member of the group named Dalton, who came from County Dublin, and there were four natives of Carlow. The latter consisted of Francis Headon of Ballyshancarragh, suspected of sheep steeling, and the three men who broke out of Carlow jail with Corcoran.[13]

The Cody and Corcoran band clearly was dominated then by individuals from the western districts of County Wexford. Their presence in south Carlow is easily explained by its immediate proximity on the other side of the Blackstairs Mountains. Indeed, members of the group took advantage of the existence of jurisdictional boundaries between Carlow and Wexford to avoid efforts by the local authorities to bring them to heel, and there appears to have been a surprising reluctance on the part of the yeomanry to pursue the band across county borders. More importantly, the group's members most certainly had ties of kinship with people on the both sides of the border. The best example of this phenomenon is the proliferation of Corcoran's residing in the southern part of Carlow, where several members of this old Gaelic family had managed to maintain a relatively high social status. In fact, a number of Corcorans were middlemen on the Kavanagh estate, and there were two attorneys by that name at Borris.[14] The strong popular support that the band received, coupled with the commonality of surnames between the rebels and members of the community in which they operated, strongly suggest such ties.

In late February 1801, Henniker ordered a large body of troops to Borris, the largest town in the southern extremity of County Carlow. Yet despite the presence of the military, the group remained elusive throughout the spring. Henniker launched a major search for the rebels in August leading a force from Kilkenny into Carlow in an attempt to surprise the gang. To the general's dismay, the premature arrival of a drummer, who had become separated from the main body, alerted the rebels. The band promptly retired across the Barrow and disappeared into Kilkenny. Henniker left a detachment at St Mullins to prevent the rebels from re-crossing the river. He also quartered a party of the Dublin militia at Rocksavage in an effort to capture members of the band whom he believed had fled into the Blackstairs Mountains. On 11 August the general crossed into Kilkenny in an endeavour to flush out the rebels hiding in the rugged area around the Rower. Simultaneously, a body under the command of a Kilkenny magistrate, Mr Foote, surrounded Brandon Hill Mountain, while a force on the Carlow side of the river swept the countryside 'searching suspected places'.[15]

These operations continued through mid-August as Henniker sent small parties to search suspected houses 'by night as by day'. On the fifteenth, fifty men were encamped near Ballybeg to deny the rebels access to the sanctuary of the Blackstairs. Simultaneously, soldiers from Graiguenamanagh moved again into the vicinity of the Rower, while others were placed to guard the river crossings. These substantial manoeuvres continued until the twenty-fourth and resulted in the capture of a solitary individual, described as 'a fellow of very bad character' who served as 'commissary' for the band. The offensive was over before the end of August, although troops were left at a number of locations.[16] Henniker's abject failure to break the band despite such a massive effort is the clearest indication of problem posed by Corcoran to the government.

As the autumn approached, the demeanour of the officers responsible for securing the region 'infested' by the gang grew more brittle. Gen. Dundas, the commander of the five-county southeastern district, held the ultimate responsibility for Carlow, and Dublin continually pressured him to eliminate the rebels once and for all. In his monthly report for September, Dundas insisted: '[E]very possible means have been used and will be continued to take, or destroy the gang, although hitherto our efforts have not succeeded.' He continued on a somewhat defensive note to state: '[N]othing in our power has been omitted that could tend to the accomplishment of this desirable end'.[17] Thus over three years after the suppression of the rebellion, this small band continued to create anxiety in the government and military, which despite their best efforts, were unable to deal effectively with the group.

In late September, Gen. Henniker and the Magistracy of Carlow requested permission to have the members of the band proclaimed.[18] A Proclamation was duly issued on 1 October offering a reward of 200 guineas each for Cody and Corcoran. Fifty guineas a head were also offered for the other sixteen members of the band.[19] This 'outlawing', combined with 'the presence of the military in all of their old haunts', finally caused the band to disperse, and several of its members fled back into their home districts of western Wexford. On 15 October authorities in Wexford learned of the presence of one such group in the Adamstown area. They passed the intelligence on to Gen. Groose, who directed detachments of the yeomanry to triangulate on the rebels from Enniscorthy, Taghmon and Wexford town. The yeomen came to grips with the group at the village of Chapel, which lay between Enniscorthy and New Ross. James Hamilton, William Reilly and Mitchell spotted a party of yeomen commanded by Capt. Richards entering the village and opened fire from the home of a man named Byrne. Greatly outnumbered, the three rebels 'retreated, repeatedly loading and firing' in the process. 'After a very desperate resistance', the yeomen killed all three men, although Hamilton, who had 'received five balls in his body', lingered for two hours during which time he threatened 'to take care of' Capt. Richards and 'set' the surviving members of the band on him.[20]

Later that day, Richard's men also captured another member of the band, Patrick Byrne, while a detachment of the Taghmon yeomanry took Moses Doyle. Local magistrates immediately requested that the latter pair be tried by court martial.[21] Thus, the Corcoran and Cody band, which was already under extreme pressure from the military in their primary area of operations, had been stripped of about one third of its operative strength. Moreover, the extreme violence of that October day graphically illustrates the mortally dangerous nature of the band's existence.

Corcoran, 1803–1804

Cody and Corcoran disappear from the historical record in late 1801, only to re-emerge in mid-1803. The lack of documentary evidence for this period may reflect a pause in the group's activities, either due to the pressure exerted by the military or as a result of the signing of the peace treaty between Britain and France. In the latter instance, the group's inactivity would demonstrate an awareness of the implications of wider political developments and strengthen the argument that Corcoran remained politically motivated. In other words, the band was awaiting a French invasion, and when this possibility was removed, albeit temporarily, they laid low. Alternatively, and more plausibly, the peace treaty may have diminished the threat posed by the gang in the eyes of the government, which ceased to take notice of its activities. In either case, it can hardly be coincidental that the paper trail stops in October 1801, when the preliminaries for the peace of Amiens were signed, only to reappear in June 1803 shortly after the renewal of hostilities in May. In any event, when the mist cleared, Joseph Cody was gone. From June 1803 on, the band is referred to as the Corcoran gang, and the same eight or nine names reappear in the reports forwarded to Dublin Castle.

Although diminished, the band had re-emerged as a force to be reckoned with. In August 1803, Mr Kavanagh observed:

> [T]he southern part of the County Carlow, near here, has long been infested with an armed Banditti of rebels and robbers, [and] has been well known to the government as in 1800 ... about ten still continue in it, well-armed and without disguise.[22]

A few weeks earlier, a party of soldiers from the 89th Regiment was escorting two deserters from the 44th Regiment (some men from this unit were believed to have joined Corcoran at about this time) to Newtownbarry. On their return the soldiers encountered a 'gentleman', who warned them that twenty to thirty armed men were waiting in ambush on the road ahead. In response, the soldiers diverted their path to the border village of Clonegall, where they billeted themselves for the night in a number of homes. Henry Wallhorn and another private bedded down in the public house of R. Nowlan. During the early morning hours of 21 June, the proprietor responding to knocking opened the door to armed men. The intruders confiscated the soldiers' weapons, wounding one of them with a bayonet in the process, and 'would have killed them' if the publican's wife had not intervened. Hugh Byrne, a member of the Corcoran band, was clearly identified as one of the responsible parties. The following day, Capt. Colclough learned that 'a party of armed men [were] drinking in a public house' at the village of Kildavin. He travelled to the pub and peered through the window. Inside he recognized members of the Corcoran band and promptly dispatched a rider to Newtownbarry for reinforcements. Before assistance could arrive, the men left the house, firing five shots in the street as they departed, and retired towards Mount Leinster. A party of yeomen arrived a short time later, and Colclough led them in pursuit of the band. Having travelled about two miles, Colclough's party heard a number of voices up ahead. The soldiers foolishly called out a challenge in the darkness, which the rebels answered with gunfire. Colclough's force responded in kind, 'but without effect'. A Sgt Jordan of Newtownbarry yeomanry was killed in the exchange. Later, the owner of the public house identified two of the men, whom he knew well, as the same pair who had conducted the arms raid on the soldiers billeted at Clonegall. The inspector of the Wexford and Wicklow yeomanry, Maj. John Beevor, confirmed: 'They belong to the gang that resort[s] to the mountains of Wicklow, Wexford, and Carlow, headed ... by a man of the name of Corcoran.'[23]

As a result of Corcoran's continued activities, Mr Kavanagh was put under increasing pressure by the government to take effective measures. During the third week of August, he rejected a proposal made by Maj. Beevor to conduct joint operations with elements of the Wexford yeomanry against Corcoran, citing the inability of the Wexford units to operate effectively at such a distance from home. Kavanagh informed Beevor that he was, however, 'intent' on 'destroying the banditti', and promised news in 'a very few days' of a 'useful attempt'. He further explained that he had received intelligence of the bands having 'garrisoned a large slated house' less than a mile from Borris. He went on to bemoan the weakness of his yeomanry corps, claiming they had only nine muskets and that the remainder of their weapons were 'fowling pieces' taken from his 'own collection'. Kavanagh was also troubled by reports that the gang numbered more than the nine men he had 'always thought'. Nonetheless, he concluded that he had formulated several plans and was confident that one 'would succeed', although he also reported that they 'were too long to commit to paper'. More ominously, Kavanagh stated, 'I shall not pretend to take any prisoners ... [or] hope that we shall escape unhurt'.[24]

Kavanagh's failure to launch an immediate attack on the band after he learned they had taken up residency in such close proximity to his own home is highly significant. It suggests that either the Corcoran band was more formidable than mere numbers would imply or, alternatively, that popular support, possibly extending to members of Kavanagh's own uniformly Catholic yeomanry corps, made it impossible for him to take effective action. Less than a week later after the above report, Kavanagh clarified his previously vague plans in another note to Maj. Beevor. He explained he had intended to 'have waylaid them in their usual passes returning from the alehouses they frequent[ed]'. Unfortunately in the interim, the Corcoran band members had 'shifted their haunts' and were 'more on their guard'. Kavanagh drew new plans, including using forty 'people of the country' who agreed 'on the first opportunity to seize the band' or, alternatively, to 'attack them at an upcoming fair'.[25] In a report written on 27 August, Maj. Beevor defended Kavanagh's lack of success against the rebels, stating, 'I believe Captain Kavanagh is as sanguine as possible, and will risk everything.'[26] Yet the very necessity of confirming Kavanagh's ardour proves that doubts existed in important quarters.

In early September, Thomas James, a member of the family of west Wexford gentry that included the notorious Orangemen John and William 'Alderman' James, wrote to the latter expressing his own opinion of the Borris yeomen. He stated that he and his corps had been out in search of the rebels on the night of 5 September and all day on the sixth. James received intelligence of the band's whereabouts and promptly moved on to St Mullins, where he learned that the rebels had once again escaped into Kilkenny. During the night of the fifth, the gang had encountered a patrol of Mr Kavanagh's yeomanry, which reportedly wounded Corcoran, Bryne and Fitzpatrick and captured Hanlon. This action, at least according to James, was not as demonstrative of the Borris corps' vigour as it first appears. Thomas James informed his brother that 'had any other corps than Mr. Kavanagh's been out on Monday every man of them would have been shot or taken, but as soon as they fired a few rounds they retreated into Borris and gave the robbers an opportunity of taking off their wounded men'.[27] More significantly, the governor of Carlow, Mr Rochfort, also addressed the utility, and less directly the reliability, of the various yeomanry corps of the region. He felt the Mount Leinster yeomanry could be 'fully relied on for their zeal and loyalty', although they suffered a severe shortage of officers. Similarly, the corps of the staunch loyalist and Orangeman Robert Cornwall could 'be fully relied on'. More cryptically, the governor observed of Kavanagh's Borris corps: '[I]t is not necessary for me to say anything respecting them.'[28]

In December, the Borris corps came under the scrutiny of the Lord Lieutenant. Earl Hardwicke called on the yeomen of County Carlow 'to use their utmost efforts to discover and apprehend Corcoran'. This request was directly forwarded to Kavanagh by William Wickham, who added, 'I am sure your active assistance will be given on this occasion, and the Lord Lieutenant [?] recommends to you to leave nothing undone.'[29] Thus, it was deemed necessary at the highest levels of government to prod the yeomen of Borris into action.

Ultimately, the inability or unwillingness of the Borris yeomanry to deal effectively with Corcoran can be attributed to the relatively unique social and religious structure of the Barony of St Mullins. At the apex of the region's social hierarchy stood the Kavanaghs, who were the largest landowners in southern Carlow. What set the Kavanaghs apart were their deep roots in the region. Descended from the last (MacMurrough) kings of Leinster, they were one of the few powerful Catholic Gaelic families in south Leinster to have retained their land during the dispositions of the previous centuries. Moreover, their 'head tenants remained totally Catholic' and, perhaps significantly, included a number of Corcorans. The middling farmers of the region were also 'overwhelmingly Catholic', and as a result, the Protestant presence in the Borris area was extremely thin.[30] The Kavanaghs were good landlords and popular with their tenants.[31] Thus, the Kavanaghs had a relationship with the community and a corresponding legitimacy in its eyes, which was unobtainable to most of the Protestant landed-elite.

Walter Kavanagh was of unquestioned personal loyalty, as is illustrated by the attack on his house that occurred during the rebellion. On the night of 25 May 1798, some 300 men were driven off with a loss of two dead and three captured. The latter were 'ordered to be hanged'.[32] A larger force under the command of Thomas Cloney, a Kavanagh tenant who regretted the necessity, also attacked Borris House in search of arms on 12 June.[33] This attack was also repulsed. Yet despite his station and influence, Walter Kavanagh was in an extremely precarious position. If he acted with vigour against the Corcoran band, which enjoyed remarkably strong local sympathy, he jeopardized his paternalistic hold on the region.

On the night of 4 November 1803, Corcoran and his men were 'drinking in Ballymurphy, only two miles from Borris'. There, 'they murdered two men', Arthur and John O'Neill. The Borris yeomanry and a detachment of the Killedmond corps gave chase the following morning, but without success. On 5 November Brigade Maj. Moore sullenly reported, 'I am sorry to say that the noted Corcoran and his gang still infest this place [Borris].' He added that the cooperation of the local population was a primary factor in the band's ability to escape.[34]

By late November 1803, as a result of the increased efforts of the authorities in Carlow and Wexford to bring them in following the deaths of Sgt Jordan and the O'Neills, the band was once again forced to move into Kilkenny. Here, they committed an act that drew an overwhelming response from the Irish government. On the evening of the twenty-fourth, Corcoran at the head of a party of twelve armed men robbed the Dublin to Waterford mailcoach near the village of Mullinavat. The rebels fired five shots, killing a horse, and then 'robed the guard and the passengers and carried off the bags of letters'. The Lord Lieutenant, the Earl of Hardwicke, 'recommended' that the governor of Kilkenny waste no time in 'assembling such magistrates and gentlemen as reside[d] most convenient to the neighbourhood where the act was committed'. These men were instructed to cooperate with the military in bringing the band to justice. Furthermore, Lt Gen. Flood, the acting commander of the forces, was ordered to send a 'general officer' to the area where the robbery occurred. This officer was to be granted 'full authority and instructions to use the most vigorous and effectual measures'. Ultimately, the government offered £100 for information leading to the apprehension of 'any of the principle offenders, who would then be 'brought to trial immediately by court martial.[35]

Hardwicke also reported the incident to the Home Secretary, Charles Yorke:

> It appears evident however that the robbery was committed by a gang commanded by one Corcoran, an old rebel who frequents the mountains between the counties of Carlow, Wexford, and Wicklow, and occasionally passes over the Barrow into the county of Kilkenny.

He continued:

> This man, like Dwyer, has hitherto contrived to elude all pursuit, very much on the same system i.e. by dispersing his men on the approach of the military, and trusting to the general attachment of the inhabitants of that wild part of the country.[36]

The Viceroy's report clearly illuminates the means by which Corcoran successfully stayed out for so extended a period. Moreover, it identifies Corcoran as an 'old rebel' and compares him to the political partisan, Michael Dwyer. Perhaps of greater importance is the fact that Corcoran and his band, although numbering less than a score of men, were deemed worthy of the attention of the highest levels of the British government.

The cause of this apparently heavy handed response on the part of the authorities only becomes evident when viewed in a political context. Mail-coach robbery was perceived as an overtly political act. Seizing the coaches disrupted the primary means of communication between the seat of government and the remainder of the country. Furthermore, the presence of political and military dispatches in the mail offered rebels a potentially vital source of intelligence. Finally, the disruption of the mail can be viewed as a symbolic attack on the authority of the central government. In 1798 the United Irishmen had seized the mailcoaches from Dublin as a signal to the outlying counties that the rebellion was under way.[37] In the rebellion's aftermath, a wave of mail robberies occurred throughout the counties most involved in the rising. These attacks invariably created apprehension and demands for effective countermeasures by both local and central authorities. Indeed, the government believed that the Mullinavat robbery was directly related to Robert Emmet's failed rebellion in July. As William Wickham explained to Gen. Floyd:

> there is every reason to be satisfied that this outrage has been effected by

an armed body of men to whom countenance and supply is given by the inhabitants of the place and neighbourhood, where it was committed, acting in furtherance of the rebellion that lately broke.[38]

Although there is no other evidence to tie Corcoran to Emmet's Rebellion, there are tantalizing hints of contact between the conspirators and the Carlow rebels. In September, Mr Richards, a moderate Wexford magistrate, reported to Wickham that he had 'as per General Groose's request ... made inquiries respecting Robert Carty'.[39] Carty was a prominent and effective officer in the rebel's Bantry regiment and served as a member of the eight-man republican directory set up in Wexford town during the rising.[40] Richards reported, 'I heard Carty was at Borris at the home of one Corcoran about two months ago [July].'[41] Carty was privy to the United Irishmen's plans in 1803, having met with Emmet and others who 'pressed' him to 'stir' the people of Wexford. Carty ultimately refused to participate in the actual rising (and in fact fled to England prior to its outbreak), later claiming under examination that he had told the conspirators the 'county of Wexford had enough'.[42] Nonetheless, it is not inconceivable that he was, at least initially, one of the emissaries sent from Dublin to test the people's willingness to rise in the weeks preceding Emmet's rebellion.

Similarly in August, Walter Kavanagh received intelligence of a 'person' having 'arrived' from the direction of Dublin on the twenty-fourth of July. This individual proceeded 'to a farmer's house near St Mullins where he met Thomas Cloney'. Cloney had served prominently as a colonel during the rebellion and, although he later denied it, was directly involved in Emmet's rebellion. Kavanagh also learned that Roger Fitzpatrick, who 'prior to [the] last rebellion [had been] the most active man in the Barony of St. Mullins, [was] now constantly busy in the same offices'.[43]

A flurry of activity resulted from the mail robbery in November. In December Mr Rochfort received a letter 'relative to the gang headed by one Corcoran', which requested that he 'call a meeting of the magistrates and gentlemen of the neighbourhood and concert measures with them'. He informed Dublin Castle that the lack of security in St Mullins could be directly attributed to the fact that no magistrates or gentlemen resided in the 'entire Barony', except for Mr Kavanagh, who in any case had recently departed for Dublin. Moreover, he went on to identify the band's primary source of strength when he recommended that the government take direct action against the population of south Carlow:

[R]ewards should ... be offered ... sufficient to induce people to give information [and the people of St Mullins] should be informed by Proclamation that if they harbour, conceal, or permit Corcoran or any of his gang, or any strangers, to remain over an hour in any of their houses or outhouses, ... they will be tried by court martial.

Rochfort further recommended the establishment of a garrison at Scullough Gap and the stationing of guards at the Barrow bridges in order to block the band's access to Wexford and Kilkenny respectively.[44]

On 13 December 1803 the Lord Lieutenant and the Privy Council issued the proclamation requested by the magistracy of Carlow, and for a second time, the band was 'outlawed'. A £500 reward was offered for the capture of, or information leading to, the apprehension of Corcoran. This document was modelled on the one that had led to the surrender of Dwyer. It also offered £100 rewards for the capture of seven other members of the band. Additional bounties of £100 were promised for the 'discovery and apprehension' of 'all persons aiding, abetting, harbouring, or assisting in the escape of James Corcoran' or any members of the band.[45]

On 28 December, two members of the band offered to surrender under the condition that their lives be spared. Hardwicke instructed Gen. Floyd to 'enter into certain conditions with the pair' with hopes that 'Corcoran w[ould] be very soon taken'.[46] 1804 found the band resorting more and more to the Kilkenny side of the Barrow as the surviving members attempted to evade the new security measures adopted by the authorities in Carlow.[47] These measures took a variety of forms. Most dramatically, Kavanagh swore 'voluntary oaths' from nearly 500 people in the Borris area on the morning of 12 January. The purport of these oaths was to 'secure Corcoran or any of his gang, should he again appear among them, or give notice so they might be secured'.[48] Additionally, Brigade Maj. Moore of the Carlow Yeomanry placed some two-hundred yeomen on permanent duty. The major, who was personally aquatinted with the Borris–Ballymurphy area, utilized the yeomen to search the bands 'known haunts'. Although several attempts to capture 'the principals of the gang' failed, the yeomen did arrest thirteen people for 'aiding [and] harbouring'. These people were initially taken to Kilkenny jail. But, 'after strict exam', two of the most important were placed in the jail at Carlow town. One of these men, Michael Joyce, was 'charged with being an unlicensed publican of Ballymurphy and [with] entertaining Corcoran and his party the night of the murder committed there [the O'Neills]'. The other prisoner, 'an elderly person' named Nancy Farrell, was charged 'with conveying intelligence to Corcoran'. Sylvester Byrne, who resided in Borris, was left in Kilkenny jail. He had been condemned to death in 1798 for his part in the rebellion, although this sentence was later commuted to transportation for life, and Byrne was ultimately granted a protection and turned free. Kavanagh knew Byrne's house 'was resorted to by the gang', and resultantly, Gen. Floyd charged him with harbouring and expressed the belief that he 'ought to be hanged'.[49]

The authorities continued to debate the best means of eliminating Corcoran once and for all. In response, Gen. Floyd ordered parties comprising an officer and twenty men posted at Killedmond, Borris and Graiguenamanagh. He then removed the remainder of the yeomanry from permanent duty. Maj. Moore disagreed with this strategy and expressed the opinion that 'there was no chance of taking him [Corcoran] without adopting the same measures as were the means of taking Dwyer ... stationing small parties of troops' throughout the effected areas. On 23 January, Maj. Moore complained of his continuing lack of success in locating the rebels and, pointedly, attributed his failure to 'the disposition of the people'.[50]

Despite the tenacious support of south Carlow's population, the noose was tightening on the Corcoran band. One member, Lawrence Brennan, was captured by the Rev. Hunt in Kilkenny on or about 27 January. The end came on Saturday 11 February 1804.[51] Under unrelenting pressure in St Mullins, the band had dispersed. Corcoran, John Fitzpatrick and Daniel Brennan slipped back into their native Wexford, where they once again sought shelter in the shadows of Killoughrum Wood. Mr Eastwood, a magistrate and the Anglican rector of the Church at Killann, learned that the men were 'harbouring' at a house less than a mile from his home. As a result of the band's presence in the area, it had been 'deemed expedient' to station twenty men of the virulently loyalist Killoughrum rangers and four of the Ross guards at Eastwood's house for its defence.[52]

Having learned of the rebels' proximity, Eastwood ordered twelve men of the rangers and two of the guards under the command of Sgt Ellison of the Ross corps to 'take the offenders into custody'. The yeomen approached the house in three bodies, but were observed, depending on the version told, by either Brennan or 'a woman who gave the alarm'. Forewarned, Corcoran's small party made a dash for the wood, but encountered three or four of the rangers, whose fire forced them to seek shelter behind a ditch. Both Corcoran and Fitzpatrick were hit early on in the engagement, the former in the hip knocking him to the ground. Yet by all accounts, the rebels continued to fight ferociously. More yeomen joined the fray. Eventually Corcoran was stuck again; this time mortally. Fitzpatrick retreated into a barn, which was then 'burn[ed] over him', and captured. Brennan, who was also wounded in the encounter, nonetheless managed to escape. The soldiers found a blunderbuss, pistol and two muskets, the latter having been 'taken from the Borris Yeomanry' around the prone body of Corcoran. One yeoman, Christian Warren, was severely wounded in the left arm 'from the many shots fired by Corcoran and Fitzgerald'. There were no other government casualties.[53] With an economy of words, the Rev. Eastwood summed up the impact of the twilight encounter as follows: '[T]hus Sir, in three hours we are so fortunate to have taken the heads of a body of ruffians that have infested this neighbourhood for five years and committed innumerable excesses.'[54]

Even in death, Corcoran continued to draw the wary attention of the regional establishment. A party of soldiers carried his body, accompanied by the wounded Fitzpatrick, to Wexford town, where both were 'lodged in Wexford Gaol'.[55] An inquest was held, the verdict of which was simply that Corcoran had 'died from wounds received from a detachment of Ross ... and Killoughrum Yeomen on the eleventh'.[56] One day later, Gen. Floyd reported to Dublin Castle that 'care was taken to identify the body'.[57] Evidence of the extent to which Joseph Corcoran had traumatized Wexford loyalists came at a meeting of the magistrates of the county held on 13 February. The sole purpose of this conclave of important men was to determine the appropriate disposal of Corcoran's remains. Considerable symbolic significance was ascribed to the corpse, for it was 'unanimously agreed' to request the hanging of Corcoran's body 'in chains as a public spectacle'. Failing this, the gentlemen decided that it would be acceptable to have Corcoran's remains 'interred in the gaol yard'. In either instance, the magistrates believed 'it would be highly injurious to the public tranquillity to have his body delivered to his friends'. Ultimately, the authorities determined: '[T]he body of Corcoran will be interred in the usual place ... for convicted malefactors in the most private manner.'[58]

News of the band's destruction was quickly sent to London. 'I have the satisfaction to acquaint you for the information of Mr Yorke, that an account was received this day of the apprehension ... of Corcoran and Fitzpatrick', wrote Evan Nepean. The Chief Secretary added: 'The arrest of these prisoners at this time is of considerable importance.'[59] By 17 February, with 'the gang being thus broken up', the military guard placed on the mail-coaches was removed.[60] Similarly on 29 February, the Commander of the Forces reported to the Lord Lieutenant that 'under the recent circumstances of the apprehension and breaking up of the gang of Corcoran, the escorts for the mail between Clonmel and Waterford' were 'no longer necessary'.[61]

The remainder of the band was taken up in short order. On the morning of 13 February, Hugh and Edward Byrne were set upon by a number of people in St Mullins. After an affray, in which the pair fired upon their assailants, Hugh Byrne was captured, although Edward managed to escape. The locals brought Hugh Byrne to Walter Kavanagh, who expressed his delight, and possibly surprise, in the 'good conduct of the country people in taking this fellow'.[62] More eloquently, Gen. Floyd commented that 'there [wa]s great satisfaction in seeing the country people thus exerting themselves in support of the laws and good order'.[63] Although this evidence of a change in the disposition of the rural population of south Carlow cannot be entirely discounted, its importance should not be overstated. It is most likely that a few individuals less fearful of reprisals, given the enhanced military presence in the region and fortified with the knowledge of Corcoran's death, took the opportunity to collect the bounty offered by the government.

A detachment of the Borris yeomanry caught up with Edward Byrne in a sand pit. After a struggle in which Byrne 'received several wounds', the soldiers took him prisoner. The Byrnes were confined in Kilkenny jail, where they joined Lawrence Brennan.[64] On 23 February, Gen. Floyd proposed trying the four imprisoned members of the gang by court martial. He further requested that the judge advocate assigned to the case by Dublin Castle arrive prior to the trial 'in order to collect facts and evidence'.[65] Edward Byrne eventually died of his wounds on 27 February. A priest urged the dying man to make disclosures about the band and its connections, yet Byrne 'confessed nothing, saying he would keep what he knew to himself'.[66]

Eventually, the government decided to try Hugh Byrne and John Fitzpatrick under civil law at the spring assizes. This alteration in plans drew a nervous response from the Mr Roth, the high sheriff of Kilkenny, Mr Kavanagh, and 'other respectable gentlemen'. The regional gentry feared the possibility that there was insufficient evidence to ensure conviction. As Gen. Floyd related, Mr Kavanagh was particularly disturbed by the prospect of Byrne and Fitzpatrick's liberation: '[T]here can be no further security for the safety ... of the inhabitants ... who have dared to set their faces against him [Byrne] and his desperate gang, which is not yet eradicated.' Floyd concurred with Kavanagh's assessment and recommended that in the event of an acquittal the pair should continue to be held on a secretary's warrant.[67]

Any perception of a transformation in the political sympathies of the rural population of south Carlow can be dispelled by the fact that the remaining shards of the gang continued to be sheltered in the Borris–Ballymurphy area. In its decimated state, the band no longer retained the ability to intimidate; and therefore, this phenomenon can only be explained by an extremely deep-rooted popular sympathy. As late as September of 1804, Maj. Moore learned of the presence in St Mullins of an armed group centred on the surviving members of the Corcoran band, Daniel Brennan and Tim Brien. These men, along with Thomas Fenton, a deserter, Henry Hays of Ballymurphy, a man named Cassidy and two others continued to be 'entertained' by individuals on either side of the Wexford–Carlow border.[68] Remarkably, it was not until 25 November 1804 that a series of reports arrived at Dublin Castle announcing the capture of Brien and Brennan by elements of the Killedmund yeomanry.[69] These two veterans of Vinegar Hill, who had been Cody and Corcoran's lieutenants and closest companions, managed to remain at large, amazingly, for more than six years. At the time of their capture they were the last active rebels in Ireland.

Conclusions

Of central importance in the examination of the Corcoran–Cody band is the question of motivation. More specifically, were they common criminals, examples of pre-political Hobsbawmian social bandits, as is argued by Daniel Gahan, or can a more overtly political agenda be established? In order to gain a fuller understanding of the group's political status it is necessary to look at the way in which contemporaries perceived the band. Although they were occasionally referred to as robbers, there is little evidence that Cody and Corcoran engaged in activities that emanated from simple criminality. Local magistrates and military officers, who were in the best position to ascertain the gang's true nature, invariably disavowed personal gain as a motivational factor. For instance, Walter Kavanagh, who bore responsibility for the day-to-day maintenance of law and order in the band's primary area of operations, reported, 'I have not heard of any robberies committed by this gang in this neighbourhood.'[70] In a like manner, Gen. Henniker stated that the band maintained a 'system of armed neutrality', in which 'they neither robbed nor would they allow others to rob'.[71] Similarly when a 'correct and ample ... account of the banditti' was forwarded to the Under Secretary Alexander Marsden in September 1801, it described Corcoran as 'neither robbing himself nor suffering his gang to do so'.[72]

In reality, the Corcoran band operated at times as a *de-facto* constabulary. The examples of this phenomenon are striking. On at least two separate occasions Cody and Corcoran captured men 'against whom examinations had been sworn for robbery'. In both instances, the prisoners were transferred to a neighbouring magistrate. The rebels later learned that a yeoman, who had previously helped them transport one of the criminals, had been 'threatened by his captain for having any intercourse with them'. In response when Cody and Corcoran captured two 'noted, desperate, advertised robbers' who had escaped from Kilkenny jail, they simply shot them.[73] Indeed while negotiating terms of surrender with Mr Kavanagh, Cody and Corcoran offered to 'atone for their misconduct by hunting and taking the heads of robbers'. Additionally, Kavanagh heard several 'comfortable and industrious farmers express obligation to them for protecting this neighbourhood [Borris] from those gangs of midnight robbers, which ha[d] infested other parts, and from which their haunts ha[d] been free'.[74] Thus, it is obvious that Cody and Corcoran band served as an alternative source of authority, rivalling and in reality more effective than, the government.

Daniel Gahan holds that the Corcoran gang 'demonstrated many of the classic characteristics of pre-modern social bandits'; therefore, S. J. Connolly's contention that banditry had disappeared from Ireland by the early eighteenth century is 'a claim which the case of the Corcoran would seem to undermine'. As evidence of the group's status as social bandits, Gahan cites the fact that the band operated in close proximity to Corcoran's home at Ballindaggan, which in turn 'provided them with the support of kin and neighbours so vital to the survival of the social bandit'.[75]

Although a number of the operational aspects of the Cody and Corcoran band do indeed mimic those of social bandits (including the utilization of mountainous terrain, the support of the local community and familial bonds within the group), there are other factors that argue for a more purely political interpretation of the band's continued resistance. Hobsbawm defines social banditry as 'little more than endemic peasant protest' that has 'next to no organization or ideology and is totally inadaptable to modern social movements'. He notes furthermore that 'the social brigand appears only before the poor have reached political consciousness', and so 'the bandit is a pre-political phenomenon'.[76] James Corcoran's status as an activist in the Society of the United Irishmen prior to the rising, as well as his participation in the rebellion itself, is demonstrative of a degree of politicization that precludes the application of the social banditry model as defined by its creator. Social banditry is an artificial construct applicable only to peasant-based societies. The economy of much of south Leinster was by the 1790s commercialized, and the region's social structure was correspondingly complex.[77] Thus, a peasant-based model, such as social banditry, is of limited utility to the study of post-rebellion Carlow and Wexford. Corcoran himself appears to have come from a family of strong farmers and was educated. He therefore fits only the loosest definition of a peasant, if indeed the term is applicable at all. More compellingly, Joseph Cody was neither an agriculturist nor a member of the community that sheltered him for years. He was a Protestant with social roots in the artisanate of Newtownbarry. The willingness of the rural population of south Carlow and west Wexford to shelter this social and religious, if not geographical, outsider weakens the argument that the band was an insular kinship-based entity.

Significantly, the government and local authorities made a clear distinction between Cody and Corcoran and the numerous gangs of armed brigands which plagued the region in the rebellion's aftermath. This distinction can be found in the language used to describe the band. As with Dwyer and Holt's cohorts, and unlike groups engaged in common criminality, the terms rebel and banditti occur interchangeably in official dispatches pertaining to the band.[78] When in October 1801, the government 'outlawed' the members of the band, the official proclamation charged the 'under named' not only with 'forming a Banditti composed of murderers, robbers, and deserters but also with 'openly avow[ing] their principles of treason'.[79] Additionally, in the account of the group's activities submitted by the local authorities in support of their request to have the band 'proclaimed', it is stated authoritatively: 'Corcoran's conduct has been that of a rebel leader, who has shaken off all pretensions to allegiance and expressed openly his expectation of a change, and an invasion.'[80] A communication from Mr Kavanagh to Gen. Henniker reported that the gang was expecting a rising in which they would partake. Obviously, this threat was taken seriously, for six months later in August 1801 Henniker reported to the Lord Lieutenant of

> the necessity of effectively destroying this gang; dangerous in case of invasion, and its consequent insurrection by instantly becoming a rallying point to the disaffected under the guidance of leaders already armed to protect the rebel, or to compel the wavering loyalists (if any such there be) to join their ranks.[81]

Clearly then, the band was perceived by the authorities as a threat to the state. In turn, this view can be attributed directly to Cody and Corcoran's status as political rebels.

Another question of major importance concerns why Cody and Corcoran were able to remain at large for so extended a period. Many members of the band were known to the local authorities, and they moved about openly during daylight hours. Yet despite extensive efforts on the part of the local yeomanry and regional military commander, Corcoran successfully evaded capture for almost six years. This ability can be explained by two factors. First, they operated in a remote mountainous region, which they knew intimately. The advantages offered by the rugged terrain of the region were clearly recognized by the magistrates who attempted to come to grips with the gang: '[T]he district formed as it is, by its nature to conceal them, and wanting a great road ... to intersect the fastness ... make it a rallying point of the disaffected.'[82] With equal frustration, Henniker observed: '[T]he situation of this part of the country remote from military protections renders fruitless any attempt with the forces under my command to surprise or effectively disperse this banditti.'[83]

Gen. Henniker concluded the above account by stating that the distances enveloped 'allowed the ill-disposed sufficient time to prepare them, and consequently they were too well secreted'.[84] Herein lay the second and essential element of the Corcoran band's survival: the protection of the local population. Fear undoubtedly played a part in the cooperation of the people, and indeed Corcoran could be ruthless. He admitted to cutting off an informer's ears, and there is a strong possibility that the killing of the O'Neills at Ballymurphy resulted from a similar offence.[85] In another report, Henniker had described Cody and Corcoran as operating 'a system of terror' which was so 'firmly established ... that no one w[ould] dare to step forward.' He further explained that the threat of 'burning and assassination' ensured the compliance not only of the 'lower orders, but even among the better sort of people in the towns as well as the country places'.[86] Indeed this ability to intimidate did not diminish with time. As late as 1803, Kavanagh declared: 'I can obtain no kind of intelligence ... for no protection I could give, would save a person known to have give such, from destruction of property and person.'[87]

Yet while intimidation alone can explain the 'contributions' and silence of loyalists, it is insufficient as an explanation for the widespread popular support the band received. Brigade Maj. Moore of the Carlow yeomanry asserted: '[T]here are many people in this part of the country who [shelter?] this gang.'[88] Even Mr Kavanagh, who understandably tried to play down the extent of Corcoran's hold on the region, acknowledged that 'there [we]re many houses where they [we]re welcome'.[89] Indeed while there may have been little choice in providing the band with provisions, the fact that 'reports concerning them [we]re so various and contradictory that they seem[ed] as if fabricated and intended to mislead and confound our operations' can only be explained by sympathy.[90] In other words, the people did not merely remain passively silent as to the gang's whereabouts; instead they served as proactive sources of intelligence and misinformation. Indeed, the rapidity with which news of government troop movements reached the rebels suggests a coordinated network of sympathizers. In explaining the fruitlessness of attempting to synchronize movements between the Borris corps and elements of the Wexford yeomanry, Major Beevor stated, 'Any movement would be immediately conveyed to them.'[91] Similarly, Lt Stone of the Killedmond yeomen found 'that in spite of the utmost secrecy ... any movement' he made 'was known to them', and Kavanagh himself complained: '[T]hey have spies everywhere.'[92]

The prevalence of disloyalty within the population of south Carlow and western Wexford was well known to the government. As Gen. Henniker noted, the 'number' of 'loyal inhabitants' in the region was 'comparatively small', and the Corcoran band was 'welcomed and protected by the majority'.[93] Moreover, this popular support had a surprising longevity. As late as December 1803, Hardwicke reported to London that Corcoran, 'like Dwyer', had 'hitherto contrived to elude all pursuit'. In turn, the Lord Lieutenant attributed this ability to Corcoran's dispersal of 'his men on the approach of the military' as well as his 'trusting to the protections which he [wa]s sure to find from the general attachment of the inhabitants of that wild part of the country'.[94]

In turn, what explains the depth of popular animosity to the state which existed in the borderlands of Wexford and Carlow? Daniel Gahan persuasively argues that part of the answer can be found in an atrocity that occurred as the Wexford rebellion wound down in late June, 1798. The government forces that pursued the rebel column headed by Father Murphy had 'perpetrated one of the worst massacres of the entire rebellion' in the Barony of St Mullins. Approximately two hundred people were slaughtered in a day-long orgy of violence on the twenty-eighth. Some of the victims were undoubtedly fleeing rebels, but the soldiers and yeomen also entered farmhouses and, regardless of guilt or innocence, killed the occupants. As Gahan notes, 'The memory of this event must have caused those who lost kin … to readily embrace and harbour a band such as Corcoran's.'[95]

Yet this interpretation fails to take into account the role of politicization as a motivational factor of the continued popular support received by the Cody and Corcoran band. Carlow, like western Wexford, was indoctrinated during the autumn of 1797 by the radical wing of the United Irishmen.[96] Upwards of 12,000 men had been recruited by the spring of 1798, making it one of the more advanced counties in Leinster.[97] In fact on 15 November, Carlow became the only county in the province to be proclaimed in its entirety. Moreover, the militancy of the movement in Carlow is demonstrated by the county committee's unanimous agreement in February 1798 to support the provincial committee's decision to arm and prepare to rise without French assistance.[98]

Evidence of a connection between the Corcoran band and the reconstituted leadership of the United Irishmen in Dublin is extremely thin. Besides the previously discussed hints of contact prior to Emmet's rebellion, there is one other episode that hints at the possibility of such a connection. In his 'confession', Hugh Byrne claimed that he and Corcoran had 'sat in committee' with a French agent in the County Wexford around the middle of January 1804. The Frenchman, John Lethang, operated in the area of Peppard's Castle on the Wexford coast and used the alias Philip Brenhan. According to Byrne, the committee, which met on Thursdays and Saturdays, was held at the home of a man named Paul Ellis who lived in the Newtownbarry area. At the meeting, Lethang promised that the French would soon effect a landing, and in the interim weapons would be landed on the Wexford coast. Additionally, Byrne stated that shortly before his death Corcoran informed him that 'he sat in a committee with a Frenchman in the city of Kilkenny ... and had prepared the greater part of the inhabitants for the attack, as they were made new United Irishmen'. Byrne's confession concludes with an account of his passage through 'the counties of Carlow, Wicklow, Wexford, and [the] lower part of Kilkenny', where he found that the 'farmers were ready to join the French'.[99]

The truth of Byrne's claims are difficult, if not impossible, to ascertain. Indeed, Gen. Floyd was initially sceptical and consulted with 'two able and active magistrates' of his acquaintance who he felt were 'intelligent and zealous men, who kn[e]w the country well'.[100] Meeting on 3 March, the three men examined 'together the declaration of Hugh Byrne' and concluded it was of sufficient merit to warrant 'measures' being 'taken on all points therein mentioned'.[101] As a result, Admiral Gardner ordered the revenue cutter, *The Swan*, to patrol the coast in order to prevent the anticipated landing of arms. Furthermore, the Lord Lieutenant 'requested' that copies of Gen. Floyd's and Admiral Gardner's reports be sent to the Home Secretary.[102] Although allowances must be made for the fact that he was a known alarmist, Hawtry White, a magistrate who lived on the east Wexford coast, did in fact confirm Bryne's account of a French spy named Lethang 'lurking' near Peppard's Castle, as 'very true'.[103]

Ultimately, there is no evidence of a French attempt to land arms. Nor is there any extant proof of the presence of a French agent in the southeast of Ireland at this late date. The informer John Boyle did operate as an agent provocateur in the guise of a Frenchmen in Kildare and Carlow prior to Emmet's rebellion and continued to serve the government in the region through 1804.[104] Alternatively, Byrne may simply have concocted the story to curry favour with his captors or as a last defiant attempt to generate fear and confusion amongst his foes. Even though a connection to Emmet most probably did not exist, it has been demonstrated that autonomous groups of rebels, with origins in the Society of United Irishmen, continued a shadow existence in several counties. The absence of coordination with the surviving republicans in Dublin in no way precludes a political orientation on the part of the Corcoran band and is in fact more representative of the breakdown in central control that occurred in the post-1798 United Irish organization.[105] Ultimately, the greatest significance of Corcoran's long-term survival is its reflection of the pervasive discontent that followed the rebellion's suppression in wide swaths of south Leinster.

Notes

1   *BNL,* 18 Mar. 1800.
2   NLI KP MS 1209, 28, Littlehales to Sir R. Butler, Dublin Castle, 6 Mar. 1800; TNA HO 100/93/188, Cornwallis to Portland, Dublin Castle, 17 Mar. 1800.

3 Ruán O'Donnell, *The Rebellion in Wicklow 1798* (Dublin, 1998), 101.

4 Roger McHugh (ed.), Carlow in '98: *The autobiography of William Farrell of Carlow* (Dublin, 1949), 217.

5 NLI KP MS 1209, 298, Littlehales to Cornwall, Dublin Castle, 28 July, 1800.

6 Names, descriptions and some accounts, enclosed in NAI RP 620/60/4, Kavanagh to Marsden, Borris, 30 Sept. 1801; ibid. 620/57/59, Colclough, near Enniscorthy, 15 Sept. 1800.

7 Ibid.

8 TNA HO 100/94/285, monthly report of Dundas, Kilcullen, 3 Dec. 1800.

9 Ibid. 100/103/12, monthly report of Dundas, Kilcullen, 3 Jan. 1801.

10 Ibid. 100/103/77, Kavanagh to Henniker, Borris, 21 Feb. 1801.

11 Ibid.

12 For Turner, see Daniel Gahan, *The people's rising: Wexford, 1798* (Dublin, 1995), 16–17.

13 Names, descriptions and some accounts, enclosed in NAI RP 620/60/4, Kavanagh to Marsden, Borris, 30 Sept. 1801; TNA HO 100/103/77, Kavanagh to Henniker, Borris, 21 Feb. 1801; NAI SOC 1020/3, proclamation outlawing Corcoran and 17 others, County Carlow, 1 Oct. 1801.

14 Kevin Whelan, *The tree of liberty*: Radicalism, Catholicism and the construction of Irish identity (Cork, 1996), 6–7; TCL Sirr Papers, MS 869/11, volume containing a list of prisoners, 1803–1805, with personal descriptions and biographical details.

15 TNA HO 100/106/261, Dundas, Carlow, 1 Sept. 1801; ibid. 100/106/262, Dundas, Carlow, 1 Sept. 1801; ibid. 100/104/71–4, Henniker to Dundas, 24 Aug. 1801.

16 Ibid. 100/104/71–4, Henniker to Dundas, 24 Aug. 1801.

17 Ibid. HO 100/106/261, Dundas, Carlow, 1 Sept. 1801; ibid. 100/106/262, Dundas, Carlow, 1 Sept. 1801.

18 NAI SOC 1020/3, Dundas to Charles Abbot, Kilcullen, 27 Sept. 1801.

19 Ibid. 1020/3, proclamation County Carlow, Carlow 1 Oct. 1801.

20 Names, descriptions and some accounts, enclosed in NAI RP 620/60/4, Kavanagh to Marsden, Borris, 30 Sept. 1801; NAI SOC 1020/3, proclamation County Carlow, Carlow, 1 Oct. 1801; NAI RP 620/59/36, Groose to Dundas, Wexford, 15 Oct. 1801; ibid. 620/59/71, Groose to Dundas, Wexford, 15 Oct. 1801; ibid. 1020/50, Henniker to Abbot, Carlow, 18 Oct. 1801; NLI Cullen Papers, MS 8339, 646–7.

21 NAI SOC 1020/50, Henniker to Abbot, Carlow, 18 Oct. 1801.

22 NAI RP 620/65/115, Kavanagh, Borris, 11 Aug. 1803.

23 Ibid. 1025/5/A, Butler to Marsden, Broomville, 22 June 1803; ibid., examination of Henry Wallhorn; ibid., examination of Michael Nowlan, publican; ibid. 1025/5/B, John Beevor, inspector of the yeomanry of Wexford and Wicklow, Newtownbarry, 22 June 1803.

24 Ibid. 1025/62, Kavanagh to Beevor, Borris, 20 Aug. 1803.

25 Ibid., 26 Aug. 1803.

26 Ibid., Beevor, 27 Aug. 1803.

27 NAI RP 620/65/102, Thomas James to Alderman James, Ballycrystal, 7 Sept. 1803.

28 NAI SOC 1025/6, William Rochfort to Wickham, Carlow, 10 Dec. 1803.

29 NLI Kavanagh Papers, MIC 7155, Wickham to Kavanagh, Dublin Castle, 8 Dec. 1803.

30 Whelan, *Tree of liberty*, 6, 7, 20, 39; also see L. M. Cullen, *The emergence of modern Ireland, 1600–1900* (London, 1981), 121–2, 202–3, 242.
31 Thomas Pakenham, *The year of liberty: The history of the great Irish rebellion of 1798* (New York, 1969), 211.
32 NAI RP 620/51–2, Gen Charles Asgill to Lake, Kilkenny, 26 May 1798.
33 Pakenham, *Year of liberty*, 211; Gahan, *People's rising*, 167–9.
34 NAI SOC 1025/25, Moore to Littlehales, Borris, 5 Nov. 1803; ibid. 1025/112, Wickham to Lt Gen Floyd, Dublin Castle, 14 Dec. 1803.
35 TNA HO 100/118/214, Wickham to the Earl of Ormonde, governor of the County of Kilkenny, Dublin Castle, 26 Nov. 1803; ibid. 100/118/216, Wickham to Floyd, 26 Nov. 1803; ibid. 100/118/211–12, Hardwicke to Yorke, Dublin Castle, 7 Dec. 1803.
36 Ibid.
37 Thomas Graham, 'Dublin in 1798: The key to the planned insurrection', in Dáire Keogh and William Furlong (eds), *The mighty wave: The 1798 rebellion in Wexford* (Blackrock, 1996), 77.
38 TNA HO 100/115/67, Wickham to King, Dublin Castle, 28 Dec. 1803.
39 NAI RP 620/66/223, Mr Richards to Marsden, 27 Sept. 1803.
40 For Robert Carty's role in the rebellion, see Gahan, People's rising, 8, 70; Kevin Whelan, 'Politicisation in County Wexford and the origins of the 1798 rebellion', in Hugh Gough and David Dickson (eds), *Ireland and the French revolution* (Dublin, 1990), 175–6.
41 NAI RP 620/66/233, Richards to Marsden, 27 Sept. 1803.
42 TNA HO 100/117/197, the examination of Robert Carty taken before Richard Ford, Whitehall, 23 Sept. 1803; ibid. 100/112/363–6, examination of Carty, Middlesex, 23 Sept. 1803.
43 NAI RP 620/65/115, Kavanagh, Borris, 11 Aug. 1803; for Cloney, also see Whelan, *Tree of liberty*, 168.
44 NAI SOC 1025/6, Rochfort to Wickham, Carlow, 10 Dec. 1803.
45 Ibid. 1030/112, Wickham to Floyd, Dublin Castle, 14 Dec. 1803.
46 TNA HO 100/115/67–8, Wickham to King, Dublin Castle, 28 Dec. 1803.
47 Ibid. 100/122/54, monthly report of Maj. Gen. R. Taylor, Kilkenny, Dec. 1803; NAI RP 620/50/47, Taylor to Wickham, Kilkenny, 3 Jan. 1804.
48 NAI SOC 1030/1, Kavanagh to Floyd, 12 Jan. 1804; ibid., Floyd to Beckwith, Kilkenny, 20 Jan. 1804.
49 Ibid., Floyd to Beckwith, Kilkenny, 20 Jan. 1804.
50 Ibid.; NAI SOC 1030/2, Moore to Littlehales, Carlow, 23 Jan. 1804.
51 Ibid. 1030/61, Floyd, Kilkenny, 27 Jan. 1804.
52 Ibid. 1030/95, Rev. Mr Eastwood, 11 Feb. 1804; ibid. 1030/11, 'Memorial of the privates in the Killoughram Yeomanry', Ballycrystal, 18 Feb. 1804.
53 Ibid. 1030/95, Eastwood, 11 Feb. 1804; ibid. 1030/11, 'Memorial of the privates in the Killoughram Yeomanry', Ballycrystal, 18 Feb. 1804; ibid. 1030/95, Gen. Waller, Wexford, 12 Feb. 1804; ibid. 1030/62, Kavanagh to Floyd, Borris, 13 Feb. 1804; ibid. 1030/111, Floyd to Littlehales, Kilkenny, 14 Feb. 1804; NLI Cullen, MS 9760, 253–4.
54 NAI SOC 1030/95, Eastwood, 11 Feb. 1804.
55 Ibid. 1030/111, 'Memorial of the privates in the Killoughram Yeomanry', Ballycrystal, 18 Feb. 1804.
56 Ibid., Floyd to Littlehales, Kilkenny, 14 Feb. 1804.
57 NLI Cullen Papers, MS 9760, 254; NAI SOC 1030/95, Waller, Wexford, 12

Feb. 1804.

58   Ibid. 1030/96, Waller to the Chief Secretary, Wexford, 13 Feb. 1804; ibid. 1030/97, Waller to the Chief Secretary, Wexford, 15 Feb. 1804.

59   TNA HO 100/124/56, Evan Nepean to King, Dublin Castle, 14 Feb. 1804.

60   NAI SOC 1030/111, Floyd to Nepean, Kilkenny, 17 Feb. 1804.

61   NLI KP MS 1018, 480, Beckwith to Nepean, Royal Hospital, 29 Feb. 1804.

62   NAI SOC 1030/62, Kavanagh to Floyd, Borris, 13 Feb. 1804.

63   Ibid. 1030/111, Floyd to Littlehales, Kilkenny, 14 Feb. 1804.

64   Ibid., Floyd to Littlehales, 15 Feb. 1804.

65   Ibid. 1030/63, Floyd to Beckwith, Kilkenny, 23 Feb. 1804.

66   Ibid. 1030/64, Floyd to Nepean, Kilkenny, 27 Feb. 1804.

67   Ibid. 1030/113, Floyd to Nepean, 18 Mar. 1804.

68   Ibid. 1030/8, Moore, Carlow, 16 Sept. 1804.

69   NAI RP 620/50/87, Floyd to Nepean, Kilkenny, 26 Nov. 1804; ibid., Moore to Floyd, Carlow, 25 Nov. 1804.

70   TNA HO 100/103/77, Kavanagh to Henniker, Borris, 21 Feb. 1801.

71   Ibid. 100/103/75, Henniker, Carlow, 24 Feb. 1801.

72   Names descriptions and some accounts, enclosed in NAI RP 620/60/4, Kavanagh, to Marsden, Borris, 30 Sept. 1801.

73   Ibid.; also see TNA HO 1000/103/75, Henniker, Carlow, 24 Feb. 1801.

74   Names descriptions and some accounts, enclosed in NAI RP 620/60/4, Kavanagh, to Marsden, Borris, 30 Sept. 1801.

75   Daniel Gahan, 'The "black mob" and the "babes in the wood": Wexford in the wake of the rebellion, 1798–1806', in *Journal of the Wexford historical society* 6, no. 13 (1990 –1991), 99, 100, n. 108; the methodology utilized in this section on social banditry is modelled directly on that used by Thomas Bartlett in his article on Michael Dwyer and Joseph Holt, '"Masters of the mountains:" the insurgent careers of Joseph Holt and Michael Dwyer. County Wicklow, 1798–1803', in Ken Hannigan and William Nolan (eds), *Wicklow history and society: Interdisciplinary essays on the history of an Irish county* (Dublin, 1994), 390–5.

76   Quoted in Bartlett, 'Masters of the mountains', 390–5.

77   For the commercialization of eighteenth-century Ireland, see Cullen, Emergence of modern Ireland and Jim Smyth, *The men of no property: Irish radicals and popular politics in the late eighteenth century* (New York, 1992), 23–32.

78   For examples of documents where the terms exist interchangeably, see NAI SOC 1025/5/A, examination of Wallhorn; names descriptions and some accounts, enclosed in NAI RP 620/60/4, Kavanagh, to Marsden, Borris, 30 Sept. 1801; NAI SOC 1020/3, proclamation outlawing Corcoran and 17 others, County Carlow, 1 Oct. 1801; TNA HO 100/104/71–4, Henniker to Dundas, 24 Aug. 1801; NAI SOC. 1020/50, Henniker to Abbot, Carlow, 18 Oct. 1801; NAI RP 620/65/115, Kavanagh, Borris, 11 Aug. 1803; NAI SOC 1030/111, 'Memorial of the privates in the Killoughram Yeomanry', Ballycrystal, 18 Feb. 1004.

79   Ibid. 1020/3, proclamation outlawing Corcoran and 17 others, County Carlow, 1 Oct. 1801.

80   Names descriptions and some accounts, enclosed in NAI RP 620/60/4, Kavanagh, to Marsden, Borris, 30 Sept. 1801.

81   TNA HO 100/104/473, Henniker to Dundas, 24 Aug. 1801.

82   Names descriptions and some accounts, enclosed in NAI RP 620/60/4,

Kavanagh, to Marsden, Borris, 30 Sept. 1801.

83 TNA HO 100/103/261, Henniker, Carlow, 12 June 1801.

84 Ibid.

85 Names descriptions and some accounts, enclosed in NAI RP 620/60/4, Kavanagh, to Marsden, Borris, 30 Sept. 1801; Gahan, 'The black mob', 101.

86 TNA HO 100/104/473, Henniker to Dundas, 24 Aug. 1801.

87 NAI RP 620/65/115, Kavanagh, Borris, 11 Aug. 1803.

88 NAI SOC 1025/25, Moore to Littlehales, Borris, 5 Nov. 1803.

89 TNA HO 100/103/77, Kavanagh to Henniker, Borris, 21 Feb. 1801.

90 Ibid. 100/104/471–3, Henniker to Dundas, 24 Aug. 1801.

91 NAI SOC 1025/62, Beevor, Borris, 26 Aug. 1803.

92 Ibid. 1025/62, Kavanagh, 26 Aug. 1803.

93 TNA HO 100/103/261, Henniker, Carlow, 12 June, 1801.

94 Ibid. 100/118/211–12, Hardwicke to Yorke, Dublin Castle, 7 Dec. 1803.

95 Gahan, 'The black mob', 100; Gahan, *People's rising*, 249–250.

96 L. M. Cullen, 'Politics and rebellion in Wicklow in the 1790s', in Hannigan and Nolan (eds), *Wicklow history and society*, 437–50.

97 Ibid. For estimates of the United Irishmen's strength in Carlow in the spring of 1798, see O'Donnell, *Rebellion in Wicklow*, Appendix four, 412.

98 Cullen, 'Politics and rebellion', 450. For the proclaiming of Carlow, also see TNA HO 100/79/346–8, an account of the several parts of Ireland that have been proclaimed by His Excellency the Lord Lt and Counsel to be in a state of disturbance or in the immediate danger of becoming so.

99 The confession of Hugh Byrne to Robert Forsayth Hutchings, enclosed in NAI RP 620/13/178/12, Floyd, Kilkenny, 2 Mar. 1804; TNA HO 100/124/81, extract of a letter from Floyd dated, Kilkenny, 2 Mar. 1804.

100 Ibid.

101 NAI SOC 1030/98, Floyd to Nepean, Kilkenny, 4 Mar. 1804.

102 TNA HO 100/124/83, Lord Gardner to Nepean, Cove, 4 Mar. 1804; ibid. 100/124/80, Nepean to King, Dublin Castle, 9 Mar. 1804.

103 NAI SOC 1030/113, Hawtry White to Floyd, Wexford, 14 Mar. 1804.

104 For Boyle, see Helen Landreth, *The pursuit of Robert Emmet* (New York, 1948), 147–8.

105 For this phenomenon in Kildare, see Liam Chambers, *Rebellion in Kildare, 1790–1803* (Dublin, 1998), 102–19. For Antrim and Down, see James G. Patterson, 'Continued Presbyterian resistance in the aftermath of the rebellion of 1798 in Antrim and Down', in *Eighteenth-century life*, vol. 22, no. 3 (1998), 45–61.

Conclusion

The significance of the period 1798–1803 has been grossly underestimated. Rather than the interlude between the great rebellion of 1798 and Emmet's final United Irish conspiracy of 1803, these years must be viewed as an integral part of a more than decade-long process of radical politicization and popular resistance. Indeed, the central fact of this pivotal period is pervasive popular alienation from the system of governance. Thus, the Anglican ascendancy and the British connection were maintained not by consent or deference, but by superior firepower. Moreover, the scale of this discontent forces us to reconsider the notion that Robert Emmet's Rebellion was a 'romantic' sacrificial rite, doomed from the onset. In reality, the broad base of popular disaffection demonstrates that Emmet could legitimately expect widespread support. The failure of risings to occur outside of Leinster on 23 July 1803 can be directly attributed to the accidental explosion at the Thomas Street Depot, which forced the conspirators to act before their preparations were complete. Poor communications and the presence of strong military garrisons in key cities ensured that the provincial radicals, who importantly had never anticipated acting without French assistance, would not rise. Yet this inactivity did not reflect apathy, or more pointedly, loyalism.

In turn, popular disaffection was the result of two interrelated processes. First, the long-term efforts of the largely middle-class leadership of the United Irishmen to disseminate their secular, Enlightenment-influenced, republican ideology to the masses appears to have taken a deeper hold than is sometimes appreciated. That continued popular resistance was concentrated in areas organized by the United Irishmen prior to the rebellion of 1798 is clearly reflective of this fact. Second, repression played a central role as a catalyst for continued resistance. Indeed, it was the persistence of counter-revolutionary violence on the part of extremists which ultimately voided the legitimacy of the state in the eyes of much of the population of Ireland. The failure of Dublin Castle's efforts – and efforts were made – to curb these brutal excesses gave the impression that they had the tacit sanction of the government. More simply, repression politicized.

It must also be recognized that rebels, be they Defenders in Ulster or United Irishmen in south Leinster, clearly distinguished between 'Ultras' and

Protestants in general. This remarkable discretion proves that sectarianism has been overstated as a motivational force in post-1798 insurgency. In turn, this leads us to the highly problematic question of confessional animosity in post-1798 society. Although the sectarian model of the rebellion of 1798 has been effectively dismantled by a number of historians over the past fifteen years, it persists in the far more limited historiography of the post-1798 period. Both Marianne Elliott and Nancy Curtin, who have done so much to clarify the picture of radical republicanism in the 1790s, see the immediate legacy of 1798 as permanent religious animosity. Elliott concludes:

> Popular disaffection was a permanent factor in Irish society after 1798 and provided a more fertile ground for United Irish expansion than at any time in the 1790s. Uncultivated by an increasingly remote leadership, however, the ground-swell flowed instead into pervasive Defenderism, and religious antagonisms were permitted to grow apace.[1]

Similarly, Curtin asserts:

> The inclusive, secular, national consciousness forged by Tone, Drennan, Neilson and their colleagues in Dublin and Belfast in the early 1790s collapsed before it had ever neared its goal...Irish Protestants, particularly those radical Dissenters in Ulster who felt threatened by what they saw as an illiberal, intolerant, popish menace, retreated from the principals of 1791 into a closer identification with Great Britain.

Moreover in Curtin's eyes, the United Irishmen inadvertently played a major part in heightening confessional animosity: 'The United Irishmen compromised their avowed non-sectarianism by exploiting and exacerbating confessional hostility.'[2]

This common focus on sectarianism is overstated. For example, it greatly underestimates the animosity that the violence of the 1790s generated in the Presbyterian population of east Ulster. In reality, the primary, if almost entirely ignored, religious tension in the region was between Anglican and Dissenter. The sectarian interpretation is further qualified the continued resistance of Protestants through 1803. On the national level, the leadership of the United Irishmen remained substantially Protestant, and the most prominent leaders of the 1803 conspiracy were, at least nominally, members of the established Church. Robert Emmet and Thomas Russell, who was in fact deeply religious, were both Anglicans. Alternatively, two of the most effective field activists in the United Irish organization were the highly respected, socially radical, Ulster Presbyterians, James Hope and William Putnam McCabe. These long-time republicans had already played an essential part in establishing the alliance between Catholic Defenders and Presbyterian United Irishmen in the North during the mid 1790s and were pivotal in the republican recruitment drive amongst the Catholic population of the counties of south Leinster in the months directly preceding the rebellion. Finally, the use of these men as agents to the predominantly Catholic districts of south Leinster prior to Emmet's rebellion, coupled with the welcome receptions they received, confirm that the sectarian case is exaggerated.

In Leinster, where the strongest case for a sectarian interpretation of post-1798 events can be made, Joseph Holt, a member of the established Church, was the most significant rebel commander in the months immediately following the defeat of the summer rising of 1798. Similarly, the willingness of the overwhelmingly Catholic population of west Wexford and south Carlow to shelter Joseph Cody, a Wexford Protestant, who actively resisted until 1801, further weakens the sectarian interpretation.

The brutalization of Irish society also emerges as a major theme of the period between 1798 and 1803. Prior to the 1790s, Ireland, despite observations to the contrary, was relatively free of excessive physical violence. Yet by 1799, a fundamental change had occurred. After 1798, the agrarian secret societies in Munster demonstrated a surprising willingness to use capital force. Earlier redresser movements were noted for their hesitancy to take human life. In a like fashion, the post-1798 Defender movement in east Ulster, although strikingly similar in many ways to the agrarian 'Steelboys' of the 1760s, also differed from its predecessors in its utilization of extreme force. What then explains this transformation? It is argued here that this phenomenon can be directly attributed to the government's creation of an environment in which capital force was increasingly the norm.

Finally, traditional Irish historiography holds that the non-sectarian republican ideology of the United Irishmen disappeared in a sea of sectarian animosity in the aftermath of the failed rising of 1798, only to reappear in the altered form of exclusive Catholic nationalism after the famine in the mid-nineteenth century. This view has been challenged in the works of Tom Garvin and M. Beames, who have attempted to establish an, albeit tenuous, ideological link between the United Irishmen and the Ribbon societies that emerged in the 1810s. In turn, the Ribbonmen merged with the Fenians in the 1860s and 1870s, eventually evolving into the I.R.B., and ultimately the I.R.A. This view acknowledges that the level of politicization of the Ribbon societies was extremely limited; and that by the 1820s they had become exclusively Catholic with a quasi-sectarian agenda. Nevertheless, this interpretation questions the view that the democratic radicalism of the United Irishmen had no direct impact on modern Irish republicanism.[3] Paradoxically, the evidence from the period 1798 to 1803 allows two contradictory interpretations of this argument. First, by demonstrating that the United Irishmen did not rapidly collapse in the aftermath of 1798, we add five years to the process of republican politicization. Moreover, the presence of Presbyterian, former United Irishmen in the Defender movement in Antrim and Down for several years after 1798 proves that, at the very least, we must push back the emergence of sectarianism in the North by several years. Alternatively, the sectarian nature of the protracted white terror, although perpetrated exclusively by extremists, not Anglicans generically, may have laid the groundwork for later religious animosity. What remains to be done is to either confirm or dispel the accepted historiographical consensus on the fate of the United Irishmen – that after 1798 or 1803, they, and with them their non-sectarian republicanism, disappeared only to re-emerge in a mythical form in the pantheon of later nationalist movements. But perhaps this rupture in the revolutionary tradition was not so abrupt. If the United Irishmen left footsteps in the sand that can be traced from the Ribbon societies through the Fenians, a more than mythical link between the United Irishmen and modern Irish republicanism will be established.

1   Marianne Elliott, *Partners in revolution: The United Irishmen and France* (New Haven, 1982), 244.

2   Nancy J. Curtin, *The United Irishmen: Popular politics in Ulster and Dublin, 1791–1798* (Oxford, 1994), 284.

3   M. Beames, 'The Ribbon societies: lower-class nationalism in pre-famine Ireland', in *Past and present*, no. 97 (1982), 128–43; Tom Garvin, 'Defenders, ribbonmen and others: underground political networks in pre-famine Ireland', in *Past and present*, no. 96 (1982).

Bibliography

Primary sources

Manuscripts

Dublin – National Archives Ireland
Byrne papers (MS 5892A)
Hutchinson papers (MS 3098)
Prisoners Petition and Cases/State Prisoners Petitions (1798–1805)
Rebellion papers (MSS 620/1–67)
State of the country papers (MSS vol. I. 1017–1032, 1080, 1091, 1092; vol. II. 3001–3960)

Dublin – National Library of Ireland
Ballitor papers (MIC 1093)
Cullen papers (MSS 8339, 9760–9762)
A description of the rising in Dublin, July 1803 (MS 14,297)
Holt letters (MSS 4770–1)
Kavanagh papers (MIC 7155)
Kilmainham papers (MSS 1014–1018, 1133–1147, 1197–1215, 1257–1259, 1278–1280, 1299–1301)
Mary Leadbeater's diaries 1790–1809 (MSS 9330–9346)
Memoirs of personalities of Emmet's rebellion (MS 10,425)
Notes, etc. compiled by J. C. M. Weale, c. 1900 towards a study of (M) Dwyer

Dublin – Trinity College Library
Cullen papers (MS 1472)
Sirr papers (MS 869)

London – The National Archive (formerly, Public Record Office)
Home Office papers (HO 100/73–124)

Contemporary newspapers

The *Belfast News-Letter*

Publications of the Historical Manuscripts Commission (Great Britain)

The manuscripts of J. B. Fortescue, esq, preserved at Dropmore. 14th report, appendix, pt. 5. 5 vols. London: Eyre and Spottiswood, 1894.

Contemporary books and documentary material

Byrne, Miles. *Memoirs of Miles Byrne*, 2 vols (Paris, 1863).

Castlereagh. *Memoirs and correspondence of Viscount Castlereagh, second marquis of Londonderry.* 4 vols. Edited by C. Stewart. London: Henry Colburn, 1848–1849.

Cornwallis. *Correspondence of Charles, first marquis Cornwallis.* 3 vols. Edited with notes by Charles Ross. London: John Murray, 1859.

Cullen, Rev. Luke. *Insurgent Wicklow 1798.* Dublin, 1948.

_____. *Statistical survey of the county of Wexford.* Dublin, 1807.

Gilbert, John. *Documents relating to Ireland, 1795–1804.* Shannon: Irish University Press, 1970.

Gordon, Rev. James Bently. *History of the rebellion in Ireland in the Year 1798.* Dublin, 1801.

Hardwicke, Earl of. *The Viceroy's post-bag: The correspondence hitherto unpublished of the Earl of Hardwicke, the first Lord Lieutenant after the union.* Edited by Michael MacDonagh. London: John Murray, 1904.

Hay, Edward. *History of the insurrection of the county of Wexford, A.D. 1798.* Dublin, 1803.

Holt, Joseph. *Memoirs.* Edited by T. J. Crocker. 1838.

Leadbeater, Mary. *The Leadbeater papers, a selection from the manuscripts and correspondence of Mary Leadbeater.* London, 1862.

McHugh, Roger (ed.). *Carlow in '98: The autobiography of William Farrell of Carlow.* Dublin: Browne and Nolan, 1949.

Moore, Sir John. *Diary of Sir John Moore.* Edited by Major General Sir J. F. Maurice. London: Edward Arnold, 1904.

Musgrave, R. *Memoirs of the different rebellions in Ireland.* Dublin, 1801.

Old Ballymena: A history of Ballymena during the 1798 rebellion. Ballymena [County Antrim], 1938.

Teeling, C. H. *The history of the Irish rebellion of 1798 and sequel to the history of the Irish rebellion. I.U.P. reprint.* Shannon, 1972.

Secondary sources

Books

Bartlett, Thomas. *The fall and rise of the Irish nation: The Catholic question, 1690–1830* (Savage, MD: Barnes and Noble Books, 1992).

Bartlett, Thomas (ed.). *Revolutionary Dublin, 1795–1801: The letters of Francis Higgins to Dublin Castle* (Dublin: Four Courts Press, 2003).

_____. and D. W. Hayton (eds). *Penal era and golden age: Essays in Irish history, 1690–1800* (Belfast: W. and G. Baird, 1979).

Bartlett, Thomas, David Dickson, Dáire Keogh and Kevin Whelan (eds). *1798: A bicentenary perspective* (Dublin: Four Courts Press, 2003).

Blackstock, Allan. *An ascendancy army: The Irish yeomanry, 1796–1834* (Dublin: Four Courts Press, 1998).

Chambers, Liam. *Rebellion in Kildare, 1790–1803* (Dublin: Four Courts Press, 1998).

Clark, Samuel and James S. Donnelly (eds). *Irish peasants: Violence and political unrest, 1780–1914* (Madison: University of Wisconsin, 1983).

Cohen, Marilyn (ed.). *The warp of Ulster's past: Interdisciplinary perspectives on the Irish linen Industry, 1700–1920.* (New York: St Martin's Press, 1997).

Connolly, S. J. *Religion, law and power: The making of Protestant Ireland, 1660–1760* (Oxford: Clarendon Press, 1992).

Cullen, L. M. *The emergence of modern Ireland, 1600–1900* (London: B. T. Batsford, 1981).

Curtin, Nancy J. *The United Irishmen: Popular politics in Ulster and Dublin, 1791–1798* (Oxford: Clarendon Press, 1994).

Dickson, Charles. *Revolt in the north, Antrim and Down in 1798* (Dublin: Clonmore and Reynolds, 1960).

_____. *The life of Michael Dwyer* (Dublin: Browne and Nolan LTD, 1944).

_____. *The Wexford rising in 1798: Its causes and its course* (Tralee: Kerryman Ltd, 1955).

Dickson, David. *Old world colony: Cork and south Munster 1630–1830* (Madison: University of Wisconsin Press, 2005).

_____. Hugh Dorian, and Breandán Mac Suibhne (eds). *The outer edge of Ulster: A memoir of social life in nineteenth-century Donegal* (South Bend, IN: University of Notre Dame Press, 2001).

_____. Dáire Keogh and Kevin Whelan (eds). *The United Irishmen: Republicanism, radicalism and rebellion* (Dublin: Lilliput Press, 1993).

Elliott, Marianne. *The Catholics of Ulster: A history.* (New York: Basic Books), 2001.

_____. *Partners in revolution: The United Irishmen and France* (New Haven: Yale University Press, 1982).

Farrell, Sean. *Rituals and riots: Sectarian violence and political culture in Ulster, 1784–1886* (Lexington, KY: University Press of Kentucky, 2000).

Foster, R. F. *Modern Ireland: 1600–1972* (London: Penguin Press, 1988).

Gahan, Daniel. *The people's rising: Wexford, 1798* (Dublin: Gill and Macmillan, 1995).

Gough, Hugh and David Dickson (eds). *Ireland and the French revolution* (Dublin: Irish Academic Press, 1990).

Hannigan, Ken and William Nolan (eds). *Wicklow history and society: Interdisciplinary essays on the history of an Irish county* (Dublin: Geography Publications, 1994).

Harvey, Karen. *The Bellews of Mount Bellew* (Dublin: Four Courts Press, 1998).

Hayes, Richard. *The last invasion of Ireland: When Connacht rose* (Dublin: Gill and Macmillan, Ltd., 1937).

Hobsbawm, E. J. *Bandits* (Harmondsworth, Middlesex: Penguin Books, 1972).

_____. *Primitive rebels: Studies in archaic forms of social movement in the 19th and 20th centuries* (New York: W. W. Norton, 1965).

Hughes, A. J. and William Nolan (eds). *Armagh history and society* (Dublin: Geography Publications, 2001).

James, Andrew. *Ninety-eight and sixty years after* (London: William Blackwood and Sons, 1911).

Kee, Robert. *The green flag, vol. I: The most distressful country* (London: Penguin Books, 1972).

Kelly, Liam. *A flame now quenched: Leitrim in the 1790s* (Dublin: Lilliput Press, 1998).

Keogh, Dáire. *The French disease: The Catholic Church and radicalism in Ireland, 1790–1800* (Dublin: Four Courts Press, 1993).

_____. and Nicholas Furlong (eds). *The mighty wave: The 1798 rebellion in Wexford* (Dublin: Four Courts Press, 1996).

Landreth, Helen. *The pursuit of Robert Emmet* (New York: McGraw-Hill, 1948).

McBride, Ian. *Scripture politics: Ulster Presbyterians and Irish radicalism in the late eighteenth century* (Oxford: Clarendon Press, 1998).

McIlfatrick, James H. *Sprigs around the pumptown* (Coleraine: Coleraine Printing Co, 1996).

Murphy, John A. Murphy (ed.). *The French are in the bay: The expedition to Bantry Bay 1796* (Dublin: Mercier Press, 1997).

O'Donnell, Ruán. *Aftermath: Post-rebellion insurgency in Wicklow, 1799–1803* (Dublin: Irish Academic Press, 2000).

_____. *Robert Emmet and the rebellion of 1798* (Dublin: Irish Academic Press, 2003).

_____. *Robert Emmet and the rising of 1803* (Dublin: Irish Academic Press, 2003).

_____. *The rebellion in Wicklow, 1798* (Dublin: Irish Academic Press, 1998).

O'Neill, Philip M. *The barrow uncrossed* (Cork: Litho Press Co., 1998).

Old Ballymena: A history of Ballymena during the 1798 (Ballymena, 1857).

Pakenham, Thomas. *The year of liberty: The history of the great Irish rebellion of 1798* (New York: Random House, 1969).

Póirtéir, Cathal (ed.). *The great Irish rebellion of 1798* (Dublin: Mercier Press, 1998).

Power, Thomas. *Land, politics, and society in eighteenth-century Tipperary* (Oxford: Clarendon Press, 1993).

Smyth, Jim (ed.). *Revolution, counter-revolution and union: Ireland in the 1790s* (Cambridge: Cambridge University Press, 2000).

Smyth, Jim. *The men of no property: Irish radicals and popular politics in the late eighteenth century* (New York: St. Martin's Press, 1992).

Stewart, A. T. Q. *The summer soldiers: The 1798 rebellion in Antrim and Down* (Belfast: Black Staff Press, 1995).

Whelan, Kevin. *The tree of liberty: Radicalism, Catholicism and the construction of Irish identity, 1760–1830* (Cork: Cork University Press, 1996).

_____. and William Nolan (eds). *Wexford: History and society – interdisciplinary essays on the history of an Irish county* (Dublin: Geography Publications, 1987).

Wilson, David A. and Mark G. Spencer (eds). *Ulster Presbyterians in the Atlantic world: Religion, politics and identity (Dublin: Four Courts Press, 2006).*

Articles

Bartlett, Thomas. 'An end to the moral economy: The Irish militia disturbances of 1793' in *Past and present*, no. 99 (May 1983), 41–64.

_____. 'Clemency and compensation: The treatment of defeated rebels and suffering loyalists after the 1798 rebellion' in *Revolution, counter-revolution and union: Ireland in the 1790s*, ed. Smyth (Cambridge, 2000), 112–13.

_____. '"Masters of the mountains": The insurgent careers of Joseph Holt and Michael Dwyer, County Wicklow, 1798–1803' in *Wicklow history and society:*

Interdisciplinary essays on the history of an Irish county, eds Hannigan and Nolan (Dublin, 1994), 390–5.

_____. 'Select documents XXXVIII: Defenders and defenderism in 1795' in *Irish historical studies* 24, no. 95 (1985), 373–94.

Beames, M. R. 'The Ribbon societies: Lower-class nationalism in pre-famine Ireland' in *Past and present*, no. 97 (1982), 128–43.

Bertaud, Jean-Paul. 'Forgotten soldiers: The expedition of General Humbert to Ireland in 1798' in *Ireland and the French Revolution*, eds Gough and D. Dickson (Dublin, 1990), 220–8.

Blackstock, Allan. 'The social and political implications of the raising of the yeomanry in Ulster: 1796–1798' in *The United Irishmen*, eds D. Dickson, Keogh and Whelan (Dublin, 1993), 234–43.

Bric, Maurice, 'Priests, parsons and politics: The rightboy protest in County Cork 1785–1788' in *Past and present*, no. 100 (1983), 100–23.

'Ceremony to remember United Irishmen held in Ballymena' [electronic publication] *RTE News*, 2 Dec. 2002. 13 July 2006 www.rte/news/2000/1202/ceremony. html.

Collins, Peter. 'The contest of memory: The continuing impact of 1798 commemoration' in *Éire–Ireland* 34, no. 2 (1999), 28–50.

Crawford, W. H. 'The Belfast middle classes in the late eighteenth century' in *The United Irishmen*, eds D. Dickson *et al.* (Dublin, 1993), 62–73.

Cullen, L. M. 'The internal politics of the United Irishmen' in *The United Irishmen*, eds D. Dickson *et al.* (Dublin, 1993), 176–96.

_____. 'Politics and rebellion in Wicklow in the 1790s' in *Wicklow history and society*, eds Hannigan and Nolan (Dublin, 1994), 411–501.

_____. 'The 1798 rebellion in Wexford: United Irish organization, membership, leadership' in *Wexford: History and society*, eds Whelan and Nolan (Dublin, 1987), 248–95.

_____. 'The political structures of the Defenders', in *Ireland and the French Revolution*, eds Hugh Gough and David Dickson (Dublin, 1990), 117–38.

_____. 'The United Irishmen in Wexford' in *The mighty wave*, eds Keogh and Furlong (Dublin, 1996), 65–78.

Curtin, Nancy J. 'Ideology and materialism: Politicization and Ulster weavers in the 1790s' in *The warp of Ulster's past*, ed. Cohen (New York, 1997), 111–38.

_____. 'The transformation of the society of the United Irishmen into a mass-based revolutionary organization, 1794–1796' in *Irish historical studies* 24, no. 96 (Nov. 1985), 463–92.

Dickson, David. 'Paine and Ireland' in *The United Irishmen*, eds D. Dickson *et al.* (Dublin, 1993), 135–50.

_____. 'Smoke without fire? Munster and the 1798 rebellion' in *1798: A bicentenary perspective*, eds Bartlett, D. Dickson, Keogh and Whelan (Dublin, 2003), 156–7.

_____. 'The south Munster region in the 1790s' in *The French are in the bay: The expedition to Bantry Bay 1796*, ed. Murphy (Dublin, 1997), 85–8.

_____. 'The State of Ireland before 1798' in *The great Irish rebellion of 1798*, ed. Póirtéir (Dublin, 1998), 15–25.

Donnelly, James S. Jr. 'Hearts of oak, hearts of steel' in *Studia hibernica*, no. 21 (1981), 7–75.

_____. 'The Rightboy movement' *Studia hibernica*, nos. 17–18 (1977–1978), 120–202.

_____. 'The Whiteboy movement of 1761–1765' in *Irish historical studies* 21, no. 81 (1978), 20–55.

Durey, Michael. 'Marquess Cornwallis and the fate of Irish rebel prisoners in the aftermath of the 1798 rebellion' in *Revolution, counter-revolution and union: Ireland in the 1790s*, ed. Smyth (Cambridge, 2000), 128–44.

Elliott, Marianne. 'The Defenders in Ulster' in *The United Irishmen*, eds D. Dickson *et al.* (Dublin, 1993), 222–33.

_____. 'The origin and transformation of early Irish republicanism' in *International review of social history*, 23, no. 3 (1978), 405–28.

Gahan, Daniel. 'The "black mob" and the "babes in the wood": Wexford in the wake of the rebellion, 1798–1806' in *Journal of the Wexford historical society* 6, no. 13 (1991), 92–110.

_____. 'The military planning of the 1798 rebellion in Wexford' in *The mighty wave*, eds Keogh and Furlong (Dublin, 1996), 109–17.

Garvin, Tom. 'Defenders, Ribbonmen and others: Underground political networks in pre-famine Ireland' in *Past and present*, no. 96 (1982), 133–55.

Gibbon, Peter. 'The origins of the Orange order and the United Irishmen: A study in the sociology of revolution and counter-revolution' in *Economy and society* 1 (1972), 134–63.

Gibbons, Luke. 'Republicanism and radical memory: The O'Connors, O'Carolan and the United Irishmen' in *Revolution, counter-revolution and union*, ed. Smyth (Cambridge, 1998), 211–37.

Graham, Thomas. '"A union of power"? The United Irish organization' in *The United Irishmen*, eds D. Dickson *et al.* (Dublin, 1993), 244–55.

_____. 'Dublin in 1798: The key to the planned insurrection' in *The mighty wave*, eds Keogh and Furlong (Dublin, 1996), 79–96.

Mac Suibhne, Breandán. 'Up not out: Why did north-west Ulster not rise in 1798?' in *The great Irish rebellion of 1798*, ed. Póirtéir (Dublin, 1998), 83–100.

McBride, Ian. 'The harp without the crown: Nationalism and republicanism in the 1790s' in an unpublished paper presented at The Folger Institute Seminar, 'Irish political thought in the eighteenth century', May/June, 1998, 10–18.

_____. 'William Drennan and the dissenting tradition' in *The United Irishmen*, eds D. Dickson *et al.* (Dublin, 1993), 49–61.

Miller, David. 'The Armagh troubles' in *Irish peasants: Violence and political unrest, 1780–1914*, eds Clark and Donnelly, (Madison, WI, 1983), 155–91.

_____. 'The origins of the orange order in County Armagh' in *Armagh history and society*, eds Hughes and Nolan (Dublin, 2001), 583–608.

Miller, Kirby A. 'Forging the "Protestant way of life": Class conflict and the origins of unionist hegemony in early nineteenth-century Ulster' in *Ulster Presbyterians in the Atlantic world: Religion, politics and identity*, eds Wilson and Spencer (Dublin, 2006), 128–65.

Munnelly, Tom. '1798 and the ballad makers' in *The great Irish rebellion of 1798*, ed. Póirtéir (Dublin, 1998), 160–70.

Murtagh, Harman. 'General Humbert's campaign in the west' in *The great Irish rebellion of 1798*, ed. Póirtéir (Dublin, 1998), 115–24.

_____. 'General Humbert's futile campaign' in *1798: A bicentenary perspective*, eds Bartlett *et al.* (Dublin, 2003), 174–87.

O'Donnell, Ruán. 'The rebellion of 1798 in County Wicklow' in *Wicklow history and society*, eds Hannigan and Nolan (Dublin, 1994), 341–78.

Patterson, James G. 'Continued Presbyterian resistance in the aftermath of the rebellion of 1798 in Antrim and Down' in *Eighteenth-century life* 22, no. 3 (1998), 45–61.

Smyth, P. D. H. 'The Volunteers and parliament, 1779–1784' in *Penal era and golden age: Essays in Irish history, 1690–1800*, eds Bartlett and Hayton (Belfast, 1979), 113–36.

Stewart, A. T. Q. '1798 in Antrim and Down' in *The great Irish rebellion of 1798*, ed. Póirtéir (Dublin, 1998), 72–82.

Tesch, Pieter. 'Presbyterian radicalism' in *The United Irishmen*, eds D. Dickson *et al.* (Dublin, 1993), 33–48.

Whelan, Kevin. 'Bantry Bay: The wider context' in *French are in the Bay*, ed. Murphy, 95–6.

_____. 'Introduction to section II' in *1798: A bicentenary perspective*, eds Bartlett *et al.* (Dublin, 2003), 97–103.

_____. 'Politicisation in County Wexford and the origins of the 1798 rebellion' in *Ireland and the French revolution*, eds Gough and D. Dickson (Dublin, 1990), 156–78.

_____. 'Reinterpreting the 1798 rebellion in County Wexford' in *The mighty wave*, eds Keogh and Furlong (Dublin, 1996), 9–36.

_____. 'The role of the Catholic priest in the 1798 rebellion in County Wexford' in *Wexford: History and society*, eds Whelan and Nolan (Dublin, 1987), 296–315.

_____. 'The United Irishmen, the Enlightenment and Popular Culture' in *The United Irishmen*, eds D. Dickson *et al.* (Dublin, 1993), 269–96.

Index

Index

CPSIA information can be obtained at www.ICGtesting.com

263363BV00004B/6/P